OLYMPUS

PRAISE FOR THE BOOK

'Eminently readable . . . pathbreaking . . . Pattanaik's language and style are fluid and comprehensible and his gift of storytelling is evident in his ability to catch and hold the reader's interest. A must-read'—*Outlook*

'In just seven odd pages [in the Author's Note], littered with his attractive illustrations, Pattanaik writes a most succinct cultural history of the world'—*Scroll*

'A veritable treasure house of intriguing tales and incisive analysis of Greek myths . . . A must-read for all those who are interested in mythology. Exuberant tales peppered with beautiful illustrations'—Usha Narayanan, author of *Pradyumna* and *The Secret of God's Son*

DEVDUTT PATTANAIK

OLYMPUS

AN INDIAN RETELLING OF THE GREEK MYTHS

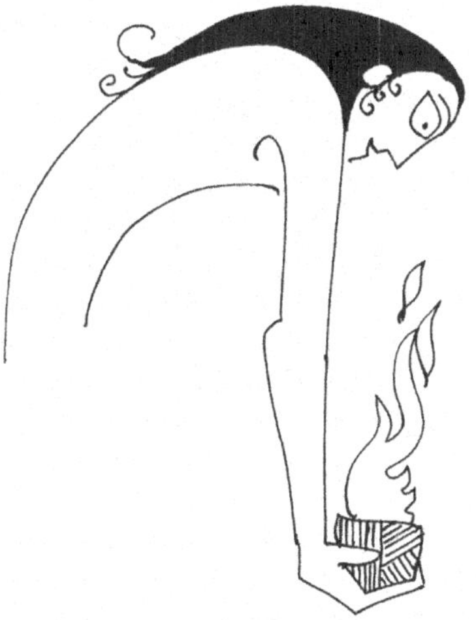

Illustrations by the author

PENGUIN BOOKS
An imprint of Penguin Random House

PENGUIN BOOKS

USA | Canada | UK | Ireland | Australia
New Zealand | India | South Africa | China

Penguin Books is part of the Penguin Random House group of companies
whose addresses can be found at global.penguinrandomhouse.com

Published by Penguin Random House India Pvt. Ltd
7th Floor, Infinity Tower C, DLF Cyber City,
Gurgaon 122 002, Haryana, India

Penguin
Random House
India

First published in Penguin Books by Penguin Random House India 2016

12 11 10 9 8

ISBN 9780143428299

Typeset in Garamond by Special Effects, Mumbai

www.penguin.co.in

I dedicate this book to Homer, Hesiod and Socrates,
and to Vyasa, Valmiki and Yagnavalkya.
Each one saw the world so differently.

Contents

AUTHOR'S NOTE

Shadows and Sunlight

Over 2500 years ago, Greek bards narrated 'mythos', stories, that sought to make sense of the world. Greek philosophers preferred 'logos', reason, to make sense of the world. For the Greek elite, the preference for logos was indicative of education; only 'barbarians' preferred mythos. From this ancient divide stems the modern preference for philosophy over mythology, concepts over stories.

This divide, however, is superficial. For both mythology and philosophy present the same idea: the former communicates through a story, along with symbols and rituals, while the latter uses precise language. Mythology creates a more visceral experience, and so appeals to everyone, not just the intellectual.

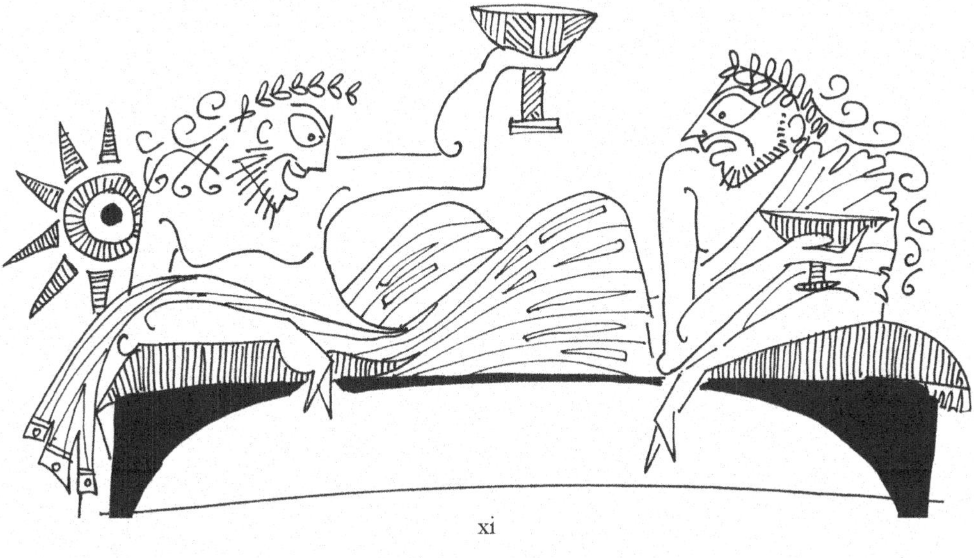

If Greek bards spoke of heroes who fight chaos and seek cosmos or order, Greek philosophers talked of shadowy caves of ignorance and the sunlit world of wisdom outside. What were shadows to a philosopher was chaos to a bard. What was sunlight to a philosopher was cosmos to a bard.

If there was a difference between the Greek philosopher and the Greek bard, it was this: the former shared what he understood whereas the latter simply transmitted what he received. But neither really abandoned the finite linear structure: from chaos to order, from shadows to sunlight, from here to there.

Greek mythology has always been at loggerheads with Abrahamic mythology, which forms the basis of Judaic, Christian and Islamic faiths. Greek mythology placed greater value on the individual contemplation of nature and culture, while Abrahamic mythology demands submission to a supernatural force.

Yet, the two have much in common: both follow a finite linear structure. Instead of chaos, Abrahamic mythology speaks of the wilderness of false gods, and instead of cosmos, it speaks of the Promised Land of the one true God of Abraham. If Greek mythology is about destination, adventure and discovery, Abrahamic mythology is about frustrated adventurers returning to a lost home.

The struggle between these two finite linear mythologies, Greek and Abrahamic, shapes much of Western thought. Modern secular thought is in fact just another 'avatar' of Greek mythology and philosophy, and this becomes evident when we see Western history as a series of attempts to define what constitutes shadows and what constitutes sunlight: many gods, one God, or no God. The West here refers to the worlds that stretch from Persia and Arabia, through Mesopotamia and the Mediterranean, to Europe—and now, America.

- Ancient Greeks sought 'theory', which means to see (orao) the divine (theoin), or the world as it is, which mirrors the Hindu concept of 'darshan'.
- Popular discomfort with mythology is rooted in the Greek disdain for the non-intellectual, and Abrahamic disdain for any alternative narratives, which informs even modern scientific education systems around the world.
- Mythology in its most primal form is constituted by rituals, from which symbols and stories emerge. These are different forms of language.
- Under colonial rule, many Indian intellectuals gave preference to the lofty ideas of the Upanishads, and mimicked the Western disdain for Puranic stories and temple rituals of the common folk.

From Greek City States to the Persian Empire

The ancient Greeks believed in 'polis', city states, not empires; in democracy, not monarchy; in consensus, not authority; and in heroes who held their own before capricious and whimsical gods, not one all-powerful God-king. For them, the Egyptians and Persians were barbarians because they did not care for reason, and chose instead to follow blindly the words of their God-king.

Greek art was individualistic and realistic, seeking to mimic reality. By contrast, art in ancient Egypt and ancient Persia was more centrally controlled royal propaganda, allowing no room for individual expression. While the human forms in Greek images showed expression and taut musculature, and were presented in action, without a frame or enforced symmetry, Egyptian and Persian images were formal, rigid and stately, and contained within frames. These Egyptian and Persian worldviews would eventually serve as tributaries to Abrahamic monotheism.

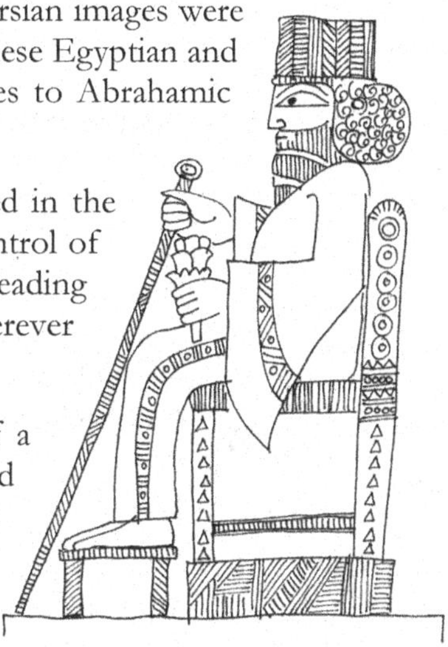

About 2300 years ago, Alexander of Macedon, educated in the Greek ways, set out to conquer the world. He seized control of Egypt and overthrew the Persian emperor. Intent on spreading Greek logos, he established cities named Alexandria wherever he went.

But eventually even Alexander succumbed to the idea of a single God-king who would bring different cultures and kingdoms under a single umbrella. He began to see himself as the unifying God-king, and his Egyptian and Persian subjects bowed to him. His own highly independent Greek companions, however, were not amused.

- The India that Alexander briefly encountered when he reached the banks of the Indus had many kingdoms, including tribal republics (jana-padas), the most powerful of which were located in the Gangetic plains. It was a world where there was tension between the world-affirming householders (yajamanas) and the world-renouncing hermits (shramanas).
- Shortly after Alexander left, India saw its first great imperial empire, that of the Mauryans, built on the Persian principle of central control, with its capital in Pataliputra in Magadha (modern-day Bihar). The first Mauryan emperor, Chandragupta, eventually renounced his throne and became a Jain monk. His grandson, Ashoka,

played a key role in popularizing the Buddhist monastic order.

- Buddhism, based on renunciation, meditation and pacifism, spread from India to Central Asia and South East Asia and eventually East Asia. Even the idea of liberation from the trap of unending rebirths reached Europe through trade routes. They influenced the monastic mystery cults of the Near East and Europe such as Orphism, Mithraism and eventually Christianity.
- Scholars believe that the Greeks introduced stone sculptures to India, however, the difference between Greek and Indian imagery is stark. Greek images are highly individualistic, asymmetrical, muscular, masculine, and the gods look imperious. Indian images are representational, symmetrical, soft, almost feminine and the gods smile and seem playful.

From Roman Empire to Holy Roman Empire

Interestingly, it was the Romans who took Greek thought to the next level. More realistic in its outlook, Rome was a city state in Italy that believed in democracy during peacetime and dictatorship during wartime. Like the Greeks, the Romans were contemptuous of the barbarians. Two thousand years ago, they established an empire that controlled the entire Mediterranean with a network of roads that allowed for the effective movement of troops to conquered lands and an efficient flow of wealth back to Rome.

Unlike the Greeks who frowned on the idea of central control and empire, the Romans sought consolidation and singularity. This happened in three phases.

In the first phase, which began nearly 2300 years ago, the Roman republic was made the centre of their world, and the idea of Rome deemed greater than any Roman citizen.

In the second phase, the Caesars made themselves permanent dictators of Rome, bypassing the democratic Roman senate, and functioned like the God-kings of yore. This happened 2000 years ago.

In the third phase that took place around 1700 years ago, when attacks from the wild Germanic tribes of the north forced the Caesars to move east to Byzantium (the 'new' Rome), the Caesar Constantine embraced Christian monotheism, wiping out all rival 'pagan' faiths.

The rise of the Holy Roman Empire, or Christendom, marked the end of a thousand years of Graeco-Roman civilization. The God of Abraham eclipsed both Greek mythos and Greek logos. The world was believed to be controlled by a personal deity, not impersonal meddlesome quarrelsome gods. Independent thinking was considered arrogant, and humility was demanded. The church became the controller and gatekeeper of all knowledge. Faith was seen as the sunlight and reason as the shadows. Later historians would call this period the Dark Ages. It would last a thousand years.

- As Christianity tightened its grip over Imperial Rome, India saw the rise of what is now called classical—Puranic—Hinduism, patronized by the Gupta kings of north India. In other words, as Greek mythology was replaced by Christian mythology in Europe, Vedic mythology transformed into Puranic mythology in India.
- The rise of Puranic Hinduism had a negative impact on the spread of Buddhism within the Indian subcontinent. As a monastic order, Buddhism did not see great value in worldly things. Puranic Hinduism, however, favoured the householder's life over the hermit's. Buddhist monasteries and caves gradually gave way to vast Hindu temple complexes, where art and culture flourished. Here, indulgence (bhoga) was as valued as restraint (yoga).
- India was known as the land of the golden sparrow because Indian merchants sought only gold from the rest of the world, which seemed to have an insatiable appetite for Indian textiles and spices.
- It is significant to note that around the same time that the Roman emperors turned Christian to prevent fragmentation of their empire, the Chinese emperors of the Sui dynasty turned to Buddhism to unify China.

From the Crusades to Enlightenment

Then, 1400 years ago, a new religion rose in Arabia—Islam. Like Christianity, it spoke of one God, Original Sin and redemption. But unlike Christianity, it saw Jesus not as the son of God, but as one of God's many prophets (another one allegedly being Alexander). The final prophet according to Islam was Muhammad, through whom the will of God was expressed and compiled in the holy book known as the Quran.

Islam spread rapidly across Persia, India, China, Africa and soon stood at the gates of Europe, via Spain. Here its march was halted and eventually reversed by the Christian leaders of Europe, who became part of what came to be known as the Western Roman Empire led by the Pope in Rome, distinct from the Eastern Roman Empire led by the emperor at Byzantium.

What followed were the Crusades, a war between the Christian and Muslim worlds, which came to a bloody end 500 years ago with the Muslims conquering Byzantium and putting an end to the Holy Roman Empire, and with it the Dark Ages.

The fall of Byzantium saw hordes of scholars and philosophers move westwards to Rome, bringing back with them the lost Greek knowledge along with revolutionary new Arab sciences. This led to the Renaissance or rediscovery of Greek ideas, and the Age of Enlightenment, which would change the world forever.

Now science was sunlight, and faith became the shadow. The authority of the church, the Pope and the Roman emperor was questioned. A single united Christendom gave way to the empires of the English, the French, the Germans and the Russians. By the eighteenth century, the idea of monarchy was being completely rejected, at first by the French Revolution and later by the formation of the United States of America.

Political change was accompanied by technological, and economic, change. European philosophers, inspired by early Arab thinkers, took Greek philosophy beyond matters of politics and society. Thus the sciences blossomed: physics, chemistry, biology, geology, botany, zoology and astronomy. A whole series of discoveries and inventions resulted in the Industrial Revolution. The printing press liberated knowledge from the control of the clergy. Sea routes were discovered. Factories were set up. Colonies were acquired. Old trading partners, such as India, gradually became the source of raw materials for the factories in Europe. Kings and their armies no longer controlled the world. Industrialists and business houses were now a force to reckon with.

- From about 1000 CE, warlords from Central Asia who had converted to Islam overran India, destroying what remained of Buddhism and shaking up Hinduism at its very foundations.
- Indians became increasingly more inward-looking: traders no longer travelled by seas to faraway lands, preferring to outsource all travel to Arabs; the status of women declined; the jati (caste) system became increasingly rigid and draconian, with some professions being considered 'purer' than others.
- Sanskrit, the language of the elite, found a strong rival in royal courts in Farsi, the language of the Persian aristocracy. This intermingling spurred an intellectual revolution: the rise of regional literature such as Hindi, Marathi, Odia, Assamese, Bengali, Tamil, Telugu, Kannada and Malayalam, and the amplification of bhakti, the discourse of passionate devotion that binds devotee to deity.
- When the Age of Enlightenment was dawning in Europe, the Mughals established their empire in India. While Europe became industrial, India remained agricultural.
- After the British overthrew the Mughals in the eighteenth century, they brought in railways and education. The railways served the same purpose as roads in the Roman Empire: enabling the colonizers to control the geography. The schools and colleges, besides creating clerks for their vast network of administrative offices, established a Western gaze in the minds of Indians, overshadowing the native gaze. The colonizers saw this as a noble act of civilizing the savages. India began to be explained using colonial templates.

From Imperialism to Nation States

Science focuses on facts and with more facts and more ways to make sense of them, scientific truth expands. Religious truth, however, remains static. Naturally, with scientific facts challenging fundamental assumptions about the material world, religious truth failed to satisfy. So scientists turned to Greek philosophers like Socrates, Plato and Aristotle for answers.

The rediscovery of Greek philosophy in Europe, however, was not accompanied by a resurgence of Greek mythology, except with a sense of nostalgia. People preferred the story of one God to the stories of many gods. This curious mixing of Greek philosophy and Christian theology resulted in a new wave of thinking that gave rise to what we now called secularism.

Secular philosophers, like the ancient Greeks, valued individual thinking, but unlike ancient Greeks, they insisted on equality and liberty of man, which were Christian values. Humanists like Kant, Rousseau and Hegel believed in the power of reason that enabled humans to break free from nature. But anti-humanists like Nietzsche, Marx and Freud questioned the very rationality of humanity, and attributed all actions to unconscious motives. If humanists defined cosmos, anti-humanists saw chaos in cosmos. Everything in life became 'problematic', a shadow, intensifying the yearning for sunlight.

In the march towards the twenty-first century, empires collapsed, colonies transformed into nation states, theories such as Evolution and the Big Bang emerged, atheism rose alongside science, technology, industrialization and capitalism, and religion came to be seen as the prime cause of fundamentalist terrorism. But seekers of social justice and human rights still function like evangelical missionaries, determined to convert the world, to drag people into the sunlight. There is talk of the 'good fight' for the 'good life'. But this quest for cosmos seems to be plunging the world further into chaos.

- In modern India, the educated elite views itself as a champion of logos and so rejects all things religious in the quest to be scientific and secular. They see the masses much as the Greeks viewed the barbarians: feudal, anti-democratic, favouring the mythos of either Hinduism or Islam. This has resulted in the infamous divide between 'India' and 'Bharat'. Bharat accuses India of being westernized, while India hopes that Bharat will be eventually modernized.

From Nation States to Globalization

Today, the West sees itself in a post-mythic, post-religious, post-structural modern world.

But the mythic eye does not agree.

Modernity firmly clings to the finite linear structure. In journalism as well as Hollywood movies, the hero myth dominates. The political discourse presents authority figures as overbearing Titans who need to be overthrown by young Olympians. Doctors look at disease as pathologies (monsters) to be overcome by medical and surgical intervention. Reaching a target in the world of business is considered an Olympian triumph. Technology is the new ambrosia, meant for all. The clash between humanists and anti-humanists, structuralists and post-structuralists mirrors the conflict between Apollonian clarity and Dionysian mysteries, over whom Zeus has to prevail.

This modern/secular/Greek worldview force-fits Hindu mythology into Greek or Christianity templates. Thus Hindu devas become 'phallic' like Hermes, and 'rapists' like Zeus, and asuras are explained as Christian demons, or Greek Titans. So the worldview establishes that India is in the shadows and in need of sunlight. It dismisses all talk of rebirth as mere superstition, failing to see the impact of this idea on the Indic mind.

Indic mythologies—Hindu, Buddhist and Jain—do not follow the linear structure that Greek storytellers (from chaos to cosmos) or Greek philosophers (from faith to reason) or Christian missionaries (from many gods to one God) or scientists and activists (from unjust feudal faith to fair egalitarian development) prefer. It has its own structure: a cyclical one.

Western mythology propagates the idea that the world is in need of changing, either by Greek heroes, or by Abrahamic prophets and kings, or by scientists, activists and capitalists. Indic mythology presents the idea that the world is constantly changing, human intervention notwithstanding. There are no heroes or villains, no oppressor or oppressed, no saviour or martyr, just different ways of looking at reality. That is why the West sees itself as masculine, active, decisive, violent and straightforward, and qualifies Indic ideas as feminine, passive, ambiguous, non-violent yet cunning.

In terms of the 'allegory of the cave', Indian sages valued the sunlight outside as well as the shadows inside. What is sunlight for some people will be shadows for others. If one is in sunlight in one context, one is in the shadows in another. The seeker is therefore encouraged to observe with empathy—rather than argue with—contrary points of view. Here, subjectivity is given as much value as objectivity, and the journey is towards plurality, not singularity. The point is not to replace false knowledge with true knowledge; the point is to expand the mind to accommodate all kinds of knowledge.

The West dismisses the Indic worldview as chaos, thus closing its mind to any new possibility but its own. Not surprisingly, there are many books by Western scholars that 'explain' Hindu mythology, but very few by Indian scholars that bother to 'observe' Western mythology.

This book is an attempt to bridge that gap.

I do not claim objectivity; I am comfortable with subjectivity and well aware of my Indian gaze. I do not fear the shadows, but I do not claim the sunlight either. I simply present my truth of Greek myths and hope it enriches, and expands, your truth. So read this book keeping in mind:

Within infinite myths lies an eternal truth
Who sees it all?
Varuna has but a thousand eyes
Indra a hundred
You and I, only two.

- The common sources of Greek mythology come from a period stretching a thousand years from the rise of the Greek city states until the transformation of the Roman Empire into the Holy Roman Empire. These sources include:
    - The ancient Greek epics of Homer (*Iliad* and *Odyssey*) and Hesiod (*Theogony*), and the Homeric hymns to the gods dating back to the seventh century BCE.
    - The now-lost Epic Cycle which included *Cypria* (the story from the marriage of Peleus till the wrath of Achilles), *Aethiopis* (the story from the death of Hector, through the attack by the Amazons and the Ethiopians, till the funeral games to mark the fall of Achilles), *Little Iliad* (which tells the story of Philoctetes and ends with the Trojan Horse), *Iliupersis* (the story of the sack of Troy), *Nostoi* (the story of the return of the Greek heroes) and *Telegony* (the story of Telegonus, Odysseus's son by the witch Circe).
    - The classical Greek plays of Euripides, Aeschylus and Sophocles dating back to the fourth century BCE as well as the writings of Greek scholars such as Herodotus, Plutarch, Pausanias and Apollodorus.
    - Roman writings, in Latin, such as Ovid's *Metamorphosis*, Virgil's *Aeneid*, Hyginus's *Fabulae* and Pseudo-Apollodorus's *Bibliotheca* composed circa the first and second centuries CE.
    - *Posthomerica* by Quintus of Smyrna, written in the fourth century CE, tells us many tales of the latter part of the Trojan War.
    - Greek mythology has been a common source of metaphors and allegories for European, and later American, poets.

PROLOGUE

The Greek Conquest

The soldiers refused to march forward. They had conquered Anatolia, Mesopotamia, Levant, Egypt, Persia and Gandhara, and were now camped on the banks of the River Indus. They were tired. They wanted to turn back before the lands they had captured devoured them.

The adventure had consumed Alexander, anyway, hadn't it? He was no longer the young Greek lad who had set out on his conquest. Now, painted in Eastern colours, wearing Eastern robes, he seemed no different from the distant, imperious God-king of Persia, surrounded by fawning courtiers. No, they would not indulge his madness any more. Enough had been done to earn him a place on Olympus. It was time to go home.

Word of these rumblings reached Alexander. 'That naked man is to blame!' his spies revealed. 'He sits on a rock staring at the sky and stars, doing nothing all day and all night. And when approached *he* asks questions. He has poisoned the soldiers' minds with strange ideas.'

Alexander's teacher, Aristotle, had told him of such men who roamed in marketplaces and questioned people, compelling them to reflect on life and their assumptions. Aristotle's teacher, Plato, had been a student of one such man—Socrates. Such men were dangerous. They threatened the social order. They were often killed. As Socrates was.

Alexander decided to investigate. He did not fear such men. He respected them. How can one man disarm an entire army, turn them away from dreams of glory, he wondered.

'What is his name?' he enquired.

The spies said, 'Unlike you, King, who became great by acquiring land, this man, and others like him, have become great by giving up everything, their lands, crowns, families, horses, cows, jewels, weapons, and even their names.'

A few days later, before dawn, without informing anyone, Alexander slipped out of his tent dressed as a commoner, and went to visit this strange person he had heard so much of. He found the man on the riverbank, naked, atop a rock, staring at the sky and the stars. He looked no older than the Greek king. But was he wise? Only that would make him a gymnosophist, a naked wise man, one of the many who wandered alone in the forests of India, about whom much was said across Gandhara and Persia. Legend had it that they could walk on water and float on air.

'What are you doing?' asked Alexander, hoping the man was familiar with his language.

'Experiencing nothingness,' said the gymnosophist, in a tongue that Alexander could understand. Alexander was impressed.

'And you? What are you doing?' asked the gymnosophist.

'Conquering the world,' replied Alexander.

'Why?'

'To be great. To be remembered for eternity. To earn a place with the gods on Mount Olympus.'

'What is Mount Olympus?' asked the gymnosophist, leaning forward, his eyes sparkling with curiosity. He loved stories.

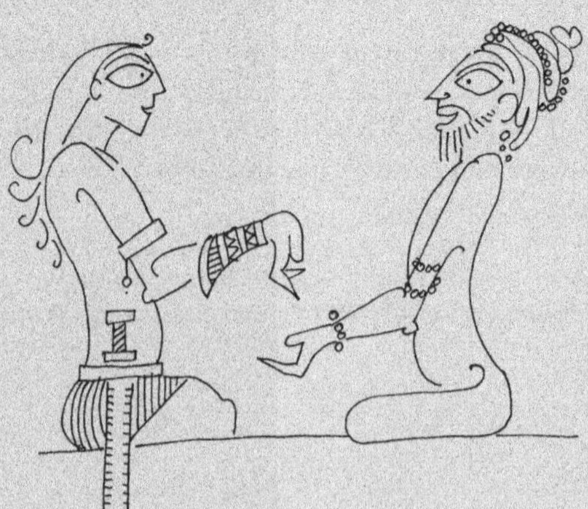

Monsoon clouds hovered above. In the distance, one could hear the trumpeting of an elephant. The sky was red, waiting for the sun. A peacock quivered in excitement. An Upanishad was about to happen between a warrior and a sage.

The battle-scarred conqueror of the world, with golden hair, transformed into a storyteller and retold tales he had heard long ago from his mother and father, servants, slaves, soldiers and tutors.

- Jain mythology speaks of three kinds of great men: the Vasudevas (heroes), the Chakravartis (kings) and the Tirthankaras (sages). Alexander mirrors a violent Vasudeva, who aspires to be a Chakravarti, a universal emperor who controls the world with his rules. The gymnosophist mirrors, or aspires to be, a Tirthankara, the sage who sees the world for what it is, in its entirety, without the desire to control it.
- Although there is little doubt that Alexander interacted with philosophers wherever he went, including India, the content of those conversations could be a later invention. Were they Jain sages, Buddhist monks, Hindu yogis? We will never know, and can only speculate.
- In India, Alexander the Great (or his representative Onesicritus) had an interview with local sages including one Dandamis (Danda-pani?), who lived near Taxila. A sage called Calanus (Kalyana?), a student of Dandamis, followed the conqueror to the West, where he died. The story of the interview and of Calanus's death are described in several sources, such as the *Anabasis of Alexander* by the Greek author Arrian of Nicomedia.
- Greek and later Roman writings describe Indian sages or gymnosophists mostly as naked and living without possessions in the forest. This leads one to conclude that they were probably shramanas or forest ascetics who gave up household life and spent all their time meditating, contemplating, and trying to overcome desires. Dandamis and Calanus could have been Vedic tapasvins, yogis, siddhas, or Jain munis or even Buddhist bhikkus.
- Porphyrus, a Roman scholar who wrote five centuries after Alexander, classified gymnosophists into two categories: the Brachmanes (brahmins?), who received knowledge from a divine source and whose leaders were appointed by other leaders, and the Shamaneans (shramanas?) who elected leaders and strove for knowledge.
- Nothingness or 'shunya' is a key concept in Buddhist thought, just as infinity or 'ananta' is a key concept in Hindu thought. From these philosophical ideas emerged the concept of zero and infinity that reached Europe by the tenth century via Arab culture. It led to a flowering of the subject we now call calculus.

BOOK ONE

Zeus

'Mount Olympus,' began Alexander, 'is where the earth touches the sky. There sits Zeus, my father, king of the gods, who rides eagles, hurls thunderbolts, and holds aloft a pair of scales to ensure there is always balance and justice in the world.'

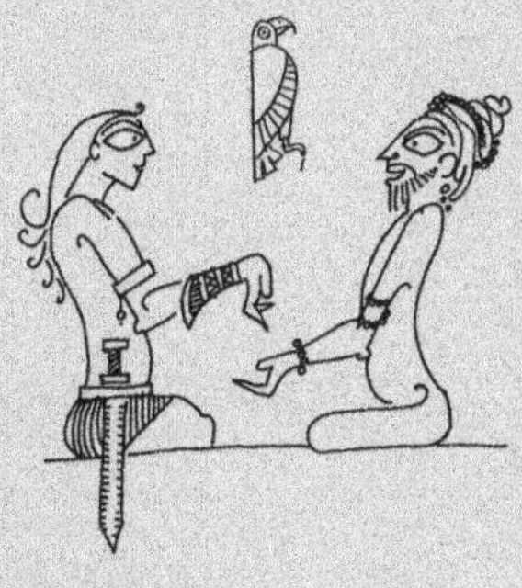

Uranus

In the beginning there was chaos: a gaping void full of darkness.

Then came Gaia, the goddess, who is earth and the arena of life.

Out of Gaia came Uranus, the starry sky. He became her lover and lay above her, clinging firmly to her.

Together Gaia and Uranus produced many children. But they were all hideous and malformed: the Hecantonchires who had a hundred hands, and the Cyclopes who had only one eye. Uranus would not let them out of Gaia's womb as they disgusted him. Then he fathered the beautiful Titans, twelve in number, but they made him insecure. And so he clung to Gaia even more firmly, refusing to let any child leave the mother's womb.

An exasperated Gaia gave the Titans a knife of flint and told them to castrate their father. None dared, except Cronus. He cut off his father's genitals, slipped out of his mother's womb, causing the sky and the earth to separate, and then cast his father's genitals into the sea.

With Cronus, time began. He would end things and start them anew.

Blood spurted from Uranus's wound. It spilled into the ocean and sprouted angry Giants and vengeful Furies, who punish crimes against fathers and mothers. The agitated bloodstained waters became foamy. From that foam emerged Aphrodite, the goddess of love, who unites the separated. With her came her son, the winged Eros, who shoots arrows of desire, and makes you long for the future and the past.

- In Hindu mythology, there is no movement from chaos to order. Nothing is permanent, neither chaos nor order; they follow each other with cyclical regularity. Our world emerges when we wake up and dissolves when we sleep, an idea presented through the story of the sleeping Vishnu.
- The Greek story of creation is traced to the epic *Theogony* (birth of the gods) by Hesiod, dating back to the seventh century BCE. This was the same time that the Upanishads were being composed in the Gangetic plains of India.
- In the creation stories of Orphic traditions, a lot of importance is given to Eros, the god of love. Scholars have linked this to Vedic hymns that refer to kama or desire as the origin of things, which takes people out of the void and darkness.
- The Greeks were clear that the origin was chaos and the purpose of the world was a movement towards order: hence the journey from chaos, through darkness and light; from Gaia and Uranus, through malformed beings towards the Titans and then the Olympians, who in turn create mortal beings with the ability to reason. These human beings are capable of overthrowing the gods—and hence comes religion.
- The separation of the sky and the earth is a key theme in many mythologies. Just as Cronus separates Uranus and Gaia in Greek mythology, Indra separates Dyaus and Prithvi in Vedic mythology.

Cronus

Cronus imprisoned his malformed brothers, the one-eyed and the hundred-armed ones, in the dark void that is Tartarus, and made himself leader of the Titans. Having thus removed all ugliness and disorderliness, he went about organizing the world and encouraged his siblings to do the same.

Titan brothers married Titan sisters. From the union of Hyperion and Theia came Helios, the sun, Selene, the moon, and Eos, the dawn.

Oceanus circled the earth, and with Tethys, he gave birth to the various rivers and streams of earth.

But when Cronus married Rhea, Gaia warned him that his children would overthrow him as he had done to his father. Consumed by fear and ambition, Cronus devoured every child that Rhea gave birth to: three daughters and two sons.

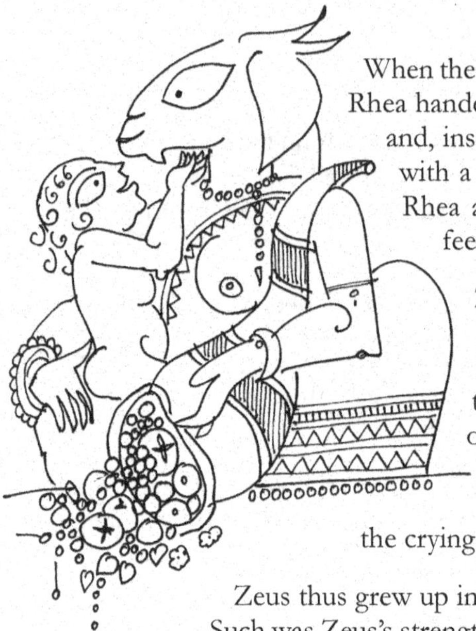

When the sixth child, Zeus, was born, an exasperated Rhea handed him over to the forest nymphs to raise, and, instead of the infant, presented her husband with a rock. Cronus, who paid little attention to Rhea anyway, swallowed the stone and burped, feeling very secure.

Zeus was placed in a cradle that hung from the branches of a tree. Suspended between earth, sea and sky he was invisible to Cronus. The dancing Kouretes, devotees of Rhea, made so much noise striking their swords to their shields and stamping their feet on the ground that Cronus never heard the crying of baby Zeus.

Zeus thus grew up in secret, on the milk of the goat Amalthea. Such was Zeus's strength that one day he broke one of Amalthea's horns, which became the horn of plenty, or the cornucopia. When Amalthea died, Zeus stretched her hide to make his shield, the Aegis.

- Chronus is identified as Saturn in Roman mythology. He is time, visualized as the Grim Reaper, or death. This connects him with Shani in Hindu mythology, associated with obstacles and delayed beginnings.
- The horn of plenty of Greek mythology becomes the always overflowing vessel, the Akshaya-patra, in Hindu mythology.
- The Titans are imagined as creating more order in the world, giving rise to new shapes and forms, from the otherwise malformed and amorphous bog that existed before. Thus, with each generation, there is a movement away from chaos and confusion towards order and clarity.
- The theme of a child threatened by his own father and so raised in secret occurs frequently in Greek mythology; Zeus's story is the first instance of this. The story of Krishna also speaks of threats to the infant Krishna from a father figure, his maternal uncle Kansa. Krishna's story was first found in the Harivamsa, composed around 400 CE, following exposure to the Yavanas or Indo-Greeks who followed Alexander and had great influence in the north-western part of India.
- Amalthea the goat is sometimes identified with the constellation Capricorn.

Zeus

When Zeus came of age, he decided to rescue his brothers. He disguised himself as a cup-bearer and offered Cronus a drink that made him vomit. Out came the rock that had been consumed in place of Zeus, followed by all the children Rhea had borne: the sons, Poseidon and Hades, and the daughters, Hestia, Demeter and Hera. They were all alive.

Though the youngest, Zeus led his brothers and sisters in a war against their father. Taken by surprise, Cronus was defeated easily and locked away in Tartarus. The victorious Zeus declared himself king and made Mount Olympus his home, which is why his siblings and he came to be known as Olympians.

Some Titans, led by Atlas, challenged the rule of Zeus. Others, like Prometheus and Epimetheus, did not, choosing instead to support Zeus. Prometheus could

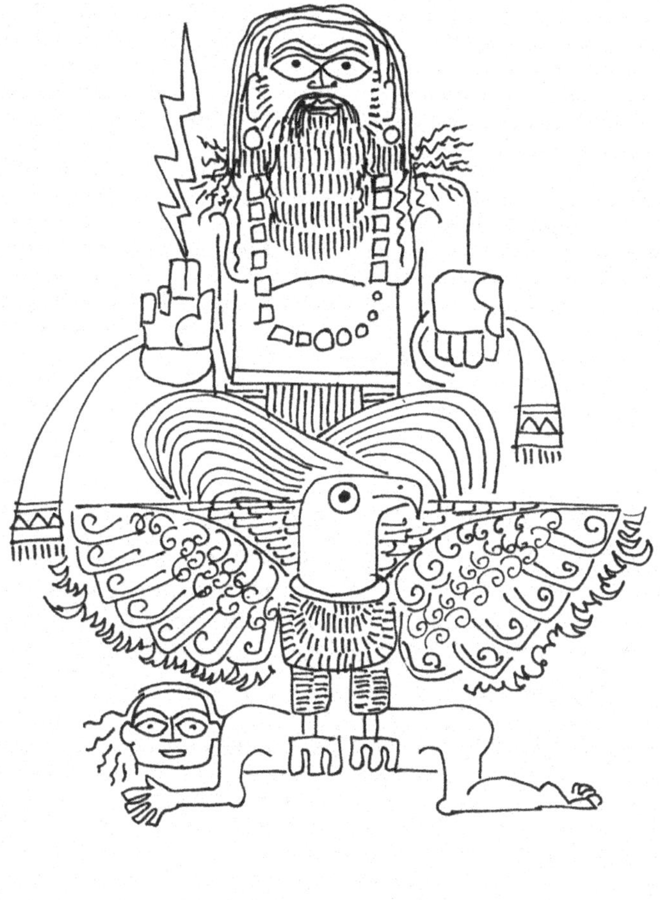

see the future, and knew that eventually Zeus would be triumphant. Atlas did not believe him, and declared war on the Olympians. This fight came to be known as Titanomachy.

In this great and very long battle, the Olympians prevailed, thanks to the thunderbolt that the Cyclopes fashioned for Zeus. The Cyclopes had never forgiven the Titans for imprisoning them and they pledged their allegiance to Zeus who liberated them.

The vanquished Titans were also cast into Tartarus. Their leader, Atlas, was made to carry the sky on his shoulders for all eternity.

- That Prometheus can see the future indicates that the ancient Greeks believed the future was predetermined. This is reinforced by the idea of prophecy. Future-gazing happens in Hindu mythology through astrology, Jyotisha-shastra.
- When European Orientalists were first exposed to the Vedas and the Puranas and read tales of war, they looked for parallels to Greek myths. They assumed that the asuras, enemies of the devas, were Titans, and that Indra, the king of the devas, was Zeus. But unlike the Titans, who are defeated and locked forever in Tartarus, the defeat of the asuras is not permanent, just as the victory of the devas is not everlasting. The Titan–Olympian war evokes a linear theme with an end while the deva–asura war evokes a cyclical theme with no final outcome.
- Tartarus is the dark void that existed before Gaia and so is chaos of chaos, and is used as a dungeon by Cronus first, and then Zeus, to confine all those who threaten their reign and disobey their rules. Eventually, it becomes the template for the Hell of Christian mythology and the Jahannum of Islamic mythology. Such a concept is not found in Hindu mythology.

Typhon

Gaia did not like the way the Olympians treated the Titans. So she created a terrifying monster called Typhon, the very embodiment of chaos, to destroy Zeus. Terrified of this creature, the gods took the form of animals and ran away. Hera turned into a cow; Aphrodite and Eros turned into a school of fish. Zeus turned into a boar and charged at Typhon. While the others ran, he stood his ground and fought the monster, hurling thunderbolts at it.

Following the defeat of Typhon, Gaia goaded some Giants, born of the blood of

Uranus, to attack Olympus. They piled mountain upon mountain and laid siege to the abode of Zeus and his siblings. But eventually Zeus broke the siege, cast the Giants into Tartarus, and became the undisputed master of the world.

Gaia then tried to poison the minds of Zeus's brother Poseidon and his sister Hera against him, but Zeus warned them against questioning his authority. In a voice that boomed across the three worlds he warned, 'If you try to pull me down from the sky, know that I will pull the earth and sea towards the sky and leave you dangling in the wind.' The Olympians never even thought of rebellion again. Zeus became overlord of the cosmos.

Gaia became quiet and distant and was eventually forgotten.

- In the Rig Veda, Indra defeats the monster Vritra. In the Jaiminiya Brahmana, there are tales of how Indra sends Kutsa to seduce and defeat the lustful ogress Dirgha-jivhi, who steals the sacred soma. These stories speak of the archetypal Indo-European hero, mirroring the acts of Greek gods and heroes. However, in Puranic times, the Goddess is the all-powerful mother of the gods, sought by Indra to defeat his enemies, the asuras.

- There are many versions of the defeat of Typhon by Zeus. In one version, the Fates feed the monster mortal food and make it weak. In another version, the monster tears away the sinews of Zeus and immobilizes him. The hero, Cadmus, distracts Typhon with the music of his pipes enabling Zeus to recover his sinews, and hence his mobility and strength, in time to destroy Typhon. Typhon is ultimately buried under the volcanic Mount Etna.
- The defeat of Typhon by Zeus mirrors the Mesopotamian epic *Enuma Elish* where Marduk defeats the monster-goddess Tiamat. It marks the end of the era of the Goddess and the rise of the patriarchal gods.
- There is an earlier version of creation, when the Goddess dominated human culture. According to this, Eurynome, the Goddess, rose from chaos, separated earth from sky, danced naked on the waters, rubbed her palms with the wind, created the serpent Ophion, mated with it and became pregnant. She then turned into a dove and laid an egg. Ophion coiled around the egg until it hatched. From the egg emerged the cosmos, the various celestial bodies. But Ophion claimed to be the creator of the world, and Eurynome banished him.
- The worship of the Goddess as the embodiment of nature is explicit only in the later phase of Hinduism, with the writing of the Devi Purana and the rise of Tantra around 700 CE. However, from Vedic times, nature is held in regard, not feared. While nature (prakriti) is seen as chaos in Greek mythology, in Hindu myths it is seen as different from culture (sanskriti), but not inferior to it. Nature is the mother (Kali), and culture is the daughter (Gauri) of humanity (Brahma).

Olympus

Zeus and his two brothers, Poseidon and Hades, divided the cosmos between them—everything except their grandmother Gaia.

Seated atop Mount Olympus, Zeus made himself the ruler of the sky, watching over the earth, hurling thunderbolts from time to time. Poseidon declared himself the ruler of the sea and the rivers, occasionally causing earthquakes. Hades became the ruler of the underworld, claiming all those who died.

Hestia, the elder sister of Zeus, became the goddess of the hearth; Demeter the goddess of life-giving grain; and Hera the goddess of the household.

With roles so clearly defined, the Olympians celebrated by eating ambrosia and drinking nectar.

- The concept of three worlds is found in most mythologies. In the Vedas, there is talk of the earth, sky and the atmosphere in between. The Puranas speak of the earth (Bhu-loka), the paradise of the gods (Swarga-loka) and the subterranean realms of the asuras and nagas (Patala-loka). In the Bible, there is earth, Heaven and Hell.
- In Roman mythology, Zeus is known as Jupiter, Hades is called Pluto and Poseidon is Neptune.
- While the world is divided amongst the Olympian gods, it is clear there is no such thing as god of earth. Earth is a goddess linked to various female divinities like Gaia, Rhea and Demeter, even Hecate. With Demeter responsible for grain, Hestia for the hearth and Hera for the household, we see the rise of human culture, and the roles assigned to women.
- Just as the Olympians have a tense relationship with the Titans, Zeus has a tense relationship with Poseidon and Hades. Consumed by envy, Poseidon causes storms and earthquakes. Similarly envious, Hades does not let the dead return to the land of the living.
- Olympus serves as the central axis of the world, the Axis Mundi, like Mount Meru or Mount Kailasa in the Hindu Puranas.
- In Hindu mythology, Yama is the ruler of the dead. He is the first human to die without leaving behind an offspring and so is eternally trapped in the land of the dead, unlike Hades who chooses to be ruler of the land of the dead.
- Hades is considered rich, as he collects tax from the dead before letting them enter the land of the dead. Coins are placed on the eyes and mouth of the dead before cremating them. In Hindu funeral rituals too, coins are sometimes placed in the hands of the dead.
- Thanatos, the god of death, is different from Hades, the ruler of the dead, just as Mrityu, the goddess of death in Hindu mythology, needs to be distinguished from Yama, the ruler of the dead.
- Unlike Hindu mythology, where there is a paranoid fear of death, and hence a yearning for amrita, the nectar of immortality that the devas possess, Greek mythology shows no such obsession. Such yearning for immortality is found in Mesopotamian mythology too, in the *Epic of Gilgamesh*. Greek heroes, however, show no such craving. Immortality is reserved for the gods, mortality for humans. The Greek way of coping with the fear of death is to live an extraordinary life that would inspire bards to compose epics. The other way is to have children, an idea encouraged by Hindu dharma-shastras too.

Iris and Arke

There were two sisters, daughters of Titans, who spanned the three worlds, from the skies above through the seas below right down to the underworld of the dead. They were Iris and Arke. Both had wings, and they took the form of rainbows.

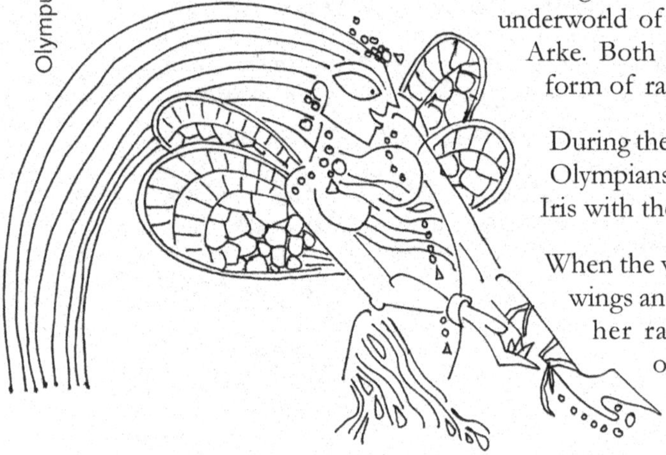

During the war between the Titans and the Olympians, Arke sided with the Titans and Iris with the Olympians.

When the war ended, Zeus tore off Arke's wings and cast her into Tartarus, causing her rainbow to fade. That is why only one rainbow is seen in the sky. The winged Iris became the messenger of the gods, whispering in the ears of heroes, kings and queens, reminding them constantly never to upset the Olympians.

- In Hindu mythology, the rainbow is called Indra-dhanush, or the bow of Indra, the sky god.
- Narada, the sage who travels between the three worlds of Hindu mythology, is popular as the gossipmonger and instigator of quarrels.
- This clear divide between old and new gods, the rejection of the old and the celebration of the new, is absent in Hindu mythology. All Hindu gods intermingle and become part of the same system.

Cybele

Once, Zeus lay on a bed of grass. And while sleeping he spilt his semen on the grass. A strange creature sprang out: it had both male and female genitalia and called itself Agdistis. Unnerved by its form, the Olympians cut out its male genitals and turned the androgynous Agdistis into the goddess Cybele.

The male genitals fell on the ground and turned into an almond tree. The daughter of a local river god ate the almonds and became pregnant and gave birth to a handsome man called Attis.

When Attis was on his way to wed the princess of Phrygia, Cybele saw him and fell in love with him. Determined not to let him marry another woman, she drove him mad. At the wedding ceremony, Attis picked up a knife and castrated himself and died as a result of the bleeding.

Cybele then restored Attis to life, and made him her consort.

- The idea of a sage or a god spilling semen on the earth and thereby fathering a child is a recurring theme in Hindu mythology as well. In the Mahabharata, Drona is born when his father spills his semen in a pot at the sight of a nymph.
- The Shiva Purana refers to Ardhanareshwara, God who is half-woman, evoking the primal androgynous being.
- The hijras of India often castrate themselves in the name of a rooster-riding goddess identified as Bahuchara Mata of Gujarat. Does this have anything to do with the Galli, the eunuch-priests of Cybele? We can only speculate.

- Cybele is linked to Gaia, Rhea, Demeter, Hecate, even the oracle. By making her a child of Zeus, this story makes her subservient to him.
- The cult of Cybele originated in Anatolia (modern-day Turkey) and spread through Greece to Rome where she came to be known as Magna Mater (the Great Mother). It is the ancient Mother Goddess cult.
- Information about Cybele comes from many sources. The earliest are Homeric hymns to the mother of gods. These hymns date back to the seventh century BCE and are attributed to Homer as they follow the same metre and style as his epics.
- In Goddess worship, the male is subservient, merely a seed-provider and protector. The female is sacred as she bears children, the next generation. Here fertility is power, indicating a time when humans were still at the mercy of the elements and not proficient in agriculture or animal breeding.
- The theme of men and women originating from a primal androgynous being is a common theme in many mythologies. In some translations, the first being created by the God of Abraham was Adam, who was androgynous, and who became male when Eve was pulled out of him.

Graces and Muses

Zeus lay with many women: Titan, Olympian, nymph, even mortal. On each, he fathered children, who were destined to be either gods or heroes.

On Eurynome, Zeus fathered the three Graces, to fill the world with good cheer. These three women were often seen dancing naked around Aphrodite and Eros.

On Mnemosyne, Zeus fathered the nine Muses, who inspired poets and artists and writers to compose works of art and music and theatre and stories to help people forget their miseries and feel joy and hope. Strange that the daughters of 'memory' would enable the production of artworks that helped people 'forget'.

Thus from Zeus came the idea of good times and creativity.

- In Hindu mythology, Saraswati embodies the Muses while Lakshmi embodies the Graces. The damsels known as apsaras are both symbols of good cheer as well as muses for artists.
- Zeus can be linked to Kashyapa, son of Brahma, who has many wives, through whom he populates the world.
- Zeus is visualized as riding an eagle and hurling thunderbolts. In Hindu mythology too, Indra hurls thunderbolts and is closely associated with the sky and rain. But unlike Zeus, he is not a father figure or ruler. It is Vishnu who rides an eagle, like Zeus, and is more like the guardian of the world. Like him, Zeus is visualized as charismatic and cunning and strong, and his consort, Lakshmi, is seen as a combination of Hera and Demeter. Interestingly, there is no concept of avatars in Greek mythology: Olympians do not take birth on earth in mortal forms.
- Muses were differentiated from each other based on what they held in their hands: a stylus, lyre, flute, globe and compass, tragic mask, comic mask, laurel wreath, scroll and veil.
- Hymen, the god of marriage, was the son of a Muse. If he did not attend a wedding, the wedding would have no inspiration and was expected to end disastrously.

Horai and Morai

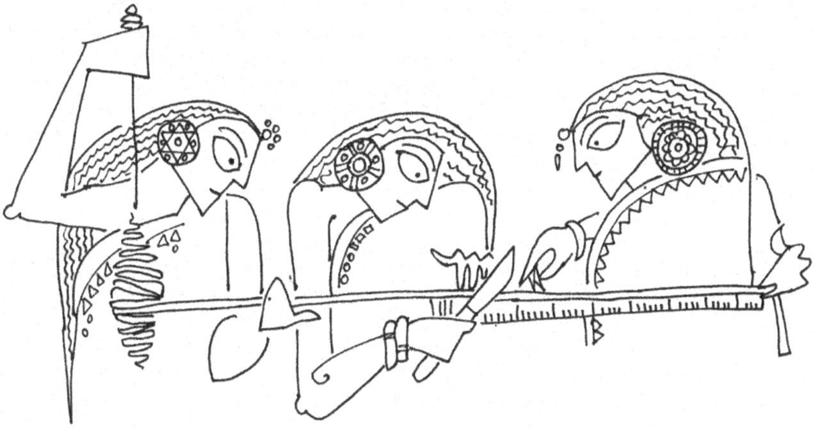

On Themis, the Titan goddess of order, Zeus fathered the Horai and the Morai.

The Horai were three in number: Eunomania who brought law, Dike who brought justice, and Irene who brought peace.

The Morai, or the Fates, were three in number who determined the fate of all beings: Clotho spun the thread of life, Lachesis measured it, and Atropos cut it, thus determining mortality.

Thus from Zeus came the idea of fairness as well as the idea of fate.

- In Hindu mythology, the role of the Fates is played by Shasthi, known as Satavai in folklore, who visits children on the sixth day after their birth and writes their fate on their forehead. But this is seen as part of 'desi parampara' or folk tradition, not 'margi parampara' or classical tradition, where fate is determined by karma, our own deeds.
- In Hindu mythology, Brahma chases his own daughter, Saraswati, like Zeus who pursues his own sisters. However, Brahma's tryst does not refer to creation of the world, but to the enchantment of the creator with his own creation.
- Why does Zeus have so many wives? This has been answered in many ways. The allegorical reason states that Zeus marries Metis (intelligence) and Themis (justice) to imbibe their qualities. The historical reason states that Zeus embodies patriarchy while the goddesses and nymphs he ravishes embody matriarchy. The etiological reason is that great heroes born of mortal women owe their greatness to their divine father Zeus.
- Nike, the winged one with golden sandals, daughter of Zeus, was the goddess of victory who placed the laurel wreath on the winner. In Roman mythology, she was called Victoria.
- In Roman mythology, Dike is called Justitia. She is visualized as blindfolded, holding scales in one hand and a sword in the other. She became the symbol of justice. The scales were also associated with the zodiac sign Libra, often used by Zeus at wartime to figure out which side had been decreed to win by the Fates. Dike who lived on earth in the Golden Age, left the earth when humans became corrupted and no longer cared for justice.
- It is debatable whether Zeus controls the Fates or submits to the Fates. In the course of Greek mythology, Zeus became the supreme controller and dispenser of justice, a forerunner to the Christian Jehovah.

Athena

Zeus pursued and made love to Metis, the Titan goddess, who had concocted the potion that made Cronus vomit. But when he learned that the child she would bear him would overthrow him, Zeus swallowed Metis whole as soon as she became pregnant.

Some time later, Zeus had a terrible headache, his head burst open and out came Athena, the goddess of crafts and wisdom. Since she had been delivered by Zeus, not Metis, Athena owed allegiance to him, and would not overthrow him. She swore to her father that she would never take a man for her husband and would serve him as a loyal daughter, ensuring his rule. Metis remained inside Zeus's body giving him good advice from within.

Though wise and patient, like all Olympians, Athena did not tolerate rivals. Once, she heard of the princess Arachne who claimed she could weave cloth better than Athena. So the goddess challenged her to a tapestry-weaving contest. The two sat at two looms and began weaving tapestries, each telling a story—Athena

of foolish mortals who dared to challenge the gods, and Arachne of vain gods who abused mortals. Both creations were equally good and so an angry Athena grudgingly accepted defeat, but then cursed Arachne that she would turn into a spider and spin webs for all eternity.

- In Hindu mythology, a child not born from the womb of a woman was called 'ayonija' and was considered special. Athena too can be called ayonija. Her rejection of sex and the pursuit of wisdom and skills mirrors the belief that household 'feminine' work is removed from knowledge and the arts. The wise sage, male or female, is expected to be celibate. Unlike Durga and Lakshmi, who are associated with power and wealth respectively, Saraswati, the goddess of knowledge, is rarely associated with the household, making her closest to Athena.
- The word arachnophobia, or fear of spiders, comes from the tale of Arachne, the princess who was turned into a spider by Athena.
- Metis embodies intelligence. By swallowing her, Zeus internalizes intelligence, which complements his brute strength by which he overpowered the Titans. This makes him a worthy leader of the Olympians.
- The denial of sexuality distinguishes some Olympian goddesses who are born of Zeus from those who were born before or with Zeus, and who celebrate their sexuality. Athena belongs to the former category: she is associated with skill and strategy but is also considered a virgin. Aphrodite and Hera belong to the latter category.
- Athena is strongly associated with the city, especially Athens. Scholars are divided on the issue of whether the name Athena is derived from Athens, or if Athens comes from Athena.
- Athena is visualized with armour: a spear and shield with the image of a Gorgon (a maiden's head with serpents for hair) and an owl on her shoulders. The owl sees all with its round eyes.
- She is often called Pallas Athena. Pallas was her childhood friend whom she accidentally killed while learning to use the sword.

Demeter and Persephone

On Demeter, Zeus fathered Persephone, who was so beautiful that she caught the attention of lonely Hades, ruler of the land of the dead. When her mother was not watching, he abducted her and took her across the River Styx, far from the land of the living, and made her his queen.

Demeter should have been happy, but she could not bear the separation from her daughter and begged Zeus to bring her back. Until Persephone was returned to her, the goddess vowed not to let any plant bear leaves or flowers or fruit.

Zeus had to use his immense powers of persuasion to make Hades release Persephone. 'She can leave provided she has not consumed anything from the land of the dead,' grunted Hades.

Unfortunately, Persephone had consumed a few pomegranate seeds while in the land of the dead. And so it was declared that for half the year she would stay with her husband, Hades, and for the rest of the year with her mother, Demeter.

- In Hindu Puranas, the earth is called Bhu-devi and all vegetation are her children, thus she is both Gaia and Demeter.
- In Europe, winter marks the great shift in seasons while in India, it is the monsoon that forms the seasonal turning point. Winter is explained as the abduction of Demeter's daughter by Hades while the monsoon is explained as Indra making love to the earth with rain and thunderbolts.
- Demeter is the goddess of the harvest. In Rome, she was called Ceres.
- Persephone, the crop, is her daughter, who rises up during harvest time but goes away in wintertime. She is depicted holding ears of corn in her hands. She is linked to the zodiac sign Virgo.
- Along with Hecate, Demeter and Persephone form the Triple Goddess: the crone, the mother and the virgin. The Triple Goddess played a key role in ancient Greek agricultural mysteries, before the rise of the Olympians.
- Demeter is never portrayed with a consort with one exception: Iasion, who lay with her, but was killed by Zeus's thunderbolt.

Poseidon

Poseidon was not very happy about ruling merely the seas. He wanted to rule the earth too, or at least some parts of it, maybe a few islands or the coastline of continents. But no matter how hard he tried, he failed. Corinth worshipped Helios, the sun god; Argos preferred Hera, the goddess of the household; and Athens venerated Athena because she gave them the olive tree, while all Poseidon gave them was salt water.

Poseidon created horses that could run like the waves on the sea, but still he did not become the preferred Olympian. And so he swore to make life difficult for everyone who lived on earth by causing earthquakes on land and storms in the sea.

He finally married Amphitrite, a sea nymph, but she avoided his company until she was convinced to change her mind by a dolphin.

Like Zeus, he often slipped out of the sea and made love to women on the shores, especially those who loved to play with seawater and pour its foam between their thighs.

Once, Poseidon made love to a young woman named Caenis and offered her anything she desired. Caenis asked that she be turned into a man. Poseidon granted her wish, turning Caenis into Caeneus, and also gave her skin that could not be penetrated by weapons. The centaurs mocked Caeneus on learning of his female origin. When they could not kill him with weapons, they crushed him under a pile of tree trunks.

- Poseidon's counterpart in Hindu mythology is Varuna who rides a dolphin, or a sea monster called makara. Varuna, father of Lakshmi, the goddess of wealth, is considered the most generous of gods, who gives humans salt and fish and seeks nothing in turn. He lacks Poseidon's cantankerous nature and has more in common with the older sea gods such as Pontus and Oceanus.
- Poseidon is depicted as holding a trident in his hand and riding waves as if they were horses or dolphins.
- In the Roman pantheon Poseidon is known as Neptune.
- The philosopher Plato tells the story of how Poseidon fathered a son, Atlas, on the mortal girl Cleito. Atlas established Atlantis which tried to conquer Athens but failed as the latter was a well-ordered city, while the people of Atlantis eventually let their avaricious human side overshadow their disciplined divine side.

Hera

Zeus took his sister, Hera, as his wife, and made her queen of Olympus. She gave him many children. There was Hebe, the goddess who serves nectar and makes everyone happy, and Eris, the goddess of strife who causes quarrels and makes everyone unhappy. There was Ares, the handsome god of war, and Hephaestus, the ugly and deformed god of craftsmanship.

Hera did not like Hephaestus because he was born with malformed feet, and cast him out of Olympus soon after his birth. He fell to the earth, and was tended by nymphs. He grew up teaching himself the art of creating instruments and artefacts out of stone, wood and metal. One day, he crafted a throne and invited all the Olympians to sit on it. Everyone admired its beauty, and the comfort it offered. However, when Hera sat on it, the chair folded upon itself and trapped Hera. Hephaestus refused to free her until she apologized for casting him away. Hera had no choice but to apologize.

- In Hindu mythology, Gauri, the domesticated form of Kali, embodies the goddess of the household. She domesticates Shiva and turns the hermit into a householder. Gauri often quarrels with him when she finds him paying undue attention to her handmaidens, but she lacks Hera's vindictiveness. Hera's jealousy is attributed to old 'matriarchal' traditions that were overrun by patriarchal tribes who adored Zeus.
- Like Ares in Greek mythology, Kartikeya, son of Shiva, is the Hindu god of war, who leads the celestial armies of the devas in battle against the asuras.
- Hera is known as Juno in Roman mythology. She holds a pomegranate in her hand, indicating her association with fertility, and rides a chariot pulled by peacocks.
- In the story of how Hera finds Hephaestus disgusting because he is lame, we see a common association in Greek mythology of beauty with order, and ugliness with chaos. This eventually led to goodness being associated with light, and evil with darkness. It reflects the human fear that is amplified when confronted with ugly, disorderly and dark spaces.
- Hera killed Lamia's children on learning of her affair with Zeus. In grief, Lamia, queen of Libya, turned into a monster who ate children while they were still in the wombs of their mother.

Hephaestus

Zeus felt sorry for neglecting the very talented, and rather useful, Hephaestus and invited him to Olympus. But Hephaestus had a condition. Unloved by his mother and ignored by his father, he demanded the most beautiful goddess, Aphrodite, as his wife. Zeus had no choice but to make this happen.

The marriage was an unhappy one. Hephaestus loved engineering, but did not understand romance. Where he measured things, Aphrodite enjoyed metaphors and music. He was a brute; she loved refinement. The goddess of love preferred the passionate and dashing god of war, Ares. 'Both are sons of Zeus, but while my husband makes weapons, it is Ares who knows how to use them in war,' she told her companions. And so, when

Hephaestus was busy in his workshop, a bored Aphrodite began inviting Ares to her bed.

Eventually, Hephaestus heard the rumours, which Aphrodite denied. Hurt and humiliated, he fashioned a special bed in secret. When the lovers lay on it, a net so fine as to be invisible fell on them, ensnaring them. There they lay for the whole world to see, Aphrodite and Ares, naked, in each other's arms, trapped by Hephaestus's net. As he had once shamed his mother, Hephaestus had now shamed his wife.

- Hephaestus's counterpart in Hindu mythology is Vishwakarma. And like Vishwakarma, he has a close relationship with the sun. If Vishwakarma is the architect of the devas, then Maya is the architect of the asuras. Both forge great weapons and build great cities.
- Hephaestus is known as Vulcan in Roman mythology. He is shown holding a blacksmith's hammer and depicted as bent, ugly and lame.
- Like Athena he is associated with skills but is considered far inferior and unpolished.
- He is closely linked to volcanic mountains, which are believed to be the workshops where he works on metal.

Aphrodite

Aphrodite was born before Olympus was established, when Uranus's severed genitals struck the sea. But some say Zeus fathered her on the Titan goddess Dione. She made people desire each other, ignoring the rules of age, gender, social status and marriage. This made her very dangerous, especially when she wore a special girdle around her waist. For then she became irresistible and could compel even Zeus to do her bidding.

Zeus's decision to get her married to Hephaestus was meant to tame her. But it only created more problems, for she refused to be bound by rules, preferring the company of Ares instead.

Once, the queen of Cyprus boasted that her daughter was more beautiful than Aphrodite. The enraged goddess made the daughter fall in love with her father, the king, and trick him into having sex. When the father discovered what his daughter had done, he decided to kill her, but she begged the gods to save her and she was turned into a myrrh tree. From this tree was born the child of incest, Adonis, the most handsome youth that ever lived. So beautiful was he that Aphrodite herself fell in love with him.

A jealous Ares sent a wild boar to kill Adonis, his rival. Aphrodite wept over her beloved's corpse and caused anemone flowers to sprout in his memory. Unable to bear the separation, she travelled to the land of the dead to bring her lover back. But Persephone, queen of the dead, refused to part with Adonis as she too had fallen in love with him.

Aphrodite declared there would be no spring unless Adonis was returned to her. And so Zeus declared that Adonis would spend one half of the year in the land of the dead and the other in the land of the living, causing winter to fall in his absence and spring on his arrival.

- In Hindu mythology, Kama, the god of love, is burned alive by a glance from Shiva's third eye. Later, Shiva discovers love in the Goddess. She is called Kamakshi, one whose eyes evoke desire. She resurrects Kama, though the resurrected Kama has no body and is called Ananga. Thus is physical love distinguished from emotional love. Kama is the Hindu Eros, and his consort, Rati, is the Hindu Aphrodite, but where Kama and Rati are husband and wife, the relationship of Eros and Aphrodite is more ambiguous, with Eros often being shown as a child in Aphrodite's arms.
- The story of the lover (Adonis) dying and being resurrected mirrors the story of the disappearing and appearing daughter (Persephone). This trope was popular not only in Greece but across the Mesopotamian region as an explanation for the change in seasons and the fertility of the soil.
- This story is found in many Latin works such as *Metamorphosis*, *Fabulae* and *Bibliotheca*.

Psyche

Psyche was so beautiful that people stopped worshipping Aphrodite and began offering prayers to her instead, unmindful of the fact that she was mortal. This enraged Aphrodite who ordered her son Eros to make Psyche fall in love with the ugliest man that lived.

Unfortunately, when Eros saw Psyche, he was so smitten by her beauty that he scratched himself with one of his arrows. He then used divine powers to secure her from her father, and take her to a secret place, far from the ire of Aphrodite. He visited her only at night, warning her that as long as she did not see him in the light, she would experience great happiness.

For Psyche, life was wonderful at night, but lonely by day, and so she begged her mysterious husband to let her family visit her. After much pleading, Eros agreed, but that was a mistake. For Psyche's sisters became so jealous when they saw her happiness that they poisoned her mind. 'Your husband may be a monster who will eat your children. How do you know?' they told her.

Influenced by her sisters, one night, Psyche lit a lamp to see the face of her husband. It was anything but monstrous. In fact, it was the most handsome face she had ever seen. As she was admiring her husband, a drop of hot oil fell from her lamp on to his face. He woke up screaming and disappeared in a rage, disappointed by his wife's lack of faith.

Consumed by guilt and sorrow, Psyche wandered the world looking for her husband. Wherever she went, she put things in order, making goddesses such as Demeter and Hera happy. But they all refused to help her, for it was forbidden for one Olympian to interfere in the affairs of another.

Finally, Psyche approached Aphrodite who treated her with contempt and set her to do four terrible tasks: sorting out a variety of grains that had been mixed together; collecting golden wool from violent sheep; fetching water from the River Styx; and securing the beauty ointment used by Persephone. Psyche succeeded each time with a little help from the gods: ants sent by Hermes helped her separate the grain, thorny bushes of Demeter collected the wool from the violent sheep, an eagle sent by Zeus fetched the Stygian water and Persephone herself gave her the ointment of beauty, which turned out to be sleep.

In the meantime, once Eros's wound healed, his disappointment turned into longing. He began searching for Psyche and eventually found her sleeping, covered with Persephone's beauty ointment. He woke her up and brought her to Olympus where Zeus decreed that the two belonged together, a decision that Aphrodite had to agree to.

Eros and Psyche were thus finally reunited. Together they created a daughter, Hedone, who became the goddess of pleasure.

- Amongst the many tales found in the Sanskrit epic Mahabharata there are the stories of Damayanti who seeks her beloved Nala who, having lost all his fortune, has abandoned her in shame, and of Savitri who brings back her husband Satyavan from the land of the dead. In these stories, as in the story of Psyche, the protagonist is a woman, and her quest is to restore lost love.
- The story of Eros and Psyche is found in artworks dating back to the fourth century BCE indicating that the story is very old, though the detailed literary version comes much later, from the Latin work *The Golden Ass*, circa the second century CE, where Eros is referred to as Cupid, and Aphrodite as Venus.
- This tale is seen as an allegory of the relationship between the human spirit (psyche) and love (eros) and has inspired scholars for centuries, including Freud. From Psyche comes the field of psychology.

Echo and Narcissus

Hera did not like that her husband continued to chase goddesses and nymphs after his marriage to her. But Zeus could not restrain himself.

Zeus sent the nymph Echo to distract Hera with long conversations. When Hera realized she was being tricked, she cursed Echo that she would only be able to repeat the last few words that someone spoke to her. Thus cursed, Echo could

find no suitor and hid in caves from where she could only repeat the final words shouted into the cave. Echo was in love with Narcissus, but he could not love this girl who only repeated words and could not hold a conversation.

Narcissus was a rather vain youth, so proud of his beauty that he rejected all his lovers, not just Echo. Nemesis, the goddess of divine retribution, caused him to fall in love with his own reflection. And so the young man spent all day and all night looking at his reflection in a pond, until he transformed into a flower.

- In Hindu mythology, the mirror is seen not just as a symbol of vanity but also as a symbol of wisdom. Shakti shows the mirror to Shiva so that he can know himself better by reflecting on his reflected image.

Leto

Once, Zeus was smitten by two Titan sisters, daughters of Coeus and Phoebe: Asteria and Leto.

Asteria resisted Zeus's advances. She flew away taking the form of a quail and plunged into the Aegean Sea where she became the floating island Delos that moved with the currents, and was difficult for sailors to locate.

Zeus then turned his attention to Leto who was more compliant. However, when news of Leto's pregnancy reached Hera, she was furious. She invoked a monster, the Python, to chase and eat Leto, and made Gaia promise that Leto would not get shelter anywhere on earth.

Pursued by the Python, a pregnant Leto ran around the earth, then jumped into the sea and swam from island to island looking for a sanctuary. Finally, she found shelter on the floating island of Delos, her own sister. There she gave birth to twins: a boy, Apollo, who was radiant as the sun, and a girl, Artemis, who was as serene as the moon.

The children had barely been born when the Python reached Delos and attacked Leto. To her surprise, the newborns raised bows, shot arrows, and killed the monster.

The children were so protective of their mother that when a queen called Niobe made fun of Leto for bearing only two children, they raised their bows and killed all fourteen of Niobe's children, seven boys and seven girls.

- Shiva's son Kartikeya fights and kills Taraka-asura a few days after his birth, much like Apollo who vanquishes the Python.
- Like Apollo and Artemis, the Hindu epic Mahabharata refers to many twin brother–sister pairs such as Kripa–Kripi or Hidimba–Hidimbi, but none are gods.
- In Greek mythology, the sun is male and the moon is female. But in Hindu mythology, both the sun and the moon are male.
- Leto was probably an ancient Cretan goddess later attached to the Olympian gods. She is also associated with Lycia, in Asia Minor, where the local peasants stopped her from drinking water from a pond, and she turned them into frogs, forever doomed to wallow in muddy water.
- Apollo is both the cause of disease and the cure of disease. Artemis is both the guardian of animals and the patron goddess of hunters. Thus the two Olympians embody opposite qualities.

Apollo

Though dashingly handsome, Apollo was unfortunate in love. The women and men he loved did not return his affections. They ran from him, turned into trees and plants, perhaps fearing his love, which was very orderly, making the world very controlled, and life rather predictable.

He fell in love with the Aetolian princess Marpessa but she chose to marry a mortal man, for she knew gods were fickle and eventually lost interest in their mortal lovers.

He burned with love for Daphne but she wanted to remain a virgin. To avoid the god's persistent attentions, she asked her father—the river god Peneus—to turn her into a laurel bush. As a sign of his eternal love for her, Apollo declared that he would always wear a laurel wreath on his head.

Apollo then fell in love with Sibyl and she agreed to be with him if he gifted her with a long life, one with as many years as there are grains of sand on the beach. Apollo made this possible but then Sibyl changed her mind and spurned him. Annoyed, he informed her that while she had been blessed with a long life, she had not been granted the gift of everlasting youth. In fact, she would spend most of her very long life bent and wrinkled and stooping over a stick, barely able to walk.

Apollo offered the Trojan princess Cassandra the gift of prophecy by kissing her on the lips. But she did not kiss him back. So the god said that while she would foretell the future, no one would believe her.

He fell in love with Coronis, daughter of Phlegyas, king of the Lapiths, and even fathered a child on her, but she in turn fell in love with a mortal man called Ischys. A white crow, left by Apollo to watch over Coronis, informed him about this. The god was so angry that the crow had not gouged out Ischys's eyes that he cursed the bird, which is why crows are now black, not white. Apollo then asked Artemis to kill Coronis. But when the princess's lifeless body was placed on the funeral pyre, Apollo heard the sound of their child come from within Coronis's womb—it was still alive. Apollo pulled him out, named him Asclepius, and gave him to the centaur Chiron to raise. Asclepius would grow up to be the god of medicine and surgery. He would save so many people from death that it would alarm Hades, and cause Zeus to strike him down with a thunderbolt.

Apollo deeply loved the Spartan prince Hyacinth who returned his affections, but sadly their relationship made the wind god Zephyrus jealous, for he loved Hyacinth too. One day, when Apollo and Hyacinth were playing with a discus, Zephyrus caused the wind to blow such that the discus turned and struck Hyacinth on his head, crushing his skull and killing him. As he breathed his last, his blood fell on the ground and turned into a flower that Apollo named hyacinth in his memory.

Apollo fell in love with a lad called Cyparissus who had a pet deer. One day, while he was out hunting, Cyparissus accidentally killed his pet deer and was inconsolable in his grief. Feeling sorry for the boy, Apollo turned him into the cypress tree whose drooping branches are forever mourning the pet deer.

- In Hindu mythology, Surya's son Revanta is often identified with Apollo. He is also identified with Artemis, for he is depicted as a handsome youth hunting on a horse, making him the god of chase.
- Plants, in Greek mythology, are often human who have transformed in their attempt to escape the unwelcome affections of a god, or death before the fulfilment of love.
- From the unhappy loves of Apollo come many plants, from the laurel to the hyacinth to the cypress. Likewise, in Hindu mythology, trysts with love create life on earth. The Brihad-aranyaka Upanishad refers to the story of Prajapati chasing Shatarupa who takes various female forms to evade him while he assumes corresponding male forms, from ant to elephant, thus giving rise to all species of beings.
- Apollo is depicted as a beardless attractive youth. While associated with sunlit clarity, order, knowledge, health and beauty, the best of what the Greek world had to offer, he was also feared for causing plagues. Apollo is also considered a god of

the arts and the leader of the Muses, and is often shown carrying a lyre that was given to him by Hermes. He is also the patron of Delphi, the seat of the oracles.

- Echo's curse is sometimes attributed to Hera, not Apollo. She realized Echo distracted her with conversations so that Zeus could pursue his affairs, and so cursed her.

Artemis

Where her brother Apollo was unhappy in love, Artemis did not yearn for it. She enjoyed the chase, the hunt, with her female companions, all of whom took a vow of celibacy.

Artemis fiercely guarded her virginity and that of her companions. When the young hunter Actaeon tried to look upon her naked body while she was bathing, she turned him into a stag, who was chased, hunted and killed by his own hunting dogs. Sipriotes, who accidentally stumbled upon the goddess as she bathed, was turned into a girl. When Orion tried to seduce one of Artemis's followers, and then turned his charms on Artemis herself, boasting that he was a better hunter than the goddess and would hunt down all the animals on earth, she got a scorpion to sting both him and his hunting dog to death.

When Polyphonte joined Artemis as a virgin priestess, the goddess Aphrodite was so upset that she cursed that the young woman would be ravished by a bear and bear it children. The sons of Polyphonte and the bear turned out to be cannibals who were eventually killed by Zeus.

Zeus took the form of Artemis to seduce Callisto, one of the goddess's virgin companions. On discovering this, Artemis drove her away, and Hera turned her into a bear. In time, Callisto gave birth to a human child who grew up to be a hunter and hunted down a she-bear, not realizing the animal was his own mother.

- In Hindu mythology, the goddess Durga rides into battle on a lion, carrying weapons in her many hands. But she is also referred to as mother. In folklore, as in the story of Kanya-kumari, a goddess often stays a virgin to retain the power to kill demons.
- In Roman mythology, Artemis is known as Diana. Artemis got her bow and arrow from Hephaestus and her hunting hounds from Hermes. She captured golden-horned stags to pull her chariot. She is associated with groves of oak trees.
- Like Athena, this daughter of Zeus was sworn to celibacy. In Hindu mythology, though, celibacy is associated with men, not women. Women are expected to be chaste.
- At Ephesus in Ionia, Turkey, there once stood a temple to a fertility goddess with multiple breasts, who was ironically identified with the virginal Artemis, but was in all probability the goddess Cybele, or Rhea.
- The three Roman goddesses Diana (Artemis), Minerva (Athena) and Vesta (Hestia) vowed to remain virgins forever. The fire of Vesta was maintained by Vestal Virgins in ancient Rome. Mars (Ares) sired twin boys on one of these women—Romulus and Remus, who became the founders of Rome.
- The scorpion sent to kill the arrogant Orion became the zodiac sign Scorpio. In some versions of the story, Artemis sends the creature to kill Orion who claims to be a better hunter. In others, Gaia sends the creature, annoyed by the hunter's masculine arrogance.

Hermes

Hermes was born from the union of Zeus and the daughter of the Titan Atlas, Maia, who hid the child in a cave to protect him from Hera's wrath.

On the first night of his birth, the child caught a tortoise and used its shell to create a musical instrument called the lyre. The next night, he stole cows that belonged to Apollo, making the animals walk backwards into his cave so that Apollo could not track them. But when Apollo complained, Hermes made peace by gifting him the lyre.

Hermes was slippery in action and sweet of tongue, and so Zeus declared he would be the god of thieves, traders, travellers and inventors. Zeus gave him winged sandals and a staff with two serpents coiled around it, as he often served as messenger to, and herald of, the Olympians. He was made responsible for taking the ghosts of the dead across the River Styx to the kingdom of Hades.

With Aphrodite, Hermes had a son called Hermaphroditus who was so beautiful that the nymph Salmacis fell in love with him instantly. She clung to him passionately while he was bathing naked in a pool and refused to let him go. Finally, the Olympians fused their bodies and turned them into a single creature with both male and female sexual parts. It was ordained that whosoever entered the pool of Hermaphroditus would also acquire genitals of both genders.

- Hermes is linked to Budh, god of the planet Mercury, and to the ability to communicate. Budh is often visualized as a combination of male and female principles.
- In Roman mythology, Hermes is called Mercury. Hermes has a winged cap and a pair of winged shoes. In his hand he holds the caduceus, a staff around which two serpents are coiled, as he conducts the living to the land of the dead.
- Just as Hermes is associated with winged sandals and a winged helmet, the Ramayana speaks of 'vimana' which is imagined as a winged chariot.
- As the god of roads and boundaries, Hermes was turned to 'herma' or a pile of stones placed at crossroads and boundaries, to which travellers would add more stones. Later, it became a pillar mounted with a head on top and a phallus on the side.
- Hermes's children included Pan whose mother ran away at his birth after seeing his goat-like legs; Priapus, the god of male genitalia; and Autolycus the thief, who was Odysseus's grandfather.
- The ancient cult of Hermaphroditus was popular in Crete and festivals involved ceremonies where men and women exchanged each other's clothes.
- The Phrygian deity Agdistis is similar to Hermaphroditus. But Agdistis is feared by the gods and is so split into male and female forms.
- The Hindu concept of Ardhanareshwara can be connected with Hermaphroditus as a composite being created from the union of male and female principles.

Pan

Hermes fell in love with a nymph called Dryope and she bore him a strange child with the legs and horns of a goat. The sight of this child caused the midwives to panic and there was complete pandemonium in Olympus, which was why the child came to be known as Pan.

Pan was a wild woodland spirit embodying the untameable side of nature. He had an insatiable appetite for sex and chased nymphs all the time. One of them, Syrinx, weary of his attentions, begged the river god to turn her into a river reed. Pan collected the reed that was once his beloved Syrinx, cut it into uneven lengths and created a musical instrument called the panpipe that he used to enchant other nymphs.

- In Hindu mythology, as in Greek mythology, there are many creatures that are part human and part animal. But while in Hindu mythology the trend is to depict such creatures as having an animal head and a human body, in Greek mythology it is usually reversed.
- In Roman mythology, Pan was called Faunus.
- Pan embodies the rural landscape that is not under the control of man.
- While fighting the monster Typhon, Pan jumped in a river and the part of his body above the water turned into a goat, and the part below turned into a fish. Thus came into being the zodiac sign Capricorn. Amalthea, Zeus's wet nurse who was a goat, is also identified with Capricorn.
- According to ancient Greek historian Plutarch, Pan is the only Greek god who died. Many Christian theologians believe this 'death of Pan' coincides with the 'birth of Christ'.
- Pan's association with untamed wilderness eventually led to his association with Satan, who is imagined as having goat legs.

Dionysus

Zeus fell in love with the mortal Semele, princess of Thebes, and fathered a child on her.

When Hera learned of the affair and the pregnancy she decided to punish Semele in the most awful way. She told the girl, 'If Zeus truly loves you, ask him to show you his godly form, not the human form he takes when he makes love to you at night.'

Thus, at their next tryst, Semele demanded that Zeus show her his godly form. Despite his warnings, she insisted on it, and Zeus showed her his godly form. It was so grandly radiant that Semele's body burst into flames.

Hermes rescued the unborn child from Semele's burning flesh and placed it inside Zeus's thigh. A few months later, Zeus 'delivered' this child born of two wombs: his mother's and father's. He was named Dionysus.

Dionysus was given to Semele's sister Ino who raised the boy, dressing him as a girl to avoid the gaze of Hera. But Hera learned the truth and drove both Ino and Dionysus mad. Ino in her madness boiled her son Melicertes alive; on discovering what she had done, she leapt to her death from a cliff overlooking the sea.

Zeus turned Dionysus into a goat and took him to faraway Asia where he was raised by nymphs. As he grew up, he discovered how to make wine from grapes, and the power of music; he made friends with all kinds of wild forest creatures. Women in particular loved his company for he inspired them to dance and sing and to challenge all rules. They called him Bacchus and themselves, the Bacchae.

When Dionysus was older and learnt how he had been cast out of his home by the machinations of Hera, he decided to return, armed with wine, music, intoxication and his new friends, the Bacchae. This meant travelling through Phrygia and then across the sea to Greece.

In Phrygia, in the spirit of amusement, Dionysus fulfilled the deepest desire of the greedy king Midas by granting him a boon: everything he touched would turn to gold. Midas was delighted with his gift until he realized that he could neither eat nor drink, for everything turned to gold at his touch. When he hugged his daughter, even she turned to a statue of gold. Midas begged Dionysus to take back the gift, which he did after a good laugh.

When it was time to cross the sea, Dionysus needed a boat. He stood on the coast until his beauty served as a beacon and drew a ship towards him. Impressed by his beauty and his gold the sailors invited him aboard. They planned to rob and then rape him, but when they tried to tie him down the knots in the ropes simply came undone. Suddenly, the mast of the ship turned into a grape-laden vine, wine filled the ship and all manner of animals and strange creatures and frenzied women appeared on the deck. Dionysus himself turned into a lion and roared lustily. The sailors were terrified and jumped into the sea, where they turned into dolphins, while Dionysus took charge of the ship.

In Athens, Dionysus met the beautiful Erigone. She introduced him to her father, the king Icarus, who welcomed Dionysus and treated him cordially. Dionysus gave the local shepherds wine, and they, in a drunken state, attacked and killed their king. Grief-stricken, the princess Erigone killed herself by hanging herself from a tree. Dionysus punished the shepherds by making their daughters commit suicide in the same manner. He then placed Erigone in the sky as the constellation Virgo.

When Dionysus reached Thebes, he expected to be greeted with open arms by the relatives of his mother. But his cousin, Pentheus, refused to indulge this new cult of wine, music and intoxication. He preferred the authoritative way of Zeus and the orderly way of Apollo, and thus prevented Dionysus from entering his city. But the ways of Dionysus enchanted the women of Thebes. They ran out of the city and into the woods, to dance and sing and drink and be intoxicated by Dionysus. When Pentheus tried to stop them, they attacked him and tore him to pieces with their teeth and bare hands.

When the madness subsided and normalcy returned, everyone in Thebes bowed to Dionysus, the god from the East. Even the gods of Olympus let him sit amongst them, for they feared his madness, though they loved his wine.

- Many scholars have mirrored the Greek binary of Apollo and Dionysus, representing structure and fluidity with the Hindu binary of Vishnu and Shiva. Like Dionysus, Shiva is the outsider god, who forces his way into the Vedic pantheon when he attacks and destroys the ritual hall of Daksha. Just as Dionysus is associated with wine, Shiva is associated with bhang or the mildly narcotic Indian hemp.

- In Roman mythology, Dionysus is called Bacchus.
- Dionysus contrasts the Apollonian order of the West, and represents chaos and fluidity, and the East. He is associated with wine and unbridled frenzied passion and orgies. He is accompanied by satyrs and wild, lustful women called maenads who tear to pieces the men who do not submit to their desires.
- Dionysus's companion Silenus is visualized as a satyr but with more horse-like features. He was always drunk but was also very knowledgeable and had prophetic powers.
- The cult of Bacchus entered Rome from Greece. Initially open only to women, it gradually became a secret cult involving drunken orgies of men and women that threatened the very stability and decorum of the Roman way of life. Seen as a counter-culture, this 'Bacchanalia' was outlawed and suppressed by the Senate. The Roman historian Livy who lived in the first century BCE writes on this rather sensational event that took place in the third century BCE.
- The cult of Dionysus was closely connected to Orphic mysteries, which in turn were linked to the gnostic (nastika?) traditions of India that spoke of mortal flesh, eternal soul, rebirth and liberation.
- Ultimately, there are twelve Olympians, like the twelve numbers on the clock, the twelve Apostles of Jesus, and the twelve Adityas of the Vedas. In each case, there is an outsider. Dionysus is the outsider in Greek mythology; in Christian mythology it is Judas; and in Vedic mythology it is Martanda.
- The list of Olympians includes Zeus, Poseidon, Hera, Demeter, Artemis, Apollo, Athena, Ares, Aphrodite, Hephaestus, Hermes and Dionysus. Hestia made room for Dionysus. Hades and Persephone, who live in the land of the dead, are not included.
- In the nineteenth century, the theory of the dying-and-returning god became very popular, establishing a connection between Dionysus and Jesus Christ: both were connected to wine, and both came to Europe from the East, facing and overpowering fierce resistance.

Prometheus

Prometheus, the Titan, told the Olympians that they needed someone to worship them and serve them. Zeus liked the idea, so Prometheus made dolls out of clay and breathed life into them. Thus was mankind created.

Prometheus taught humans to forage and hunt for food. He taught them agriculture and herding and fishing. And, much to Zeus's delight, he taught them to make oblations to the gods.

Humans offered Zeus a choice of offerings: bones wrapped in fat, or beef wrapped in ox stomach. In other words, something bad in the guise of something good and something good concealed within something bad. Zeus accepted the former, and on realizing he had been tricked, decided to punish mankind by taking away fire, for creatures who could trick the Olympians into accepting a bad offering could one day overthrow them.

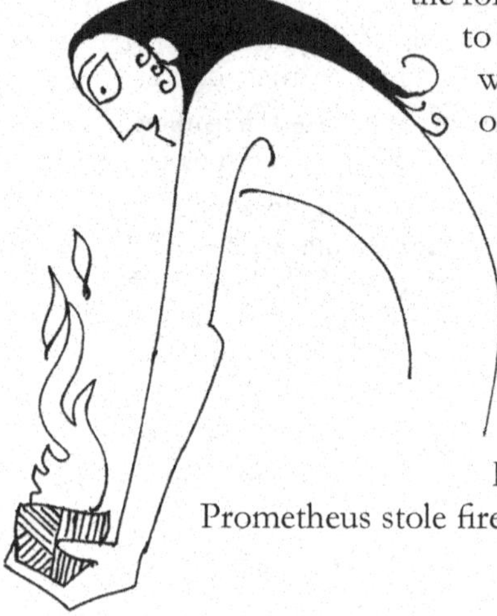

Without fire, humans lived like animals, unable to cook meat or ward off predators, unable to clear dense forests for settlements or combat the darkness of the night. Prometheus begged Zeus to reconsider and forgive them. But Zeus remained unmoved.

Finally, when Zeus was not looking, an exasperated Prometheus stole fire and gave it back to humanity.

As the smoke from the hearths of human homes rose to Mount Olympus, Zeus became very angry. Enraged by Prometheus's insolence, he grabbed him by the neck, tied him to a rock and ordered his eagle to eat the Titan's liver all day long. But since Prometheus was immortal, the liver regrew at night and the torture resumed the next day—eternal suffering for one who dared disobey Zeus.

- Prometheus embodies forethought and his brother Epimetheus embodies afterthought. In Hindu mythology, a similar theme is expressed through the characters of the intuitive Bhrigu, who serves the asuras, and the rational Brihaspati, who counsels the devas.
- The Vedas speak of a 'pra-math', a thief. And Vedic myths mention the theft of fire by Matarisvan. Probably these stories have a common Indo-European root.
- The story of Prometheus draws attention to the Greek divide between the divine and the human. The Olympians both admired and feared humans.
- Prometheus has for centuries embodied the trickster who defies authority to enable the ascent of humanity and suffers for it.

Pandora

Zeus asked Hephaestus to create a woman using clay. He asked Aphrodite to bless her with beauty and Athena to give her womanly skills like cooking and weaving. He named this woman Pandora and sent her to Epimetheus who lived with mankind.

Though they were brothers, Epimetheus was the very opposite of Prometheus. While the latter thought before acting, the former acted before thinking. Epimetheus fell in love with Pandora and brought her to live with humans, all of whom also adored her.

Pandora carried a box with her, a gift from Zeus. 'Don't open it until I tell you to do so,' the Olympian had told her. But Pandora could not contain her curiosity and opened it anyway. Out came disease and sorrow and envy and greed and gluttony, and all the things that plague humanity. Pandora shut the box quickly, but it was too late; the damage was done.

The only thing that stayed within the box was hope, which would propel humanity forward.

- The story of Pandora comes from the seventh century BCE *Theogony* of Hesiod.
- Pandora's tale is seen as the patriarchal corruption of the 'all-giving' Goddess of pre-Olympian times.
- Originally, Pandora carried a jar. But mistranslations in the sixteenth century turned the jar into a box.
- Both Greek and Biblical mythology hold women responsible for the suffering of humanity. Both Pandora and Eve take decisions that cause havoc. In Hindu mythology, women are not blamed for the suffering of mankind, but the female form embodies temptations that distract the celibate hermit. In Buddhist mythology, all seekers are warned to stay away from the daughters of Mara, the demon of desire.

Tartarus

Zeus was clear that anyone who disobeyed him would be brutally punished, as Prometheus was. Most of those who offended Zeus found themselves in Tartarus, beyond the River Styx, suffering for all eternity. These included the audacious Ixion, the guileful Sisyphus and the treacherous Danaids.

Ixion, king of the Lapiths, spun forever on a wheel of fire in Tartarus. His crime: he did not respect the rules of hospitality. He invited his father-in-law to his house to receive his bridal price, and killed him instead. When invited to Olympus for a feast, he tried to rape Hera herself.

Sisyphus was made to roll a boulder all day to the top of a mountain, only to find it rolling down at night. Thus he was trapped forever in a monotonous meaningless task. His crime: though a king and a navigator, he was deceitful, crafty, known to kill his own guests and use the secrets of the gods as currency in negotiations. In exchange for having a spring to flow in his kingdom, Sisyphus told a river god the whereabouts of his daughter, the nymph Aegina, who had been abducted by Zeus. This infuriated Zeus and he decided to imprison Sisyphus in Tartarus. But Sisyphus was so crafty that when Thanatos, the god of death, came to chain him, he tricked the god into chaining himself by asking him to demonstrate how the chain worked. The chaining of Thanatos meant no one died on earth, which angered the gods, especially Ares, the god of war, who finally released Thanatos, and dragged Sisyphus to Tartarus.

The Danaids were forty-nine sisters who were made to fill water in a vast tub using a perforated pot. Their crime: on their wedding night they killed their sleeping husbands, the sons of Aegyptus, on their father's instruction.

- In Hindu mythology, the Garuda Purana describes various types of hell or naraka depending on the nature of the crime. But Tartarus is not just about common crimes, it is about hubris that affects the cosmos and so earns the displeasure of Zeus. It shows those suffering to be wilful agents of chaos who threaten harmony.
- Being forced to perform a thankless, meaningless, monotonous task was the greatest punishment for the Greeks, and often the result of angering the gods.
- In Hindu mythology, the material world goes through repetitive, senseless, purposeless cycles: all humans are thus Sisyphus. Wisdom is finding meaning through it.

Deucalion

Zeus noticed that humans, created and nurtured by Prometheus, were foul and cruel and more interested in fighting each other for wealth and power than in offering oblations to the Olympians. Worse, they had begun to doubt the power of the Olympians.

Once, when Zeus was visiting him, Lycaon, the king of Arcadia, decided to check if the Olympian was indeed a god and so, along with the flesh of animals, served him the flesh of a human, his own son, thus breaking the rules of hospitality and the rules against cannibalism.

Enraged, Zeus decided to destroy all humanity with a great flood. He caused the oceans to overflow and the rivers to swell and the rains to fall until the entire earth was covered with water. All living creatures, plants and animals and humans, were destroyed in this flood.

But then Zeus found floating on these waters a chest, within which were a man and a woman, the only survivors of the flood. The man was Deucalion, son of Prometheus, and the woman was his wife Pyrrha, daughter of Pandora. Like his father, Deucalion had foresight and had known that one day Zeus would lose his patience with humanity and devastate the earth. And so the couple had hidden in a wooden chest, and stayed safe and dry while the waters deluged and destroyed everything else.

When the waters subsided, Deucalion and Pyrrha came out of the chest and begged for mercy at the shrine of Zeus that stood nearby. Taking pity on them, Zeus said, in a rather cryptic way, 'Throw the bones of your grandmother behind you and you shall establish a new line of humanity who will be as wise as you.'

The bones of their grandmother? Where would the couple find them? Then Deucalion realized what Zeus meant, and along with his wife began gathering rocks from the ground and throwing them over their shoulder, for the earth was their grandmother and the rocks were her bones.

The rocks thrown by Deucalion became men and those thrown by Pyrrha became women. These men and women, born after the flood, were the new line of humanity, fire controllers, who respected the Olympians and offered them oblations.

From this race of men would be born heroes, who would defy the limitations imposed on them by the Olympians. Some would become gods themselves, grudgingly admired by the Olympians. Others would earn a place in the heaven of heroes, Elysium, located in the underworld across the River Styx, reserved for those who live extraordinary lives. Those who upset the gods would be cast into the dark void that was Tartarus. The rest, the ordinary, the mediocre, would spend the afterlife in the shade of the Asphodel fields.

- In Hindu mythology, Brahma is the grandfather of humanity—there is a biological connection. But there is no such connection in Greek mythology. The gods create humans from clay. In later myths, they are created from the earth by sowing the seeds of dragons and other monsters.
- Some of the crimes that Zeus abhorred were the ill treatment of guests and human sacrifice.
- Deucalion's survival in the box reminds us of the tale of Noah's Ark found in the Old Testament of the Bible, and of Utnapishtim who survives the flood of the Mesopotamian gods.
- Augustine of Hippo who lived in the fourth century CE took the tale of Deucalion as historical fact, and considered him a contemporary of Moses. In medieval times, Deucalion's flood was dated to around 1500 BCE, a regional flood that followed the more global flood witnessed by Noah.
- Deucalion and Pyrrha had a son called Hellen from whom all the Hellenic tribes of Classical Greece arose: the Achaeans, Ionians (from whom come the Persian word 'yunan' and the Sanskrit 'yavana' that describes the Greeks), Dorians and Aeolians.

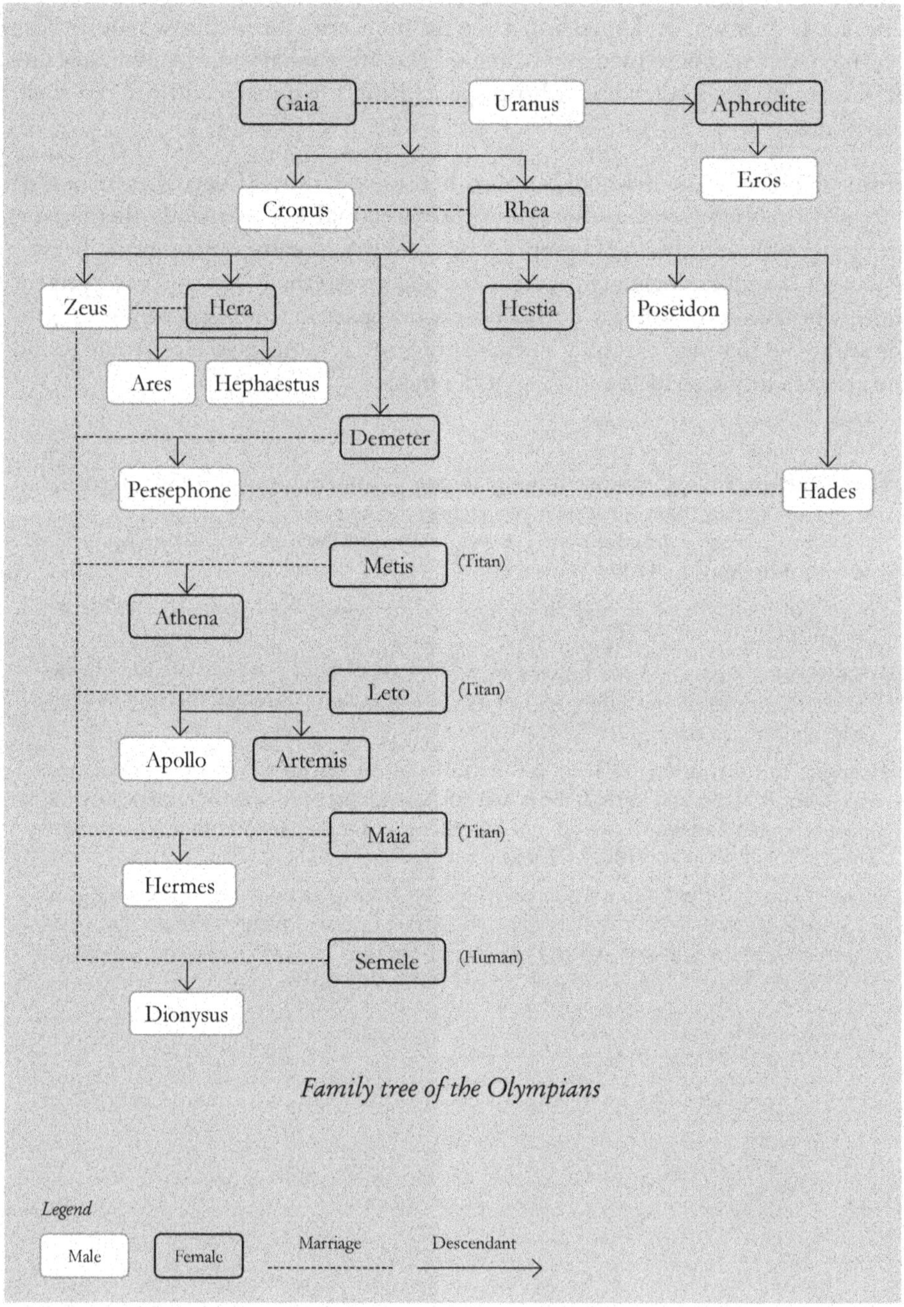

Family tree of the Olympians

BOOK TWO

Minos

'Zeus reminds me of a king struggling to maintain order, contending with the violence of those who came before him, the quarrels of those around him, and his suspicion of those who stand below him,' said the gymnosophist. 'I can feel his struggle to harmonize the intellectual Athena with the passionate Aphrodite, the lucid Apollo with the intoxicated Dionysus.'

'How interesting! You see the Olympians inside you,' said Alexander. 'I see them outside. In Crete, ruled by Minos, I find Dionysian mysteries, and in Athens, ruled by Theseus, I find Apollonian clarity.'

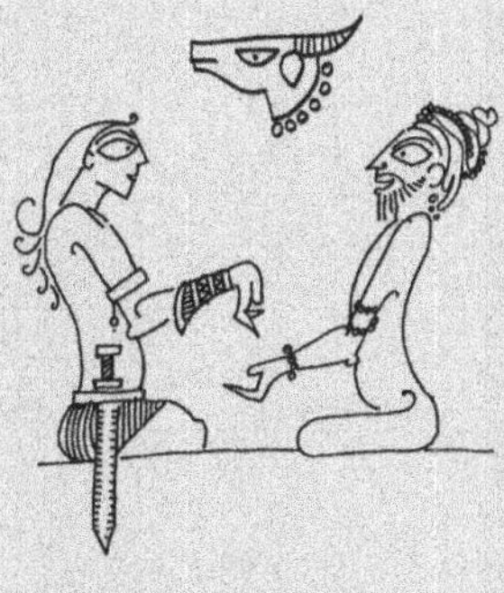

Io

Zeus demanded that the king of Argos give his daughter Io to him. The king dared not refuse a god, even though he knew his actions would upset Hera, for Io was her priestess and was expected to be faithful to the goddess.

As Zeus was enjoying Io's company, he saw Hera approaching and, fearing for Io's safety, immediately turned her into a cow.

But Hera was not fooled. She knew that the cow was not really bovine but a woman who had caught Zeus's fancy. She told her faithful minion, the giant Argus, to watch over this cow, for sooner or later she would revert to her human form for the pleasure of Zeus.

Argus had a hundred eyes. And at any time, at least one pair was always open, so he could watch Io night and day. Nothing she did escaped his sight. Finally, Zeus sent Hermes to play his lyre until Argus shut all his eyes and fell asleep. Hermes then beheaded the sleeping giant and let Io escape.

Hera was furious. She placed the eyes of Argus, who had served her so well, on the tail of a peacock.

Then she sent a gadfly to sting Io and chase her around the world, giving her not a moment to rest. Io fled from Europe into Asia through a sea route that came to be known as the Bosphorus, or the path of the cow. She ran through lands that would later be known as Phrygia, Phoenicia and Egypt. Everywhere she went, she gave birth to Zeus's children, who would rule these lands.

- The peacock is linked with a tale of infidelity in Hindu mythology too. Rishi Gautama discovers his wife, Ahalya, in the arms of Indra, the king of the devas. He curses that Indra will sprout a hundred eyes on his body so that he can 'see' where his senses lead him. Eventually these eyes are placed on a peacock's tail. A peacock's feathers are used to ward off the 'evil eye' in many Hindu rituals.
- Io is identified with the Egyptian goddesses Hathor and Isis.
- From Io descend many Greek heroes like Perseus, Cadmus and Heracles.
- Io is the name given to one of planet Jupiter's moons.

Europa

One of Io's many sons, the king of Phoenicia, had a daughter called Europa, who often took care of her father's cows and bulls. Zeus saw Europa and, enamoured of her, he decided to seduce her.

He took the form of a white bull and walked towards her while she was gathering flowers. When she touched him, he lowered himself, inviting her to sit on him. As soon as she climbed on to his back, he ran into the sea, carrying her with him, jumping over the waves until he reached the island of Crete.

There he ravished her, and in time she gave birth to three sons: Minos, Rhadamanthus and Sarpedon.

- Ancient cattle-herding civilizations revered the bull for its virility, which could not be tamed unless it was castrated and thereby stripped of virility. In the Indus Valley civilization, we find seals with the image of the bull. In Hindu mythology, Shiva rides Nandi, a bull. In Jain mythology, the first Tirthankara is known as Rishabha, which means bull, and his symbol is the bull as well. Even Buddha was addressed as a bull amongst men.
- The story of Europa is as old as Homer's *Iliad*, which was probably composed around 2800 years ago. The name Europe comes from Europa, and at first it was used for parts of Thrace. It began to signify the entire continent only from around 1200 years ago, when it referred to the western part of the Holy Roman Empire that was Latin, and led by Charlemagne, and distinct from the eastern, Greek part.
- The European Union currently acknowledges Europa, mother of Europe, through its website and currency notes.
- Rationalists believe that Europa was a Phoenician princess who was kidnapped by bull-worshipping Minoans.
- One of the moons around planet Jupiter is named Europa.
- A rare earth element, europium, is named after Europa.
- As a bull, Zeus connects Asia (Argos) to Crete, while as a cow, Io connects Greece to Asia (Lycia, Phoenicia) and Africa (Libya, Egypt). These tales thus establish a connection along the eastern half of the Mediterranean Sea. The western half is the theatre where the adventures of Heracles, Odysseus and Aeneas take place.

Pasiphae

Minos drove both his brothers out of Crete—Rhadamanthus because he was popular with the people, and Sarpedon because they both loved the same boy, Atymnius.

Then, to prove he was worthy of the crown, Minos prayed to Poseidon and asked him to send him a bull from the sea as a sign of his support, promising to sacrifice it to the sea god himself. Pleased, Poseidon let a bull emerge from the sea; Minos, however, liked the animal so much that he decided not to sacrifice it.

An angry Poseidon caused Pasiphae, Minos's wife, to fall in love with the bull and want to have sex with him. To seduce the bull, Pasiphae had the inventor Daedalus build her a model of a cow with a compartment within which she could hide. The bull mistook the contraption for a real cow and responded as Pasiphae wished, giving her pleasure and getting her pregnant. Thus was born a terrible beast called the Minotaur, who had the body of a man but the head of a bull and an appetite for human flesh. The creature embodied the falsehood of Minos, the shame of Pasiphae and the anger of the Olympians.

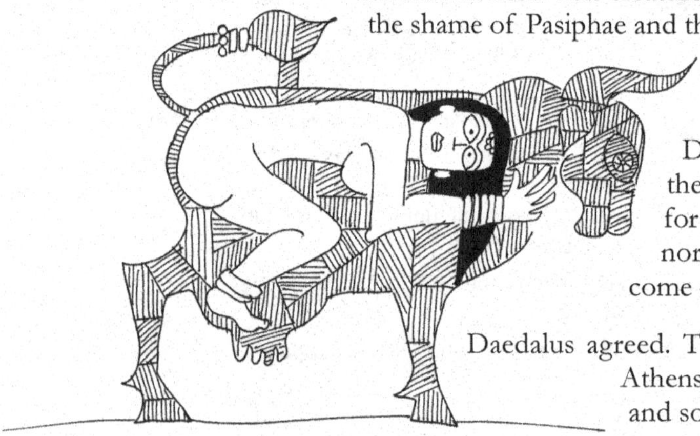

Embarrassed by the creature, but terrified of killing it, Minos asked Daedalus to build a labyrinth under the palace that would serve as home for the Minotaur. Neither the monster nor those who entered it would ever come out.

Daedalus agreed. The inventor had fled his home in Athens and had been given shelter in Crete, and so was obliged to both his hosts.

- In Jain and Buddhist stories, queens often dream of celestial creatures like elephants, horses and bulls entering their womb, an indicator that the child they have conceived will be a great king or sage. However, in these stories, the queens are never shown as desiring the animal; nor is there an instance of a god approaching a queen in the form of an animal.
- The story of the bull emerging from the sea reveals how, in ancient Greece, royal power and legitimacy were derived from the Olympians.
- The island of Crete, home of the Minoan civilization, was famous for rituals and sports that involved dancing around bulls and leaping over them.
- Pasiphae was seen to be related to the witches of the East, known for their enormous sexual appetite, and this story of her copulating with a bull captured the Greek imagination.
- Pasiphae had given her husband Minos a potion by which his semen would turn into

scorpions in the vaginas of his mistresses. Thus she forced him to be faithful to her. But Minos ordered the inventor Daedalus to design the world's first condom, using a goat's bladder, by which he could protect his mistresses.

- When the ruins of Crete were discovered, many archaeologists searched in vain for the mythical labyrinth. Finding none, they concluded the palace itself with its many rooms and corridors may have inspired the tale.
- Minotaur is a word created by combining two words: Minos and Taurus (which means bull).

Androgeus

Minos and Pasiphae had another son called Androgeus, a handsome lad who went to Athens to participate in games held in honour of Athena. There he won many prizes and many admirers. Envious of his prowess, the Athenians asked him to fight the Cretan bull, which killed him.

Minos did not think that the fight was fair. In fact, he was convinced that Aegeus, king of Athens, had murdered his son in jealousy, and so he led an attack against Athens. When that was not successful, he asked his father Zeus to strike the city with pestilence and famine until they agreed to do as he bade them: 'You have taken the life of one son of Minos. Now you must give life to the other son of Minos. Send seven boys and seven girls every nine years into the labyrinth of Minotaur.'

Aegeus had no choice but to agree.

- This story of Minos's vengeance comes from the second-century Latin work *Bibliotheca* (meaning library), a vast collection of Greek myths written by one Apollodorus. This is almost a thousand years after the epics of Homer and Hesiod.
- Rationalists believe that Minos was a title, and perhaps referred to a great line of kings that ruled Crete. These kings had a navy that held sway over the Mediterranean

and so were much hated by the Greeks, especially Athenians.

- Mahish-asura, the buffalo-headed demon of the Hindu Puranas, reminds us of the bull-headed Minotaur. But the story of Mahish-asura dates back to the seventh century CE while that of Minotaur was known at least a thousand years before in the Mediterranean.

Aegeus

Long ago, the oracle at Delphi, who could understand the whispers of the Fates and the Olympians, revealed to Aegeus, king of Athens, a puzzle. Aegeus shared the oracle's cryptic words with his friend, Pittheus of Troezen, who deciphered it to mean that Aegeus ought not to get drunk that night for then he would father a great hero, who would also be his killer.

Pittheus did not share the meaning with Aegeus. Instead, he got Aegeus drunk, and forced his daughter, Aethra, to have sex with him that night. That same night, instructed by Athena, Aethra waded across the sea to a nearby island where she was possessed by Poseidon. As a result of her intimacies with a man and then a god, Aethra became pregnant.

While leaving Troezen, Aegeus placed his sword, shield and sandals under a huge boulder and told Aethra, 'If you bear a son and he is strong enough to push this boulder aside and find this sword of mine, tell him to travel to Athens and find his father.'

Sure enough, Aethra gave birth to a son called Theseus who grew up to be strong enough to push the boulder aside and find his father's sword, shield and sandals. When Aethra told Theseus about his father, he decided to visit Athens. Pittheus tried to stop his grandson, for he knew Theseus would be the cause of his father's death, but Theseus was in no mood to listen.

- Stories of sons, raised by single mothers, who inherit their father's strength are found in Hindu mythology too as in the case of Bharat, son of Shakuntala, who is raised in the forest, and is as strong as his father Dushyanta.
- Like most Greek heroes, Theseus has two fathers, one mortal and the other immortal. Theseus's divine father is Poseidon, making him the nemesis of Minos, who broke his word to Poseidon and incurred the god's wrath.
- The trope of a father asking his pregnant wife to send the child to him only if he is a 'worthy son'—Theseus proves his worth by lifting the boulder to find his father's sword—is a recurring theme in folklore, one that we see even in the tenth-century Persian tale of Rustom and Sohrab found in the *Shah Nama*.
- The prophecy of a son killing his own father is also a recurring theme in Greek mythology.
- Theseus, the son of Poseidon, was destined to rule Athens, a city that refused to make Poseidon their patron god and chose Athena instead, for he offered them seawater and she gave them the olive tree.

Theseus

Normally, people would travel from Troezen to Athens by sea, avoiding the land route that was full of violent highway robbers. But not Theseus. He travelled by road, outwitting all the thieves along the way and subduing all the scoundrels who plagued the land. Six of these are worthy of mention.

First was the lame thief, Periphetes, who would beat up unsuspecting travellers with his bronze club.

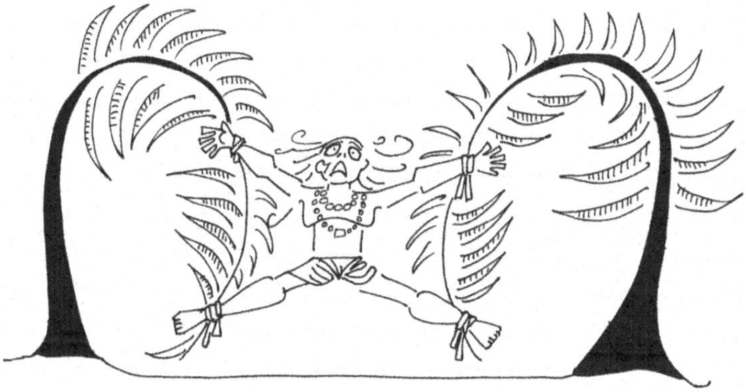

Second was Sinis, who would tie his victims between two pine trees that he would bend simultaneously and then release, causing the hapless victims to be torn apart.

Third was Phaea, an old woman who would set upon travellers her man-eating pig.

Fourth was Sciron who would kick people off a cliff after tricking them into bending down to wash his feet.

Fifth was Cercyon who challenged people to a wrestling match and then killed them after defeating them.

Sixth was Procustes who invited travellers to spend the night in his home where he stretched the legs of short travellers till their knees snapped, or cut off the feet of tall travellers so that they fit the bed in the guest room.

By the time Theseus reached Athens, he had won the support of its people. And when he showed the sword to Aegeus, he was hugged and welcomed as the prince of Athens.

Sadly, it was the year to send the tribute of seven boys and seven girls to Crete. Theseus, never one to shy away from a challenge, decided to be part of the tribute. 'Fear not, father, I will come back alive,' he said.

The sails of the ship that took tribute to Crete were always black. 'Replace these with white sails when you return, my son,' said Aegeus.

- In the Mahabharata, Bhima earns a reputation for himself by saving common people from the excesses of the rakshasa Baka, to whom villagers had to send a cartload of food every month: the demon would eat the food, as well as the cart driver and the oxen pulling the cart. In the Bhagavata Purana, Krishna makes Gokul and Vrindavan safe by killing various troublemakers who attack the village in the guise of animals, and sometimes as forest fires and thunderstorms. These acts of protecting the village make them heroes, as in the case of Theseus.
- Theseus is a founding hero who overpowers forces of previous religions, embodiments of chaos, to establish the Olympian order.
- Theseus's Six Labours make him a forerunner of Heracles who was asked to perform twelve labours.
- The killing of thieves and establishing order in Athens led to Theseus being identified with establishing democracy in Athens.

Ariadne

Upon his arrival in Crete, as luck would have it, Ariadne, the daughter of Minos and Pasiphae, fell in love with Theseus. Determined to save him, the princess went to Daedalus and asked his advice. Daedalus said, 'Theseus may be strong enough to kill the Minotaur, but no man is skilled enough to find his way out of my labyrinth. Tell him to take a ball of thread and tie one end around his waist and let the ball of thread unravel behind him, marking the path he takes into the maze. After killing the monster, he can trace back his path out of the labyrinth by simply following the thread.'

Theseus did as advised and traced his path into the labyrinth with the ball of thread. The way was littered with bones, remains of Athenian boys and girls who had been sent as tributes over the years. After a long-winding journey through dark, smelly, cavernous corridors, Theseus finally came face-to-face with the dreaded monster. The two wrestled for a long time. Finally, Theseus exhausted and overpowered the Minotaur. Finding his way out was easy, thanks to Ariadne's thread. When Theseus emerged from the labyrinth triumphant with the head of the Minotaur in his hand, Minos had no choice but to let him go.

As a peace offering, Minos gave his daughter Phaedra as wife to Theseus, much to the irritation of Ariadne, who also insisted on travelling to Athens with the man she loved.

Theseus, however, abandoned Ariadne on the island of Nixos, and proceeded home with only Phaedra by his side. Why did he do that? Perhaps because he did not really love Ariadne. Or perhaps because she had already been promised to Dionysus, and Theseus of Athens had no intention of angering the god of wine and madness.

Giddy with victory and love, Theseus forgot to replace the black sails of his ship with white ones. An anxious Aegeus assumed his son had been killed by the Minotaur and, grief-stricken, jumped from the cliffs into the sea. The prophecy of Aegeus being killed by his own son was thus fulfilled. From that day, the sea near Athens came to be known as the Aegean Sea, after Aegeus.

- In traditional Hindu lore, a hero's success depends on three factors: shakti (strength), yukti (strategy) and bhakti (devotion). Theseus succeeds not only because he is strong but because, thanks to Ariadne, he has strategy, and thanks to his parentage, which includes an Olympian, Poseidon, he has the support of celestial forces.
- Theseus's journey from Crete to Athens is the journey from Dionysus to Apollo, from intuition to rationality, from fluidity to structure.
- The clash of Minos and Theseus is also the clash between a son of Zeus and a son of Poseidon. But Zeus cannot help Minos for he broke his word, a grave crime in the eyes of the Olympians.
- Theseus abandons Ariadne on learning that she is dedicated to Dionysus. In popular lore, on Athena's advice, he leaves her while she is sleeping.
- In Etruscan art, Dionysus is often depicted with his consort, Ariadne, who bears him children who embody grapes and wine.
- Ariadne was probably an ancient mother goddess whose cult was first linked to the hero Theseus, and later with the god Dionysus.
- Theseus, a son of Poseidon, kills the Minotaur, the offspring of the bull sent to Crete by Poseidon.
- The ship of Theseus was kept in Athens for centuries. Over time, each rotting piece of the ship was replaced by a fresh one. Eventually, every inch of the ship came to be made of materials that were not part of the original. Was this ship then truly the ship of Theseus? This was the famous paradoxical question raised by Greek philosophers.

Perdix

After Theseus's departure from Crete, Minos learned about the ball of thread he had used to get out of the labyrinth. The idea could not have been Ariadne's; she was not that smart. The idea had to be that of Daedalus, who had built the labyrinth. Since the inventor was originally from Athens it was quite possible he wanted to help the handsome Athenian prince.

Daedalus had to leave Athens after he committed a terrible crime. He was upset when he discovered that his young nephew, Perdix, was a better inventor than his own son, Icarus. In fact, people said that the nephew had the potential to outshine even his talented uncle. In a fit of jealousy, Daedalus pushed Perdix to his death from the roof of his house. He then fled with Icarus and sought refuge in Crete.

- Jealousy is a common theme in Hindu mythology too. Ravana is jealous of his brother, Kubera, who builds the golden city of Lanka. Duryodhana is jealous of his cousins, the Pandavas, who build the city of Indraprastha.
- Daedalus is the archetypal skilled craftsman who is said to have invented carpentry.
- Athena saved Perdix and turned him into a bird, a partridge that avoids building nests in high places.
- A crater on the far side of the moon is named Daedalus.
- The journal of the American Academy of Arts & Sciences is called *Daedalus*.

Icarus

Minos, angry with Daedalus's treachery, had him imprisoned in a tower. To escape, Daedalus designed wings for himself and his son, Icarus, using bird feathers and beeswax. Father and son strapped on the wings, jumped out of the tower and began flapping until they were able to glide on the wind like birds. They made it out of the city, out of the island and over the sea.

But then Icarus grew too confident and felt the urge to fly towards the sun. As he flew higher, the beeswax in the artificial wings began to melt. The feathers came undone and he fell into the sea and drowned. Daedalus could do nothing to save his son and so flew alone to faraway Sicily.

- In the Ramayana, we hear the tale of the vulture brothers Jatayu and Sampati, who challenge each other to fly higher. Sampati spreads his wings to stop Jatayu from flying too close to the sun and burns his own wings in the process. The now-flightless Sampati stands on the ocean shore and is able to see Lanka with his keen eyesight.
- Daedalus embodies maturity in an artist while Icarus embodies impetuousness.
- The story of men riding high only to be struck down is an oft-repeated motif in Greek mythology: Icarus falls when he flies too high, Phaeton is struck by a thunderbolt when he tries to fly his father's sun-chariot, and Bellerophon is struck down when he tries to fly towards Olympus on his flying horse. These were seen as acts of hubris, excessive pride that makes people forget their place in the cosmos, thus causing chaos.
- In Sumerian mythology, Etana is the equivalent of Icarus. He rode towards heaven on the back of an eagle, seeking a magical herb, but then looked down and lost his balance.
- People who are dangerously over-ambitious are said to suffer from an Icarus complex.
- Perdix, whom Daedalus envies, is turned into a bird by the gods, while Icarus, whom Daedalus loves, cannot fly with his man-made wings. Perdix flies up and survives, while Icarus tumbles down and dies.

Daedalus

Minos was determined to find Daedalus. So he sent his spies to kings around the Mediterranean Sea with a puzzle: How did one thread a spiral shell? It was a problem that Minos knew no one other than Daedalus could solve.

Sometime later, news came that the king of Sicily had succeeded. Someone in his court had told the king to tie a thread to an ant, make it enter one end of the shell and lure it out the other end with a drop of honey. Minos was pleased, for only Daedalus could have thought of that.

He demanded that the king of Sicily hand over the inventor. The king agreed and invited Minos to a banquet where Daedalus would be presented to him. Before the banquet he asked his beautiful daughters to give Minos a bath. As soon as Minos got into the tub, the king's daughters, guided by Daedalus, poured boiling water on Minos and scalded him to death.

- Just as Minos uses a puzzle to draw out Daedalus from his hiding place, in the Hindu epic Mahabharata, Damayanti gets spies to use puzzles to locate her husband, Nala, who abandoned her in the forest.
- Minos had reason to be angry with Daedalus: he helped Minos's wife Pasiphae have sex with Poseidon's bull using a lifelike statue of a cow; and he told Minos's daughter Ariadne how Theseus could escape the labyrinth with a simple ball of string.
- It was important for Athenians to tell the story of how the great king of Crete was killed by an Athenian as there was historical rivalry between them over control of the waters and trading routes of the Mediterranean.
- After his death, Minos was made the judge of the dead, along with his brother, Rhadamanthus, and his half-brother, Aeacus. Rhadamanthus judged the easterners; Aeacus judged the westerners; Minos had the casting vote.

Antiope

Meanwhile, in Athens, with Phaedra by his side, Theseus established democracy, a new form of governance where the authority of the king was tempered by the collective wishes of the people.

In times bygone, the priest-king was obliged to take care of the city, ensure its security and its prosperity, and in exchange he received the obedience of the people. Now Theseus created an assembly, the polis, where people spoke their mind and decisions were taken by consensus. This balanced the excesses of the king, and helped him choose a course of action when he could not make up his mind.

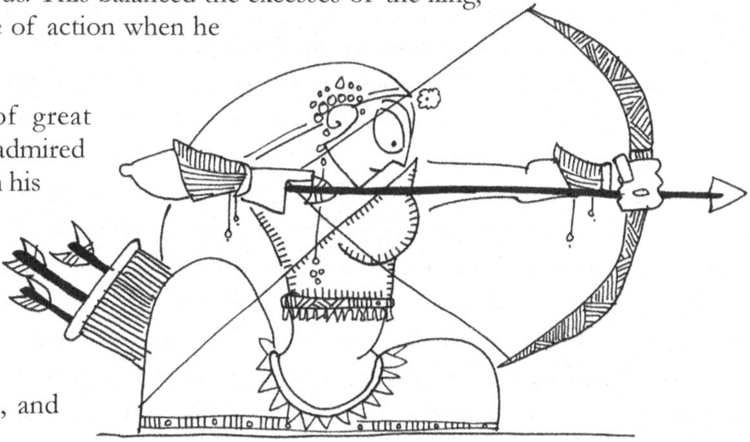

What followed was a period of great harmony. Everyone in Athens admired Theseus. Instead of fighting with his neighbouring kings, he took the novel step of inviting them to an assembly so that everyone could live together in amity.

It was in this period that Theseus encountered the tragic Oedipus, and helped him die in peace, burying him secretly near Athens. Later, he also buried the Seven who were killed when they attacked Thebes. Thus, Theseus and Athens became renowned for generosity and humanity.

But good times make heroes restless. And so was the case with Theseus, who longed for adventure, and thus decided to visit the land of the Amazons.

The Amazons lived in the east, in Asia. They were female warriors who used men only to procreate. Any male offspring were returned to the fathers but the female ones were kept and raised as Amazons. Theseus offered himself to the queen Antiope and she bore him a son, Hippolytus. Father and son were then asked to leave but Theseus decided he would take Antiope with him, and abducted her.

The enraged Amazons chased him to Athens and launched an attack on the city. During the fight, they realized that their besotted queen was fighting on the side of the Athenians. The Athenians managed to push the Amazons back, but not before one of the attackers' arrows killed Antiope, the woman who was once their queen.

- Plutarch wrote in the first century CE about how Theseus established democracy in Athens, and identified Romulus of Rome with Theseus.
- In Hindu mythology, Krishna belonged to the Yadu clan which had no kings, but where decisions were arrived at through consensus by a council known as Dasarhi.
- In Indian folklore, there is a reference to stri-rajya, or the land of women, where no man may enter. It is ruled by Pramila and is sometimes called kadali-vana, the banana grove. The only man who succeeds in entering this place is Matsyendra-nath, the great yogi, who is enchanted by the women there until he is rescued by his student, Goraksha-nath.
- A battalion of female warriors guarded Chandragupta Maurya. The Greek ambassador Megasthenes identified them as Amazons.
- Amazon means 'without a breast'. This tribe of women supposedly cut off their right breasts to enable them to shoot arrows better. Amazons were said to live in the East, probably in Turkey or Scythia (Persia), or in Africa.
- In the *Alexander Romances*, fantasy adventure tales based on the life of Alexander that became popular in Europe in medieval times, Alexander meets and gives a child to the Amazon queen named Thalestris.

Hippolytus

Antiope's son, Hippolytus, grew up to be a handsome man, but he decided to serve Artemis and live as a virgin. This upset Aphrodite, who caused Theseus's first wife, Phaedra, to fall in love with her stepson. Phaedra invited Hippolytus to her bed, and when he refused, she accused him of trying to rape her.

An angry Theseus invoked Poseidon who sent a monster from the sea to startle the horses pulling Hippolytus's chariot, causing him to fall from it. Hippolytus's feet got entangled in the reins, and as the horses bolted, he was dragged along the ground. His head smashed against the roadside rocks and he died.

On learning that Theseus had caused Hippolytus's death, a guilt-ridden Phaedra killed herself. By the time Theseus learned the truth it was too late.

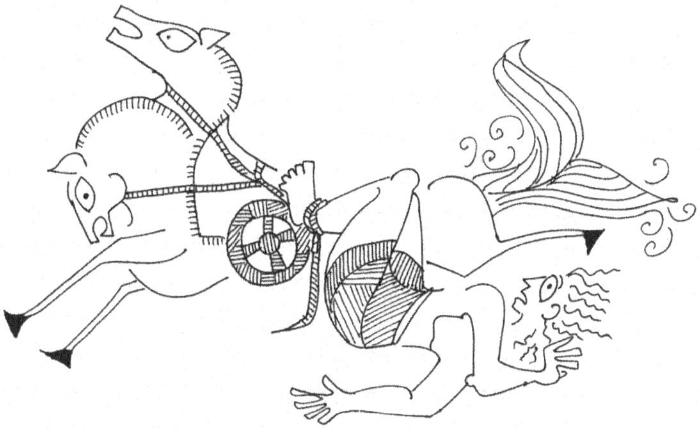

- The story of a king's wife falling in love with a stepson is a recurring theme in Indian folklore as well. In India's Nath traditions, we find the story of Chaurangi-nath whose hands and feet were cut off and who was thrown into a dry well after he was falsely accused by his stepmother of desiring her. By the grace of the Nath sages, he became a sage himself with magical powers and eventually forgave his stepmother.
- In some versions of this tale, Artemis resurrects Hippolytus with the help of Asclepius, the divine healer, and he becomes part of a cult where girls who are about to get married offer hair as proof of their chastity.
- The desire of a stepmother for her stepson is called the Phaedra complex in psychoanalysis.

Pirithous

Following the death of his wives, Antiope and Phaedra, and his beloved son, Theseus lost all interest in governance. But then an unlikely friendship reignited the spark of adventure.

It so happened that Pirithous, king of Lapiths, was getting married and Theseus had been invited to the wedding feast, as had many kings, gods and even centaurs.

Centaurs were creatures that had the body of a horse but the torso of a human; an unruly bunch, they were so smitten with the bride that they tried to kidnap and rape her, but were stopped by the noble Theseus.

A fight followed between the centaurs and the Lapiths, with Theseus fighting alongside Pirithous. The two succeeded in killing the centaurs. Comradeship and victory sparked an unlikely friendship between the noble king of Athens and the not-so-noble king of Lapiths.

When Pirithous's wife died during childbirth, he sought comfort in the company of his friend Theseus, also a widower. One day, both decided to help each other find new wives.

'Help me abduct Helen, daughter of Zeus, who is being raised in Sparta. I have been told she is the most beautiful woman in the world,' said Theseus. Pirithous agreed, and the two of them went to Sparta and kidnapped Helen, who was still a little girl.

'I too want a daughter of Zeus as my wife. Athena and Artemis would not be interested, but maybe Persephone, wife of Hades,' said Pirithous.

So the two friends made their way to the underworld to achieve this audacious feat. A furious Hades imprisoned both of them and tied them to chairs from which they could not get up. Years later, during his journey to the land of the dead, Heracles managed to free Theseus, but not Pirithous.

When Theseus came back to the land of the living, and returned to Athens, the citizens refused to let him enter. For in his absence, the city had been threatened by war. The twins Castor and Pollux had raised an army of Spartans and marched to Athens to rescue their sister, Helen. Luckily the noble Akademos had prevented war by pointing the brothers to the place where Helen had been hidden. They found Helen being cared for by Theseus's mother, Aethra. Seeing Helen cling to Aethra, the brothers decided to take Aethra with them to Sparta to serve as their sister's slave. The Athenians blamed Theseus for causing the Spartans and, before them, the Amazons to attack their city and banished him from Athens.

So a homeless, wifeless, childless, motherless Theseus wandered across Greece, from city to city, until one of the kings, tired of his smugness, or perhaps jealous of his fame, pushed him over a cliff and he fell to his death in the sea.

- In Hindu mythology, securing wives by abducting them is called rakshasa-vivah, and by rape is called pisacha-vivah.
- The battle of the centaurs and Lapiths is a popular theme in Graeco-Roman art. The deformed, monstrous centaurs symbolize uncontrollable lust.
- The tragic end of Theseus is the result of his restlessness in a life of peace, and his arrogance and pride, or what the Greeks called hubris. It is his pride that makes him crave unattainable women like the queen of the Amazons and the young Helen, daughter of Zeus. Their hubris is the downfall of many heroes, for it draws the attention of Nemesis, the goddess of divine retribution. It is not a coincidence that Nemesis is the mother of Helen in some versions of her story.
- Theseus's mother Aethra serves Helen as a maid and accompanies her to Troy, from where she is finally liberated by her grandsons, Demophon and Acamas, sons of Theseus and Phaedra, who come to Troy with the Greek army.

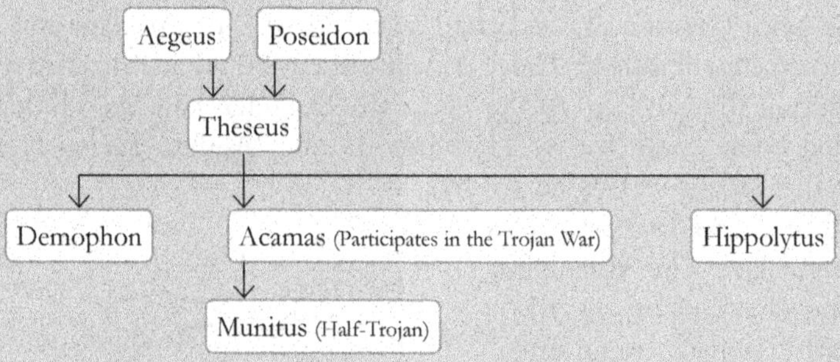

House of Theseus

BOOK THREE

Oedipus

'The arrogance of man is a terrible thing, born of a feeling of inadequacy. It goads men towards ambitions that ensure their downfall,' said the gymnosophist, thinking of the fall of Minos and Theseus.

'My teachers called this hubris, which we see even in those of aristocratic birth who think they are entitled to more. The oracles ask us to submit to the thread spun by the Fates, over which even the gods seem to have no control,' said Alexander. 'The Fates make fools of men, display our helplessness, and turn us into tragic heroes, like Oedipus.'

Cadmus

Cadmus was told by his father to go in search of his sister, Europa, and not return until he had found her. He scoured beaches and grottos and mountains but found no trace of her. Eventually, he gave up the search and decided to make Greece his home.

He went to the oracle at Delphi who advised him to find a cow with the image of the moon on its side, and walk behind it until it sat down exhausted. The place where the cow sat down would be his home.

Cadmus followed the oracle's instructions and found near where the cow sat down a river that was guarded by a dragon. Cadmus fought the dragon and killed it, not realizing that the creature belonged to Ares and anyone who slayed it was doomed to suffer a curse for generations.

Athena advised Cadmus to sow the teeth of the dragon in the soil. From it sprang a race of hostile and fully armed warriors. Cadmus threw a rock amongst them, causing them to quarrel and fight with each other, until only five survived.

These five joined Cadmus to found the citadel of Thebes.

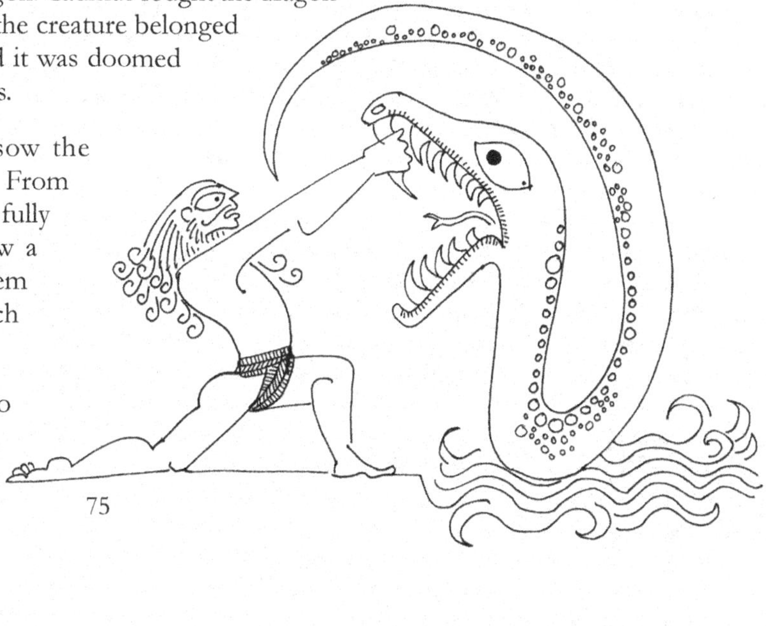

- Cadmus looks for Europa, while Castor and Pollux look for Helen. Brothers are thus seen as guardians of sisters, a theme also found in Hindu mythology, where Dhristadyumna keeps a lookout for the welfare of Draupadi, Balarama and Krishna watch over Subhadra, and Yama over Lakshmi.
- Cadmus is the mythic founder of Thebes though many have tried to prove he was a historical figure, a migrant from the Near East. Herodotus calculated that Cadmus lived 1600 years before his time, in 2000 BCE. But the Phoenician script, from which the Greek script came into being, was developed only around 1000 BCE.
- The city of Al-Qadmus in Syria is named after Cadmus.
- The phrase 'Cadmean victory' means a victory that involves ruin. Cadmus, while establishing his city, sends his people to fetch water from a river whose guardian dragon kills them. Though Cadmus slays the dragon, it is only after it has claimed the lives of those who were supposed to live in the city Cadmus was building.
- Cadmus brought the Phoenician script to Greece. The alphabet was sacred in Greece for it recorded the feats of heroes and thus granted immortality to great men. While the oral tradition depended on humans, the written tradition broke free from such dependence. This distinguishes Greek culture from Indic culture where until recent times, greater value was placed on the oral tradition.

Harmonia

Zeus felt sorry for Cadmus, who had failed in his mission to find his sister. So he decided to give him a wife: Harmonia.

All the gods were invited to the wedding of Cadmus and Harmonia. Amongst them was Hephaestus, who gave Harmonia a necklace as a wedding present. This necklace was cursed: it would cause madness, strife and suffering for generations in the House of Cadmus. Hephaestus did this cruel thing because he believed Harmonia was the child born of the union of his wife Aphrodite and her lover Ares.

So it came to pass that Harmonia's son Polydorus died at an early age. Polydorus's son, Labdacus, was killed by Dionysus's followers for criticizing their god. In this period of turmoil, Nycteus, father-in-law of Polydorus, served as regent of Thebes. Labdacus's son, Laius, was sent to Pisa, where he was raised in the House of Pelops.

- The idea that the quarrels of the gods (Hephaestus, Aphrodite, Ares) result in strife on earth (misfortune in the House of Cadmus) has no parallel in Hindu mythology. However, the idea that the deeds of ancestors (Cadmus killing Ares's dragon) impact the lives of future generations (Polydorus, Labdacus) has parallels in Hindu mythology. In the epic Mahabharata, because Yadu disobeys his father Yayati, his descendants are cursed with death should they wear the crown and become kings themselves. Thus Yadu's descendants, Krishna included, never crown themselves as rulers.
- Harmonia, daughter of Ares and Aphrodite, brings harmony, while Eris, daughter of Zeus and Hera, known to Romans as Discordia, beings disharmony.
- Cadmus was deeply troubled by the ill fortune that clung to his family and he blamed it on the dragon he killed to establish Thebes. Since the gods seemed to love a serpent so much, he wished to become one. The gods obliged. Harmonia clung to the serpent and begged the gods to turn her into one too. In art, Cadmus and Harmonia are often depicted as a pair of serpents.

Nycteus and Lycus

King Nycteus had a daughter called Antiope, who was a Maenad, a follower of Dionysus, whom Zeus ravished in the form of a satyr. Thus disgraced, a pregnant Antiope ran away from Thebes and married Epopeus of Sicyon.

Unable to bear the shame, Nycteus killed himself. His brother, Lycus, then became regent of Thebes in his place. To avenge his brother Lycus attacked Sicyon, killed Epopeus and dragged Antiope back home. On the way, she gave birth to twin boys in a cave in the middle of a forest, but was forced by her uncle to abandon them.

In Thebes, Antiope suffered the cruel treatment meted out by Lycus's wife, Dirce, for years until she managed to escape. She found her children, the twin boys Amphion and Zethus, in the cave, being raised by hunters. Amphion, son of Zeus, had grown up to be a fine musician while Zethus, son of Epopeus, was a herdsman.

Antiope roused her sons to wage war against her uncle who had treated her so badly. The brothers waged war and defeated Lycus, and forced him to declare the brothers the new rulers of Thebes. They would have killed Lycus, but Hermes forbade them to. So they turned their attention to his wife, Dirce, tormentor of their mother. They tied her hair to the horns of a bull and let the animal drag her to her death.

- Rape is not a common theme in Hindu mythology. It is associated with villains, not gods. In the Bhagavata Purana, Kansa is conceived when his mother is raped by a gandharva, so the mother curses that this child of rape will be killed by a true descendant of Yadu. In the Ramayana, Ravana rapes Rambha who curses Ravana that if he forces himself on a woman his head will split into a thousand pieces.

In the Mahabharata, King Danda rapes Araja, the daughter of Shukra, as a result of which he is cursed: his kingdom will be consumed by a sandstorm and turned into a wilderness called Dandaka-aranya.

- As the word 'rape' evokes violence, some authors prefer the phrase 'seduction by the gods'. But in many of these stories, the women resist the advances of the gods, who do not take kindly to being spurned and take the women by force, in which case it is not seduction, but rape.
- Satyrs have human torsos and the hind legs of a goat. That Zeus takes this form explains the close association Antiope has with Dionysus in the Greek tradition. She is often described as a Maenad.
- Fathers killing themselves because their daughters have brought shame to the family is common in patriarchal societies where women are seen as property. Antiope's disobedience is threefold: through her relationships with Dionysus, Zeus and Epopeus.
- Antiope bears two sons: one divine and one mortal. Amphion is the son of Zeus while Zethus is the son of Epopeus. Amphion, the musician, is contemplative, while Zethus is the active herdsman. They are like the Dioscuri, two brothers, horsemen, worshipped as a pair for good luck and protection. The theme of a woman bearing twin children, one by god and one by man, one immortal and one mortal, is a popular theme in Greek mythology.
- Antiope, the Theban princess, mother of Amphion and Zethus, must be distinguished from Antiope, the Amazon, mother of Hippolytus.

Amphion and Zethus

Amphion and Zethus decided to build walls around Thebes. While Zethus, the herdsman, used his beasts of burden to carry the rocks, Amphion used his song and music to make rocks move. The wall that encircled Thebes was famous for its seven gates.

Amphion married Niobe who bore him seven sons and seven daughters. Unfortunately, Apollo and Artemis killed them because Niobe dared to mock Leto, the mother of the twin Olympians, declaring that as she had borne more children she was more fertile than Leto. Driven by grief, Amphion attacked Apollo, and was also slain.

Zethus married Thebe who bore him one son, but in a fit of madness, she killed her own son and then killed herself, driving Zethus to commit suicide.

Thus the rule of the twin sons of Antiope came to an end.

Lycus, now old, then sent for Laius, son of Labdacus, who had been raised in Pisa, in the House of Pelops, to return home and rule Thebes.

- The rivalry of Leto and Niobe over who has more children mirrors the rivalry seen in the Mahabharata between the two wives of rishi Kashyapa. Vinata, the mother of all birds, has two children who she hopes will be greater than the many children of Kadru, the mother of snakes.
- Sappho's poetry suggests before they became mothers, Leto and Niobe were once the best of friends.
- Niobe displays hubris and so invites the wrath of Leto for disrupting the cosmos.

Jocasta

Laius returned to Thebes bearing a curse: for he had broken the rules of hospitality in Pisa when he ravished Pelops's son, Chrysippus.

Crowned king, he married Jocasta but was clear that he wanted no children, for he was cursed, and the oracles of Delphi had warned him that his son would kill him. But Jocasta was determined to be mother. She got Laius drunk one night and forced him to have sex with her. In due course, she gave birth to a son.

Laius bound the newborn's ankles and pierced them with a hook, just as a hunter pierces the feet of hunted game, and gave him to his gamekeeper with instructions to take the child to the forest and hang him from a tree as food for animals. Luckily, the infant was found by another hunter, who gave him to the childless king of Corinth who raised him as his own.

They named the child Oedipus, meaning 'large feet', since his ankles were swollen.

Oedipus grew up blissfully unaware that he was adopted, until one day a beggar called him a 'foundling'. He decided to find out the truth by consulting the oracle at Delphi. However, the oracle told him something even more horrifying: 'You will kill your father and marry your mother.' Hearing this, Oedipus, determined to change his fate, decided not to return to his parents' house in Corinth.

- Homosexual, or homoerotic, love is a consistent theme in Greek mythology: Zeus and Ganymede, Apollo and Hyacinthus, Minos and Atymnius, Theseus and Pirithous. But it was not always reciprocated as we learn in the story of Laius and Chrysippus.
- In the Bhagavata Purana, Kansa kills his newborn nephews, the sons of Devaki, to save himself from imminent death. This mirrors Laius's fear that compels him to kill his own son. In the story of Perseus, his grandfather tries to kill his mother, Danae, as it is foretold that she will give birth to his killer.
- Laius does not want to have sex with his wife. It is not clear if this is because he prefers men or because he wants to avoid fathering a son who, it is prophesied, will kill him.
- The overpowering nature of fate and prophecies and the helplessness of man before this cosmic force is a key theme in the story of Oedipus.

Laius

As Oedipus travelled far away from the house of his parents, he came upon a bridge that was wide enough for only one chariot to pass. He had almost crossed the bridge when a man rode on to the bridge on his chariot from the other side and demanded right of passage.

'It will be faster if you just wait and let me pass,' said Oedipus, but the man on the chariot, a king no doubt, was too arrogant to wait for a commoner. He blocked Oedipus's passage and demanded that he turn back instead. When Oedipus refused, the man swung his whip and lashed at him.

A fight ensued, and the man on the chariot perished. Oedipus ran away, not realizing the man he had just killed was Laius, king of Thebes, his father.

- In ancient mythologies, the right of passage over a narrow bridge is a key trope that shows the conflict between pride and humility. In the Mahabharata, Vasistha's son Shakti demands right of passage but the king Saudasa refuses to give it to him. So Shakti turns Saudasa into an ogre. The ogre then attacks Shakti and kills him.
- Laius is buried where he is murdered and his kingdom is cursed because his murderer is not punished.

The Sphinx

Laius had been on his way to the oracle at Delphi to figure out how to save Thebes from the menace of the Sphinx, a creature with a woman's head, a lion's body and vulture's wings that guarded the entrance to the city. She did not let anyone pass through the gates unless they answered her riddle correctly, but allowed people to leave. If this continued, Laius had realized, the city would either starve to death, as no farmer or shepherd or trader could enter, or be deserted, as its hungry citizens would be forced to flee.

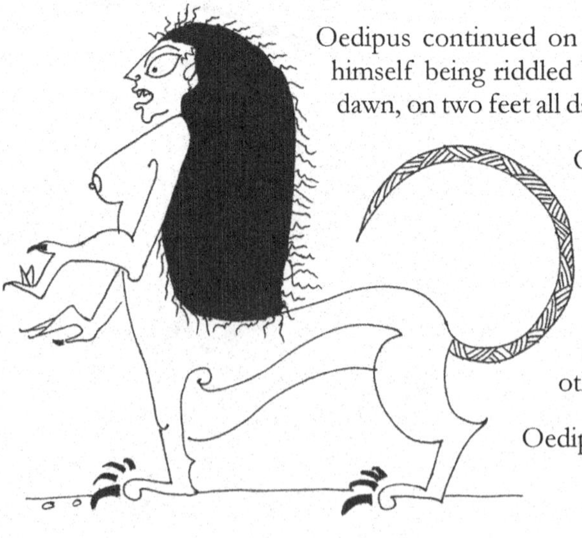

Oedipus continued on his path and reached Thebes and found himself being riddled by the Sphinx. 'What walks on four feet at dawn, on two feet all day, and on three feet at dusk? Answer or die!'

Oedipus answered, 'Man, who crawls on all fours as a child, walks on two feet for most of his adult life, and then stoops over a stick in old age.'

The Sphinx was furious. She asked another question, 'Who are the sisters who give each other birth? Answer or die!'

Oedipus answered, 'Day and night, of course.'

Accepting defeat, the Sphinx killed herself. The joyful Thebans hailed Oedipus as the saviour of the city.

Soon news reached Thebes that their king had been killed in a duel on the way to Delphi. 'Let us make Oedipus, saviour of our city, our new king. Let him marry Jocasta, the widow of Laius,' the people shouted. And so it came to pass that Oedipus married Jocasta, not realizing that she was his mother.

- In Hindu mythology, a sphinx is called purusha-mriga or vyagra-pada, half-human with the legs of a lion or tiger. They are known to be devotees of Shiva.
- In the Mahabharata, Yudhishtira is asked questions by a yaksha or forest creature that takes the form of a heron. For each correct answer, the creature promises to bring one of Yudhishtira's dead brothers back to life. Thus failure to solve the riddle of the yaksha results in death, a theme similar to the riddle of the Sphinx.
- In Greek mythology, the gods have human form. All creatures who are not fully human are survivors of an earlier mythology. Half-human and half-animal creatures like Pan were seen as remnants of chaos.
- The Sphinx was depicted as a woman with the haunches of a lion, the wings of an eagle and a tail made of a serpent. She was a child of Typhon, like many monsters of Greek mythology such as the Chimera and Cerberus.
- In ancient Egypt, sphinxes were said to guard tombs and temples, and protect their mysteries. The presence of the Sphinx in Greek mythology suggests close contact with ancient Egypt through trade.
- The Greeks considered the Sphinx as being of foreign origin, from Ethiopia.

Tiresias

Unlike Laius, who avoided her bed, Oedipus loved Jocasta very much and gave her four children: two boys and two girls. Theirs was a happy family for nearly twenty years.

But then the city was struck by an epidemic. When the Delphic oracle was consulted, she said the gods were angry as the killer of Laius had not yet been caught and punished. Oedipus swore he would do it.

'But no one saw who killed my poor husband,' said Jocasta.

'Let us invite the blind seer Tiresias who sees more than mortals do,' Oedipus suggested. It was a decision he would regret.

Tiresias was not born blind. The son of a shepherd and a nymph, he once struck dead the female of a pair of copulating serpents. As a result, he became a woman and lived as one for seven years before coming upon another pair of copulating serpents. This time he killed the male and was transformed back into a man.

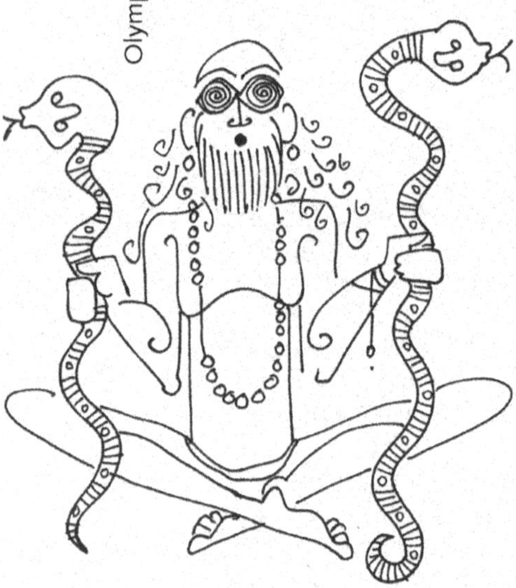

Tiresias was the only person in the world to have had sex both as a man and as a woman and so only he knew the answer to the question which eluded even Zeus and Hera: 'Who gets more pleasure during sex: men or women?' Tiresias answered that women do.

Zeus laughed and said perhaps that was why men were unfaithful to their wives, to compensate in quantity what could not be achieved in quality. Hera, however, was not amused and she directed her rage at Tiresias, making him blind. Zeus felt sorry for Tiresias and touched his ears. As a result, the blind Tiresias could hear the language of birds and animals and know what no humans would ever know. And he knew who had killed Laius.

- The desire to know the future is an indicator of humanity. All cultures have people who speak of the future. In Hindu mythology, kings often consult sages and astrologers to know what the future has in store.
- Tiresias is the archetypal soothsayer in Greek mythology.
- Tiresias is blind and hermaphroditic, indicating his connection with the invisible world of spirits—he can see things that others cannot see, hear things that others cannot hear, and move between spaces that are out of bounds for others.
- In some stories, Tiresias is blinded as he stumbles upon a pond where Athena is bathing naked. He sees her nakedness and so is cursed to lose his sight. On the intervention of his mother, Athena cleans his ears so that he can understand birdsong and practise divination.

Creon

'Laius was killed by his own son who then married his own mother. You, Oedipus, are the son of Laius, and Jocasta, your wife, is also your mother. This disgusts the gods who therefore have cast the spell of disease on the city of Thebes,' revealed Tiresias.

Oedipus refused to believe him. 'My father and my mother live in Corinth. I may have killed Laius and married his widow, but he was no father of mine.'

Messengers were sent to Corinth. The king had died and his widow was not ashamed to reveal the truth: Oedipus was an adopted child, found hooked to a tree in the forest by hunters.

Unable to handle the truth, Jocasta killed herself.

Oedipus's sons, Eteocles and Polynices, mocked their father, even as he mourned the death of his wife. 'So should we call you our father or our brother?' they said. Worse, at the funeral meal, they offered him the haunches of the sacrificed animal instead of the shoulder that was meant for the king. Angry, Oedipus muttered a curse that his sons would never get along and would kill each other.

Full of disgust and shame and heartbreak, Oedipus blinded himself with the pin of Jocasta's brooch, for what good are eyes that cannot see the truth?

But that was not punishment enough. Creon, Jocasta's brother, drove Oedipus out of Thebes for only with him gone would the epidemic that plagued Thebes end.

- The story of Oedipus led Sigmund Freud to construct the Oedipus complex: the unconscious repressed male desire to compete with the father for the mother's affections. Indian psychoanalysts have argued that in India, the story reveals a Yayati complex: the repression of sons by their fathers. The Yayati complex is the opposite of the Oedipus complex.

- In Euripides' play *The Phoenician Women*, Jocasta does not kill herself.
- The story of Oedipus is one of fate, free will and tragic flaw.
- It is ironic that Tiresias who is blind can see more than Oedipus who has eyes. That is why Oedipus blinds himself, for he cares not for human eyes that do not reveal the truth and instead present delusions.

Oedipus

Abandoned by his people and his sons, despised for committing patricide and incest, the blind Oedipus—once a king and husband and father—wandered all over the land, shunning the company of people, fearful of their reaction if they discovered his identity. Only his daughters, Antigone and Ismene, stood by him, serving him without judgement.

After many years of wandering, he came to Colonus, a grove near Athens, that was sacred to the Furies, ancient spirits who punish those who disrespect their parents.

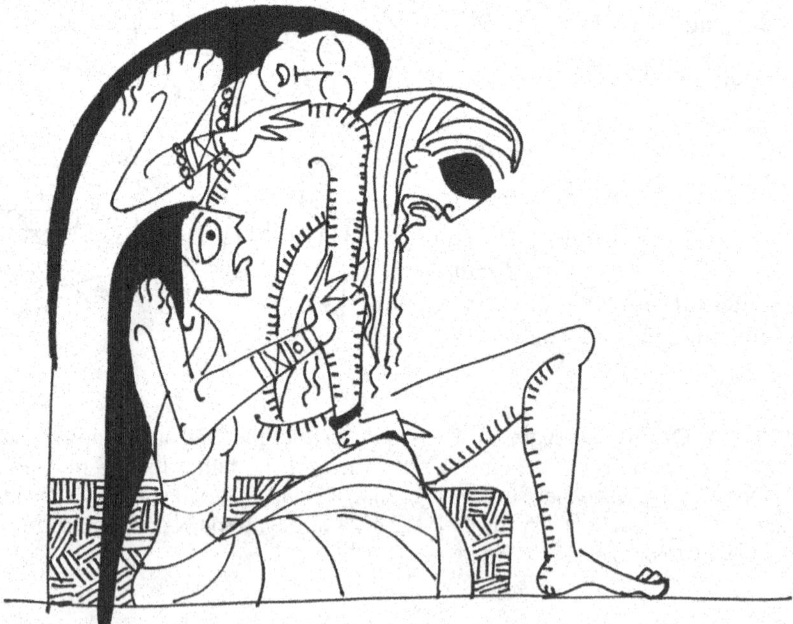

'This is a good place to die,' Oedipus told his daughters.

The guardians of the grove tried to drive Oedipus away but he insisted on meeting their king, Theseus. When the king arrived, Oedipus revealed his identity and begged Theseus to let him die there. The king, feeling sorry for Oedipus, agreed. Only then did Oedipus reveal a secret: 'It has been foretold that the land where I am buried will always stand safe, never succumbing to any assault by its enemies.'

- The idea of fate is found in both Greek and Hindu mythologies. But while the gods determine man's fate in Greek stories, in Hindu tales it is the outcome of our own past actions which attract boons and curses.
- If in the play *Oedipus Rex* Oedipus is shown as wanting to challenge and escape fate, in *Oedipus at Colonus* there is resignation, or rather acceptance of the idea that fate is a necessity and inescapable.
- While Oedipus's sons fight over Thebes, his daughters take care of him; thus ancient playwrights and mythmakers presented the tendencies of the two genders.

Eteocles and Polynices

After throwing Oedipus out of the city, his two sons began fighting over the throne. Finally, it was decided that each brother would rule the kingdom alternately for a year, beginning with Eteocles in the first year.

Unfortunately, after he ruled as king for a year, Eteocles—with the support of Creon—refused to hand over the crown to his brother. A furious Polynices declared war on Thebes, raising an army of seven commanders—each ordered to attack one of the seven gates of the city.

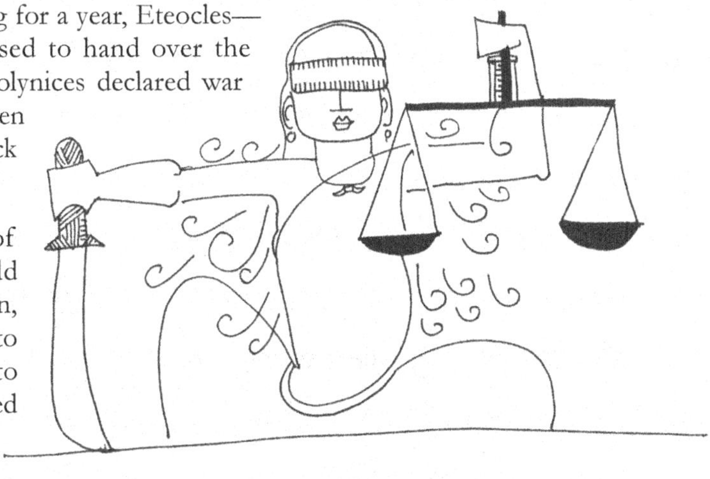

It was around this time that news of the powers Oedipus's grave would grant the land reached Thebes. Creon, now regent, rushed with Eteocles to meet Oedipus. They begged him to return and protect the city threatened by the armies of Polynices, but Oedipus refused to indulge the opportunists.

Then Polynices came to his father, purportedly seeking his blessings. While Creon wanted Oedipus to be buried within the walls of Thebes, Polynices wanted to bury Oedipus outside. For Polynices hoped that the power of Oedipus's grave would help him defeat his brother, Eteocles, who had been declared king of Thebes by Creon.

Oedipus was disgusted as to how those who rejected him while he was alive wanted control over his grave. And he was not even dead yet! He refused to forgive his sons and reiterated his curse that his two sons, who had humiliated him and driven him out of Thebes, would die at each other's hands.

Both Creon and Polynices tried to force Oedipus to change his mind by dragging Antigone and Ismene back to Thebes with them. But Theseus thwarted their attempts. In gratitude, Oedipus told Theseus to follow him deep into the woods to the spot where he would die. 'Bury me and keep the location of my grave secret so that no one can desecrate it. May it protect Athens forever.'

And so Oedipus, rejected by his sons and his subjects, finally died alone and in secret, genuinely mourned only by his daughters. Theseus, who buried him, never told the world where the grave stood, for the sake of Oedipus and Athens.

- If the Ramayana is about following rules, then the Mahabharata is about breaking rules. This epic contrast is mirrored in Greek mythology through the cities of Athens and Thebes. Athens is seen as a place where boundaries and roles are strictly adhered to while Thebes is where there is transgression, allowing for themes of incest, rape, murder and hubris.
- At Colonus, Oedipus is no longer a tragic figure but a hero sought after by two forces, those inside Thebes and those exiled from the city. When he dies, it is in secret and only Theseus knows his gravesite. Those who first mocked him, then sought him, do not ever find him.

Antigone

Polynices raised an army of seven commanders, each of whom was to storm and take control of one of the seven gates of Thebes. The attack, however, was unsuccessful; all seven commanders were killed.

Then Polynices fought his brother Eteocles and ultimately these two sons of Oedipus ended up killing each other.

Creon was declared king of Thebes. He ordered that Eteocles's body be brought into the city and buried with full honours. Creon also decreed that Polynices, who had raised an army against his own city, did not deserve a burial and that his body would rot in the battleground outside the city walls, to be claimed by wolves and vultures. Thus while one son of Oedipus was given due respect, the other was stripped of all dignity.

Antigone and Ismene, Oedipus's daughters, who had returned to Thebes after the death of their father, mourned both their brothers. Unlike Creon, they believed that both sons of Oedipus deserved to be given decent burials, not just the one. But Creon refused to change his mind: the traitor Polynices who had disrespected Thebes deserved neither honour nor a proper burial.

Ismene submitted to the will of the new king but not Antigone. She defied Creon,

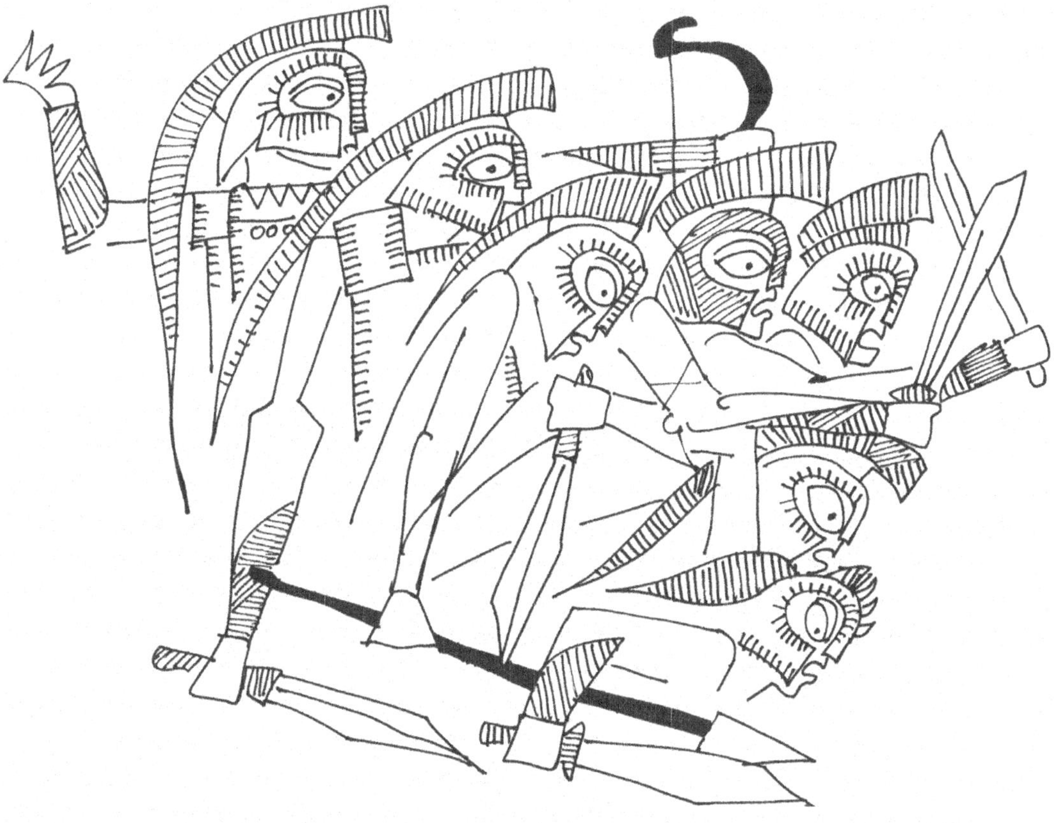

walked out of the city at night, and cremated her brother with full honours on her own on the battlefield. When this was discovered, she was arrested and Creon ordered that she be buried alive.

Rather than submit to Creon, the defiant Antigone hanged herself. Creon's son, Haemon, who was engaged to marry Antigone, could not bear the loss of his beloved betrothed and took his own life. In despair, Haemon's mother also killed herself. Thus, Creon found himself all alone as a result of attempting to impose the will of the city over the wishes of family members.

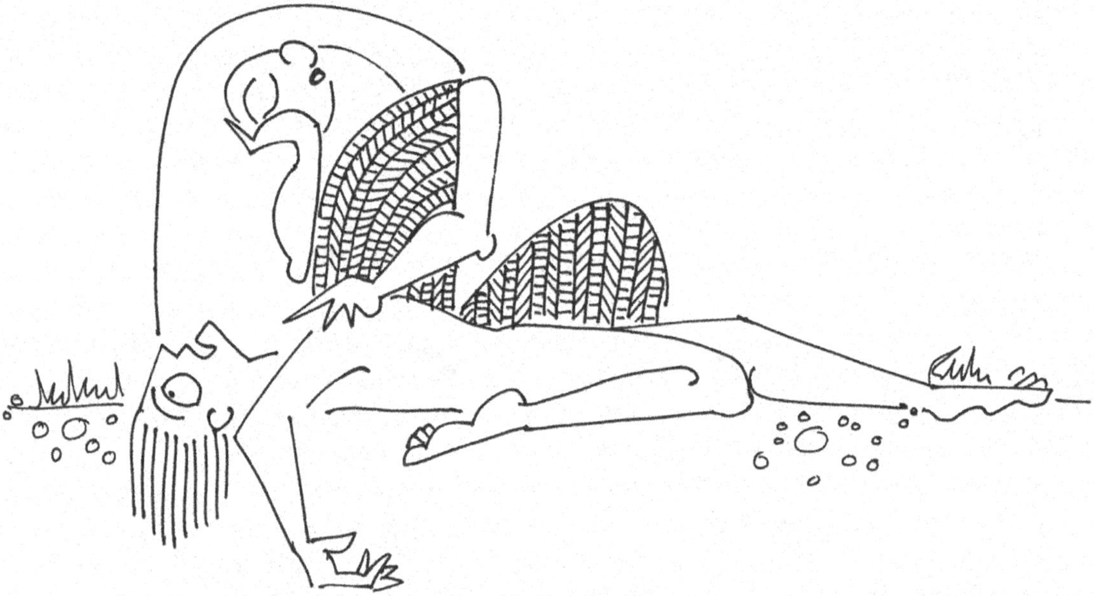

- Conflicts between the rules of the city and the rules of nature dominate Hindu thought too. The Sama Veda classifies all its melodies into forest songs and settlement songs. In the forest, there are no rules, no ruler, no regulating authority. In the city, there are rules, rulers and regulating authorities. Which is better? The freedom of the forest, where no one helps anyone, or the rules of the city, where the strong are expected to help the weak?
- Antigone embodies the heart while Creon embodies the head. She is all about compassion where he is all about rules; she symbolizes feminine 'divine law' and he, masculine 'human law'.

Epigoni

Each of the seven commanders who had attacked one of Thebes's gates and failed had a son. These sons grew up and called themselves the Epigoni. They attacked the city and razed it to the ground, and with that Thebes, established by Cadmus, ceased to exist.

- Greek mythology informs us how Thebes came into being and how it collapsed; Hindu mythology describes the rise and eventual demise of Dwarka. Both cities were established by refugees: Cadmus, who is searching for Europa and cannot go back home; and Krishna, who is escaping the wrath of a Jarasandha determined to destroy Mathura. Both cities are annihilated by war: the Epigoni devastate Thebes; and the civil war of the Yadus, together with the curse Gandhari—mother of the fallen Kauravas—hurls on the Yadus, destroys Dwarka.
- The second Theban war led by the Epigoni takes place ten years after the first Theban war, between the sons of Oedipus. It is the great war of the Greeks before the Trojan War. Both Apollodorus and Pausanias tell the story of the war.
- The *Epigoni* is an epic that formed a part of the Theban cycle. Only the first line of the epic survives today: 'Now, Muses, let us begin to sing of younger men.' The story was also the subject of a tragedy written by Sophocles.

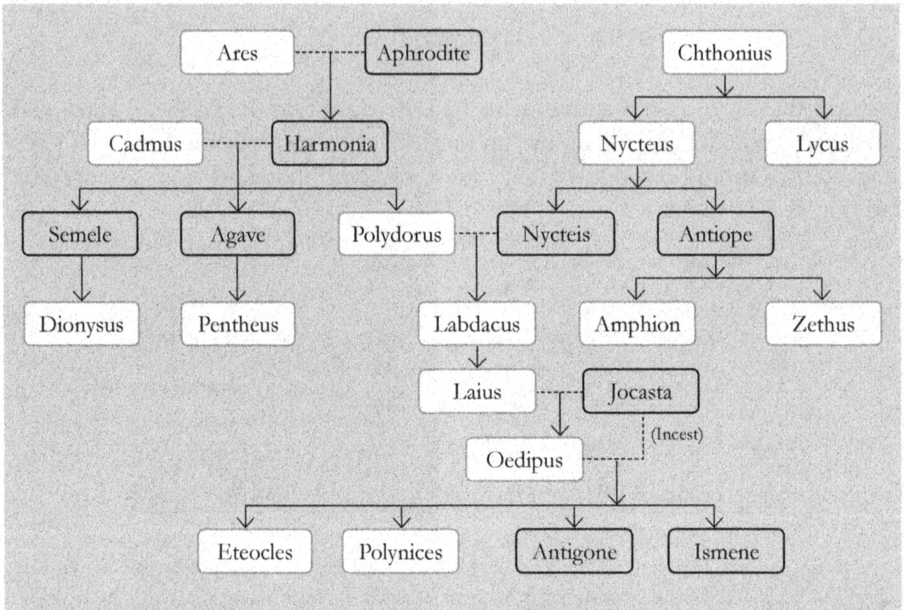

House of Cadmus

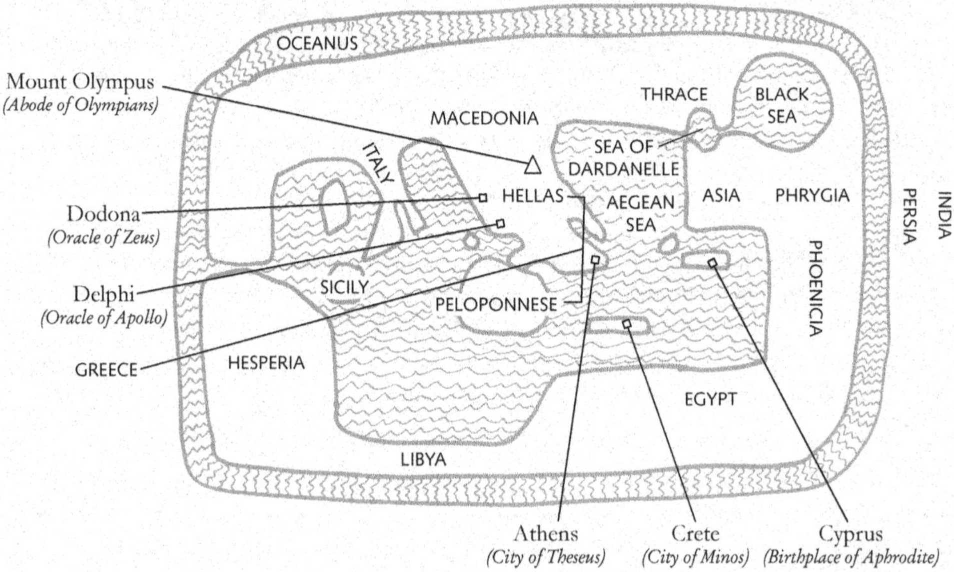

Mythological Map of Ancient Greece
(Representational, not drawn to scale)

BOOK FOUR

Heracles

'Are you a child of the Fates or a victim of hubris, Alexander?' asked the gymnosophist.

'Sometimes I think I am a child of destiny. At other times I think I am just ambitious. So I don't know. Does anyone really know? All I seek is a place in Elysium, the heaven of heroes, in the land of the dead, beyond the Styx. Or maybe even a place in Olympus, amongst the gods. For that is what was given to Heracles. He too was torn between hubris and the Fates. And he too, like me, was a son of Zeus.'

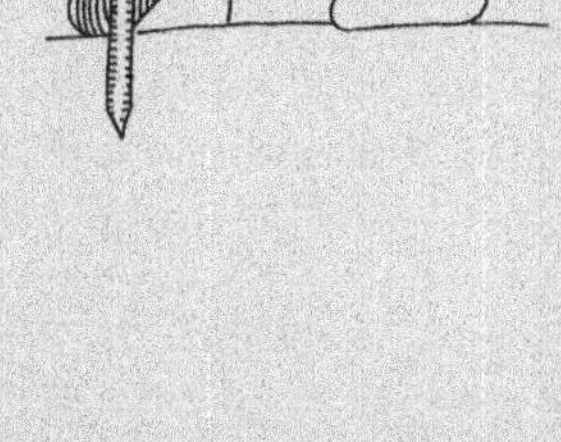

Danae

Heracles was a son of Zeus. His mother, Alcmene, was the granddaughter of Perseus, who was also a son of Zeus. Perseus's mother, Danae, had descended from Io, who had been seduced by Zeus long ago.

It was foretold that Danae's son would kill her father, Acrisius, king of Argos. And so Danae was locked in a tower, away from all men. But her father couldn't hide her beauty from the gods. Danae caught the eye of Zeus who made love to her in the form of a shower of gold that streamed into the room along with a shaft of sunlight. Soon after, she gave birth to a son whom she named Perseus.

When Acrisius discovered Danae had given birth, he was so upset that he put her and Perseus in a box and threw it into the sea. After drifting for days, the box was found by a fisherman called Dictys who gave refuge to the abandoned mother and son.

- In the Mahabharata, Kunti invokes the sun god Surya who approaches her as sunlight. The child born from their union is abandoned—placed in a basket and set afloat on the river. But Vedic gods need to be invoked by women who want to bear their children. It is only in rare instances that one hears of a god making love to a woman without her permission, as in the tale of Agni who is enchanted by the wives of the Sapta Rishis, but is warned against acting on his desires by his wife Svaha.
- The theme of a son or grandson destined to kill his father or grandfather is a recurring one in Greek mythology. It starts from the rivalry between Uranus and his son Cronus, and then Cronus and his son Zeus. This actually symbolizes the fear of the previous generation that it will lose its relevance to the next generation. Although it is inevitable, but the old still resist.
- Danae is the name given to an asteroid.

Perseus

Dictys had a brother, Polydectes, who wanted to marry Danae. She, however, kept him at bay saying that she would do so when Perseus grew up. When Perseus came of age, she had another excuse: not until he made his own fortune. So to get rid of Perseus and secure Danae, Polydectes challenged Perseus to bring him the head of Medusa.

The reckless Perseus accepted without thinking too much about it. He then learned the dreadful truth about Medusa: she was a Gorgon, with snakes for hair, and anyone who laid eyes on her turned into stone.

Luckily for Perseus, the Olympians were more than willing to help this son of Zeus.

Athena told Perseus to consult the three grey witches, the Graeae, to determine the whereabouts of Medusa. These three grey sisters shared a single

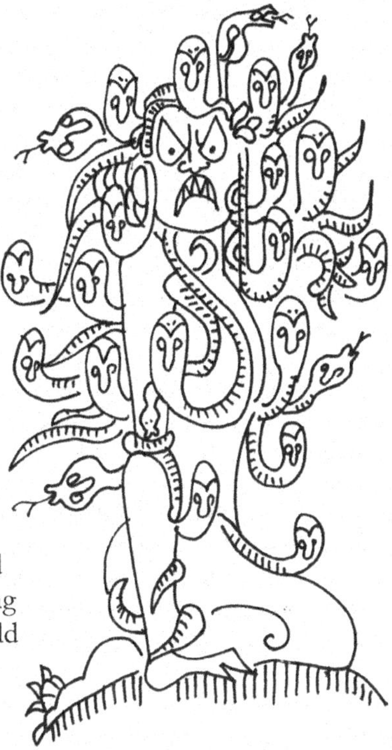

eye between them and could see everything. As the sisters passed the eye between them, Perseus grabbed it, rendering the sisters sightless, and refused to return it until they told him where Medusa was.

Hermes gave Perseus a pair of winged sandals, a helmet that belonged to Hades and made the wearer invisible, a polished bronze shield, a sharp and firm sword and a pouch from Hephaestus.

Guided by Athena, Perseus approached Medusa while she slept. He came flying using his winged sandals so that his footsteps would not wake her up, and instead of looking at her directly, he observed her reflection in the shiny bronze shield. Medusa, however, did wake up; but she could not see Perseus as he was wearing Hades' helmet. All the Gorgon saw was a sharp and strong sword come at her with tremendous speed and before she could react, her head had been severed from her neck. Perseus then put the head in his pouch and proceeded homeward.

- Perseus owes his success to the Olympians. Such tales of heroes who are helped by gods and goddesses are seldom found in Hindu mythology, where the heroes are gods themselves, or they contain a divine spark. They may even be avatars, finite manifestations of the infinite divine.
- The Gorgons were three sisters of whom only one, Medusa, was mortal. Their name means 'dread'. Their parents were ancient marine deities: Phorcys and Keto. Gorgons were probably linked to ancient Mother Goddess mystery cults and later became monsters with the rise of the Olympian gods. These were primal deities who descended from the ancient god of the oceans, Pontus, a child of Gaia.
- According to the Roman poet Ovid, who lived over 2000 years ago, Medusa was a beautiful woman who was seduced or raped by Poseidon in the temple of Athena. Athena therefore cursed her to grow snakes instead of hair and made her so hideous that everyone turned to stone when they saw her face.
- From the blood of Medusa, spilt when she is beheaded, rises Pegasus, the flying horse, who plays an important role in the story of Bellerophon.
- In ancient times, amulets with the face of Medusa were used to ward off evil spirits.

This was known as the Gorgoneion. Alexander the Great's shield also bore this image.

- Medusa has come to represent many things, from fear of maternal sexuality to feminine rage to nihilism.

Andromeda

On the way home, in Aethiopia, Perseus saw a girl chained to a rock. It was Andromeda, whose mother Cassiopeia had foolishly claimed that her daughter was more beautiful than the Nereids, sea nymphs. Furious, the Nereids had sent a monster to destroy the kingdom, and would spare it only if Andromeda was offered to the monster as a sacrifice.

As the monster rose from the sea to claim Andromeda, Perseus rushed to her rescue, coming between her and the creature. He waved the severed head of Medusa at the monster, turning it to stone. Andromeda could not believe her good fortune. As reward for his valour, Perseus asked Andromeda's father, King Cepheus, for her

hand in marriage. Cepheus could not refuse, but there was a problem. Andromeda was betrothed to marry another, and the suitor did not like Perseus trying to claim his bride-to-be. He attacked Perseus along with his friends. Outnumbered, Perseus waved Medusa's head before them, and they too turned to stone.

- Andromeda, Cassiopeia, Cepheus and Perseus are all constellations identified by Graeco-Roman astronomers such as Ptolemy. Hindu mythology is also full of stories that can be connected to constellations, such as the story of the seven sages, the Sapta Rishis, who are linked to the Great Bear, and their estranged wives, the Krittikas, who form the Pleiades or Seven Sisters.
- Cassiopeia displays hubris, or extreme pride, when she boasts that her daughter is more beautiful than a goddess, whether the Nereids or Aphrodite herself.
- The image of Perseus fighting a monster to save a damsel morphs into the idea of the knight in shining armour fighting the dragon to save the damsel in distress, which becomes a metaphor for Chaoskampf, German for the human struggle against chaos for order.

Acrisius

Perseus returned home with his bride and the head of Medusa, which he used to turn his mother's suitor Polydectes to stone, leaving Danae free to marry the simple fisherman Dictys, who had helped raise her son. Perseus gave the Gorgon's head to Athena who placed it on her shield.

When Danae told Perseus who he really was, he decided to go to Argos and meet his grandfather. But fearing death at the hands of his grandson, Acrisius abandoned Argos before Perseus arrived, leaving the crown for him.

Years later, Perseus was invited to participate in the funeral games of a local king. During the games, Perseus threw his discus further than any of the other athletes, much to the delight of the audience. In fact, he threw it so far that it hit someone in the audience—an old man who died on the spot. Everyone recognized him as Acrisius, who had come to the games to secretly watch his grandson compete. Thus fate had its way.

However, for the crime of killing his grandfather, Perseus had to abandon the city of Argos. Luckily for him, the king of Tiryns was in a similar situation. And so the two kings exchanged their positions.

As king of Tiryns, Perseus built a new city nearby, on the spot where his cap fell near a mushroom. Since the word for both cap and mushroom in Greek is 'myces', the new city came to be known as Mycenae.

- Acrisius cannot escape what is prophesied. He must submit to fate. The three Fates, who may or may not be influenced by the Olympians, especially Zeus, determine his destiny. On what basis is fate decided? On the basis of keeping order or cosmos, and avoiding chaos. This is very distinct from the idea of karma found in Indic mythologies, where fate is a reaction to previous known and unknown actions.
- In the Greek world, the act of killing demands a ritual cleansing which involves exile, participating in ritual funeral games, or performing tasks ordained by oracles, who speak the will of the gods. Similar ideas of cleansing are found in Vedic as well as Puranic literature too. Indra has to cleanse himself by doing austerities for the crime of killing Vritra; Ram has to cleanse himself for the crime of killing Ravana; and the Pandavas have to cleanse themselves for the crime of killing the Kauravas. Taking a dip in the Ganga to wash away sins is a kind of ritual cleansing.

Alcmene

Perseus had three sons. One became the king, the second sired a boy called Amphitryon while the third fathered a girl called Alcmene.

Amphitryon and Alcmene fell in love but, following a disagreement, Amphitryon fought and accidentally killed Alcmene's father, as a result of which he had to leave Mycenae and take refuge in the city of Thebes. Alcmene followed her beloved and married him as soon as Creon, the king of Thebes, ritually cleansed Amphitryon of the crime of killing his own uncle.

On the couple's wedding night, Zeus took the form of Amphitryon and made love to the bride first and then the real Amphitryon made love to her. As a result of this, Alcmene bore two children, one divine and one mortal: Heracles, the son of Zeus, and Iphicles, the son of Amphitryon.

Heracles was named on Athena's advice in the hope that Hera would not hate a child named after her. Athena then took the infant Heracles and, without revealing his identity, asked Hera to nurse him. As goddess of the household, Hera loved doing this, but to her irritation the child suckled so hard that the pain was unbearable.

She yanked him away from her breast, but by then he had consumed enough of Hera's milk to become very strong.

Hera was extremely upset at how she had been tricked by Zeus and Athena and swore to make Heracles' life miserable, even though he was named after her and she had nursed him. She sent serpents to kill the infant Heracles in his cradle. But the child simply caught hold of the snakes, squeezed the life out of them and shook them around like a rattle.

Heracles grew up to be a great warrior, skilled in the art of fighting with a sword, a lance, a club, a bow, on the ground and on a horse-drawn chariot. He was even taught music but he hated it so much that he accidentally killed his teacher with a musical instrument.

In his youth, Heracles went hunting and killed a lion. The beast had been ravaging the kingdom of King Thespius and had proved notoriously difficult to catch. A very pleased Thespius sent all fifty of his daughters to make the young man happy. Instead of choosing one, Heracles made love to all of them, for he was as virile as he was strong.

- The Greek Heracles is the same as the Roman Hercules.
- The story of Heracles suckling Hera's milk forcefully echoes the story of Krishna sucking milk and eventually the life out of the demon Putana's breasts. Like Heracles, Krishna faces many threats to his life when he is a child and he grows up to be strong and virile, loved by many women, leading many scholars to suggest that the Krishna lore was inspired by the story of Heracles.
- The drops of milk that spurted as Hera pulled Heracles away from her breasts turned into the Milky Way.

Megara

King Creon was happy with Heracles whose heroic deeds had brought great fame to the city. He was even happier when Heracles got rid of the Misyans, who were forcing the Thebans to pay them annual tribute. And so he let Heracles marry his daughter, Megara. Heracles and Megara had many children, and lived happily.

However, Hera could not bear to see Heracles happy. Every night she whispered in his ears that he was an ordinary human, not a hero, not worthy of being called a son of Zeus. She told him how his father Amphitryon had been thrown out of Mycenae for killing his uncle, and how Amphitryon's cousin, the mediocre Eurystheus, was the ruler of his ancestral kingdom, wielding more power than Heracles ever would. Slowly, she made Heracles feel insecure and invalid, and drove him mad. And in his madness, Heracles picked up his club and smashed the heads of his own children. A horrified Megara, unable to understand what was happening, picked up her youngest child and tried to run away. But Heracles picked up his bow and shot her and his youngest son dead.

When the madness waned and sanity returned, Heracles realized what he had done. Inconsolable in his grief, he went to the oracle at Delphi for advice, where he was told that the only way to be cleansed of his terrible crime was to fulfil ten tasks assigned to him by his uncle, Eurystheus, ruler of Mycenae.

- The madness of Heracles mirrors the madness of Nala and Yudhishtira, described in the Mahabharata, who cannot control themselves while gambling and end up losing their entire fortune. The Greeks blamed this on the Olympians, while the Mahabharata blames karma (the outcome of past deeds) and kala (the whimsical nature of time).
- In some stories, Megara is not killed and she marries Heracles's nephew, Iolaus, son of Iphicles.
- Iolaus served as charioteer, companion and lover of Heracles. This was part of a socially acknowledged erotic relationship between an adult male (the erastes) and a younger male (the eromenos) usually in his teens.
- In Euripides' play *Heracles*, dated 400 BCE, Heracles returns from Hades and finds

Lycus trying to kill his father, wife and children. He slays Lycus and rescues his family, but then Hera drives him mad. He thinks he is killing Eurystheus and his soldiers, when he is in fact murdering his own family members. In the play, Theseus tries to argue that even gods do unspeakable things, but Heracles remains inconsolable.

- A hero was needed to destroy the old remnants of chaos and establish Olympian order. Hera chose Eurystheus while Zeus chose Heracles. Hera therefore hated Heracles.
- The tension between Heracles and Hera is perhaps a reflection of the rise of the patriarchal male gods of Olympus who overshadow old goddesses like Gaia, Rhea and Hecate. Hera tries to delay Heracles' birth, makes his birth difficult, sends snakes to kill him and eventually drives him so mad that he kills his wife and children. He fights back with the help of Zeus and Athena, drinks her milk and acquires superhuman powers, and ultimately ends up winning her admiration through his courage, resilience and persistence.
- Any task requiring great effort is called a 'Herculean' feat.
- Creon, king of Thebes, is brother-in-law (and uncle) of Oedipus, and father-in-law of Heracles. He must not be confused with Creon, king of Corinth, who wishes to be Jason's father-in-law.

Eurystheus

Where Heracles was strong and smart, Eurystheus was weak and dull, but as fate decreed, the extraordinary Heracles was powerless before the ordinary Eurystheus. In fact, Eurystheus was so insecure before Heracles that he first hid in a great bronze jar. And later, he refused to see Heracles, choosing instead to send him the list of tasks through a messenger, Copreus.

The first task was to kill the Nemean lion. This was no ordinary lion, as Heracles discovered when his arrows did not even scratch the lion. So Heracles had to wrestle the mighty beast with his bare hands; he used the creature's own claws to rip out its entrails. Heracles then used the lion's impenetrable skin as his cloak and its scalp as headgear.

His second task was to kill the Hydra, a monster that lived in a swamp and had multiple heads. Each time a head was cut off, two more appeared. Finally Heracles came up with a solution. After he chopped off a head, his nephew Iolaus would use a torch to burn the severed neck thus cauterizing the wound, not letting it sprout new heads. Thus he was able to cut off all the heads of the monster, without letting new ones appear.

For his third task he had to capture the golden-horned Ceryneian hind or deer that was sacred to Artemis, alive. So he chased the deer until it was too exhausted to run, then picked it up, threw it over his shoulders and brought it before Eurystheus.

Heracles' fourth task was to trap the wild boar of Arcadia, also known as the Erymanthian boar. Heracles succeeded in his task by driving the beast into snow.

For his next task, he was told to clean the Augean stables, which were the dirtiest stables in the world, full of dung and rotting hay. Heracles cleaned them in a day by simply diverting two rivers through them.

The sixth task was to rid a lake of the bronze-beaked Stymphalian birds which had made the lake so filthy that no one could drink its water. Heracles used bronze kettledrums given to him by Athena to create a loud noise for such a long time that the birds could not even hear their own mating calls. They were so frightened that they took flight and refused to return.

His seventh task was to capture the Cretan bull. Heracles easily subdued it, but the real challenge was to bring it from Crete to Mycenae across the sea. Heracles made the bull swim and like Europa, long ago, sat on the animal's back and travelled back home.

The eighth task was to steal the wild man-eating mares of Diomedes, king of Thrace. Heracles seized them by making them eat their own master, Diomedes, after which they became calmer.

The ninth task required Heracles to travel to the land of the Amazons and acquire the girdle of Queen Hippolyta for the pleasure of Eurystheus's daughter. The

Amazons feared that Heracles, like Theseus, would take away their queen and so attacked him. In the fight, Hippolyta was accidentally killed while Heracles escaped with the girdle.

Heracles's tenth and final task was to fetch Geryon's cattle for which he had to travel west towards the Atlantic. As he crossed the Libyan desert the heat became so unbearable that he shot an arrow at the sun. The sun god, Helios, feeling sorry for him, gave him a chariot that enabled him to travel west more easily. Heracles placed rocks, known as the Pillars of Heracles, on the European and African sides of the channel that connected the Mediterranean Sea and the Atlantic Ocean. To capture the cattle, Heracles had to first defeat Orthus, Geryon's two-headed dog, and then Geryon himself, who had three heads, three chests, three pair of arms, and so wore three helmets, carried three shields and three spears. Heracles then herded the cattle back to Eurystheus's court, taking the long overland route from Spain through France, Germany and Italy to Greece. Often Hera would send gadflies to scatter the cattle away but Heracles would always find them, though it took him over a year to return home.

- Many Greek travellers such as Megasthenes, Greek historians such as Diodorus, and Roman philosophers such as Cicero were convinced that Pataliputra was built by Heracles during his journey East, as part of his many labours. Some equated Krishna's feat of killing the multi-hooded snake Kaliya with Heracles's feat of killing the multi-headed Hydra. Others saw Balarama as Heracles, for he was renowned for his strength as well as his temper. Also, like Heracles, Balarama is associated with a club (musala, in Sanskrit). Many have traced the name Heracles (or Herakles) to Hari-kula-esha, or 'lord of the Hari clan', and it probably refers to Balarama who was fair, not to Krishna, who was dark.
- As the great-grandson of Perseus, Heracles could have been king of Mycenae, but Hera delayed his birth until his uncle Eurystheus, a mediocre man, was born. Hindu mythology also has a story where a delay in birth results in loss of kingship. In the Mahabharata, Gandhari conceives a child first, but by the grace of the gods, Kunti delivers her child first, and so it is Kunti's son Yudhishtira who has a greater claim on the throne than Gandhari's son Duryodhana.

- The final fixed list of the labours of Heracles comes from an epic poem, now lost, written by Peisander in 600 BCE.
- A crab tried to stop Heracles from killing the Hydra, and was rewarded by Hera, who placed the crab in the stars as the constellation Cancer.
- Bucephalus, Alexander the Great's horse, was said to have descended from the man-eating mares of Diomedes.
- During his adventures, Heracles visited many lands. In Egypt, the king captured him and tried to sacrifice him to the gods. Heracles broke his chain and killed the king instead.
- The labours as they progress become increasingly tougher and later, demand that Heracles travel further and further away from Greece, for Eurystheus was convinced that Heracles, who like him was a descendant of Perseus, was a more worthy contender for the throne of Mycenae.
- Heracles is identified in art by his lion-skin cloak and his olive-tree club. The lion killed by Heracles becomes the zodiac sign Leo.

Hesperides

When Heracles had performed all the tasks set for him, Eurystheus argued that he had completed only eight labours, not ten. Had he not taken the help of his nephew, Iolaus, to cauterize the necks of the Hydra? Had he not got two rivers to wash the Augean stables, which meant he had not done the job himself? Thus two more tasks were given to Heracles: fetching the apples from the Garden of the Hesperides, also known as the Apples of Joy, and then capturing Cerberus, the three-headed dog of Hades, ruler of the land of the dead.

Heracles did not know where the Garden of the Hesperides was and had to wrestle Proteus, the shape-shifting old man of the sea, to learn the location. Proteus told Heracles that only Atlas, the Titan who held up the sky, knew where this garden was located, for the Hesperides were his daughters.

When he found Atlas, Heracles offered to relieve the Titan of his burden for a short while. In exchange, he asked that Atlas bring him the apples from the Garden of the Hesperides. Atlas agreed. Mighty Heracles held up the sky while Atlas went to fetch the apples. But on his return, the Titan changed his mind. 'You keep holding the sky. I will deliver the apples wherever you tell me,' he said.

Heracles realized that unless he came up with a clever idea, he was trapped. So he told Atlas that he did not mind holding up the sky forever, and then requested Atlas to hold the sky for just a moment while he placed a pillow on his shoulders as padding. Though strong, the Titan was not very smart, and so he agreed. As soon as Atlas was holding up the sky again, Heracles picked up the apples, thanked him and made his way back to Greece.

- Trickery is an important part of a hero's kit in Greek as well as Hindu mythology. Hanuman, the monkey-god, who plays a key role in the Ramayana, is both strong and smart, often using trickery to solve problems. Once, while travelling across the sea, a demon called Surasa insisted he enter her mouth before proceeding further. Knowing this to be a trick, Hanuman reduced himself to the size of a fly and zipped in and out of the demon's mouth before Surasa could snap it shut. Thus, having satisfied her condition, Hanuman moved on.
- Hesperides is derived from Hesperus, or the evening star Venus. It is associated with the nymphs of the sunset who tend to the apple tree of happiness that grew from the gift of a branch given by Gaia to Hera on her wedding day.
- The nymphs who tend to the apple tree at Hesperides are the daughters of Atlas.
- The Apples of Joy associated with Hesperides is the very opposite of the Apple of Discord that Eris uses to cause the Trojan War.
- 'Golden apples' perhaps refer to oranges that were unknown in Europe and the Mediterranean until the Middle Ages. They were first cultivated in China.

Cerberus

Heracles' final task was to capture and bring back Cerberus, the hound of Hades. This meant crossing the River Styx and entering the land of the dead. Undaunted by the prospect, Heracles made his way there. Hades, who had been impressed by the many tales of Heracles' valour, was pleased to meet him and allowed him to take the hound to the land of the living. But he had one condition: Heracles would have to use his bare hands and no weapons.

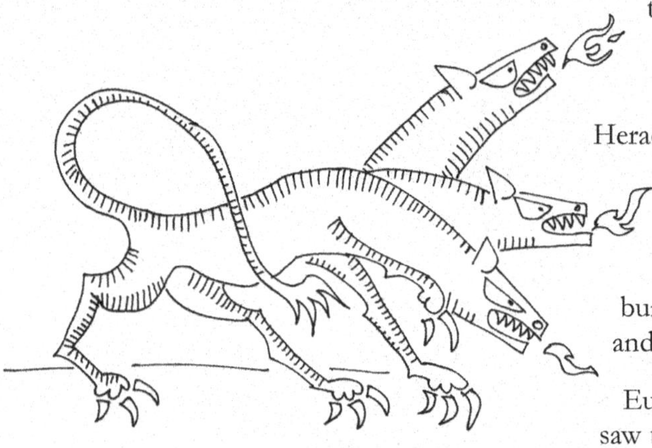

Heracles approached the hound with trepidation but soon realized that even Cerberus's fangs and claws could not tear the thick and strong cloak made from the hide of the Nemean lion. Using the lion-skin, he bundled up Cerberus, put him in a bronze jar and took him to Eurystheus.

Eurystheus removed the lid of the bronze jar, saw the terrible Cerberus and realized Heracles had finished the last, and toughest, task assigned to him. And so he declared that Heracles had been cleansed of the crime of killing his wife and children.

- After killing Kansa, upon Devaki's request, Krishna travels to Yama-loka, the land of the dead, and brings back his long-dead brothers to the land of the living so that Devaki, their mother, can see all her eight sons together. Thus Hindu gods also travel to the land of the dead fearlessly.
- During his trip to Hades, Heracles liberates Theseus who was trapped there along with his friend Pirithous who had planned to abduct Persephone and was punished for his audacity.
- Just like the Hydra, the Chimera and Orthus, the two-headed dog who guarded the cattle of Geryon, Cerberus was the offspring of Typhon. Thus, in Greek mythology, monsters are born of primal beings who embody chaos.
- The twelve labours of Heracles are sometimes identified with the twelve constellations that make up the zodiac. The crab, the bull and the lion he kills are clearly three of them: Cancer, Leo and Taurus. Sagittarius is his teacher, Chiron, whose death he causes accidentally.

Chiron

During his journey to the land of the dead Heracles met the Titan Prometheus, trapped in Tartarus, suffering unending misery, his liver being eaten all day by an eagle only to regenerate itself at night.

Heracles killed the eagle and broke Prometheus's chains, but when he tried to take him out of Tartarus, he was stopped by Hades. 'A life for a life,' Hades said. 'You must give me an immortal who is willing to take this Titan's place.'

Heracles remembered his teacher Chiron, a centaur, blessed with immortality. Long ago, he had injured his teacher, shooting him accidentally with an arrow dipped in the venomous blood of the Hydra. The wound had not healed and Chiron was doomed to suffer this injury for all eternity. If he took Prometheus's place, he would no longer suffer bodily pain, for those who lived in Tartarus had no bodies. They were shades, shadows of the living.

The centaur readily agreed and so Hades let Prometheus return to the land of the living and Chiron walked in Tartarus forever, suffering no bodily pain.

The Olympians were impressed with Heracles' smart thinking. They cast Chiron in the stars as the constellation Sagittarius, the wounded teacher.

Zeus, though, was not very happy about Prometheus's release until the Titan told him a secret, 'You desire the sea nymph Thetis. Beware, for a child born of her will be greater than the father.' An insecure Zeus was grateful for this foresight and so forgave Prometheus finally.

- There is only one Hindu tale which mirrors the Greek idea of eternal suffering: that of Ashwatthama, son of Drona, who is cursed by Krishna to live forever with a body covered in sores, never experiencing the peace of death, because he tried to kill an unborn child, the only surviving descendant of the Pandavas. He still lives, they say, suffering his unending punishment.

- The idea of bargaining with immortality as a currency is a repeated theme in Greek mythology. Prometheus can leave Tartarus only when the immortal Chiron takes his place. Pollux shares his immortality so that he and his mortal twin, Castor, are always together.
- Heracles has a tense relationship with centaurs. Once when visiting his friend Pholus, a centaur, he accidentally opened a jar of sacred wine whose scent caught the attention of other centaurs, who joined the party, drank unwatered wine, and got so drunk that they attacked Heracles. In the ensuing fight, Pholus ran away, Chiron suffered a never-healing wound, and many centaurs died.

Omphale

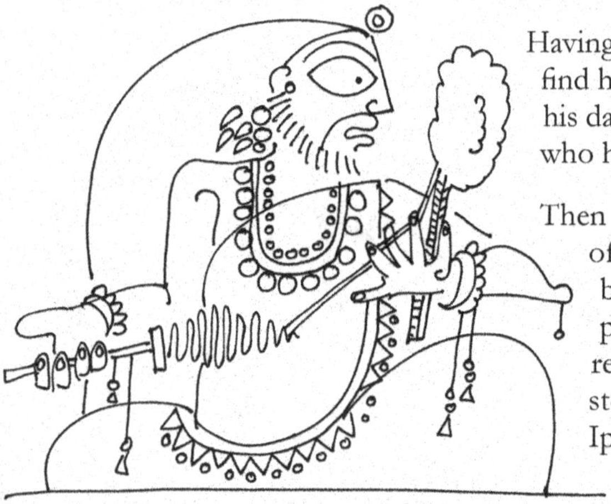

Having been liberated by Eurystheus, Heracles decided to find himself a wife. But no man was willing to give him his daughter and no woman was willing to marry a man who had killed his own children.

Then Heracles learned that Eurytus of Oechalia was offering his daughter, Iole, to any man who could beat him and his sons in an archery contest. Heracles participated in the contest and won, but Eurytus refused to give him his daughter. Angered, Heracles stole Eurytus's cattle and killed his youngest son, Iphitus, who, ironically, admired him greatly.

As punishment for this crime, Heracles had to spend three years as a slave to Queen Omphale of Lydia. And she delighted in not just making him her lover, but also dressing him up as a woman.

- The idea of a Greek hero wearing women's clothes for the pleasure of an oriental queen disturbed many Greeks who were comfortable with man–boy love but not cross-dressing. In contrast, Hindu mythology is full of tales where Hindu gods cross-dress for the pleasure of their mothers and wives. In temples, Krishna is often made to wear the nose-ring of his beloved Radha, and tie his hair in a plait.

- There were lost comedies of how Heracles is forced to wear women's clothes and spin thread while Omphale wore his lion skin cloak and held his olive-wood club.
- Lydia is modern-day Turkey. Long has the West held the view that the East emasculates men as evinced in the tale of Omphale cross-dressing Heracles.

Deianira

Finally, Heracles managed to get a wife in Calydon. Her name was Deianira. But marrying her was not easy. He had to first defeat the river god Achelous who also wanted to wed her.

Heracles and his new bride decided to make their home in the city of Trachis. On the way, they had to cross a river. Heracles could swim across it, but not his bride. Nessus, a centaur, offered to carry Deianira across on his back. Heracles accepted and put his bride on the centaur's back before swimming across the river himself. When he reached the other bank, he saw that Nessus had stopped in the middle of the river and was fondling his wife, intent on raping her. Furious, he shot a poisoned arrow at Nessus, fatally wounding him.

As he was dying, Nessus looked at the innocent Deianira and whispered, 'My blood is a love potion. Apply it on your husband's clothes and when it seeps into his skin he will love you so much that he will never even think about killing you as he did his first wife.'

Using the centaur's dead body as a raft, Deianira reached the other shore. But she also collected some of his blood to induce love in her mad but strong husband, of whom she was more than a little scared.

- Hindu mythology has horse-headed beings known as Kimpurushas, but rarely creatures whose torso is that of a horse, like the centaurs of Greek mythology. From the mouth of horse-headed beings such as Hayagriva, Vedic wisdom is transmitted to sages.
- Many post-Buddhist artworks found in Bodh Gaya, Sanchi and parts of Odisha have images of centaurs, suggesting a Greek influence.
- Centaurs are known for their wild lascivious nature. Chiron, the wise teacher, is an exception. In art, heroes are often depicted fighting centaurs, as in the battle where Theseus fights centaurs alongside Lapiths.

Iole

After several years of being happily married, Heracles decided to avenge the insult inflicted on him by Eurytus of Oechalia who had denied him a wife. He raised an army and ransacked Oechalia, killing Eurytus and managing to secure

Iole as his concubine. Iole tried to escape by jumping from the ramparts but her robes ballooned like a parachute and she fell safely to the ground, with no hope of escaping from Heracles.

Though Heracles insisted that Iole was merely a concubine, not a wife, Deianira was not so sure. She decided to use the blood of the centaur Nessus to rekindle passion in her husband. She smeared it on his cloak, expecting profusions of love when he draped it; instead he screamed in agony, for the blood of the centaur was poisonous and it burned his skin and his flesh.

Heracles realized he would soon die. Too proud to be killed by another, he decided to take his own life. He climbed on to a pile of wood and asked the warrior Philoctetes to set it aflame.

As the fires rose, Zeus looked down from heaven and, deciding that Heracles was the greatest of his sons, picked him up and brought him to Olympus. Here he was reconciled with Hera and given in marriage to Hebe and allowed to live like a god. Those on earth who searched his pyre for his bones found none.

- Though Heracles is compared with Krishna, the similarities are superficial. Heracles is a tragic hero-son of Zeus, while Krishna is God on earth, trying to enlighten humanity.
- One recurring motif in the story of Heracles is that he is denied what he feels he deserves: a happy married life with Megara, the throne of Mycenae on which sits the lout Eurystheus, payment after washing the Augean stables, payment after saving Hesione from a sea monster sent by the gods to devour her, and the hand of Iole after winning Eurytus's archery contest.
- Euripides' play *Heraklides* tells the story of Heracles's children who are taken by his nephew, Iolaus, to Athens to protect them from Eurystheus. But the king of Athens cannot protect them as the oracles tell him that only the sacrifice of a young maiden to Persephone will ensure victory against Mycenae. The king refuses to sacrifice any Athenian and so Heracles' daughter Mecaria offers herself to save her siblings. After her sacrifice, a war is fought, in which old Iolaus miraculously regains his youth and captures Eurystheus alive. The Athenians refuse to execute him as it is against their law but Eurystheus, humiliated in defeat, tells them to do it as it is prophesied that he will return as a guardian ghost of the city and protect Athens from the Spartans.
- After Eurystheus's death, the throne of Mycenae passed on to Atreus, son of Pelops.

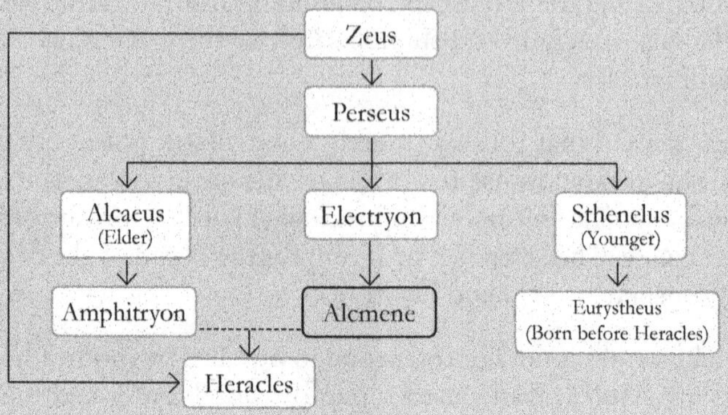

House of Perseus

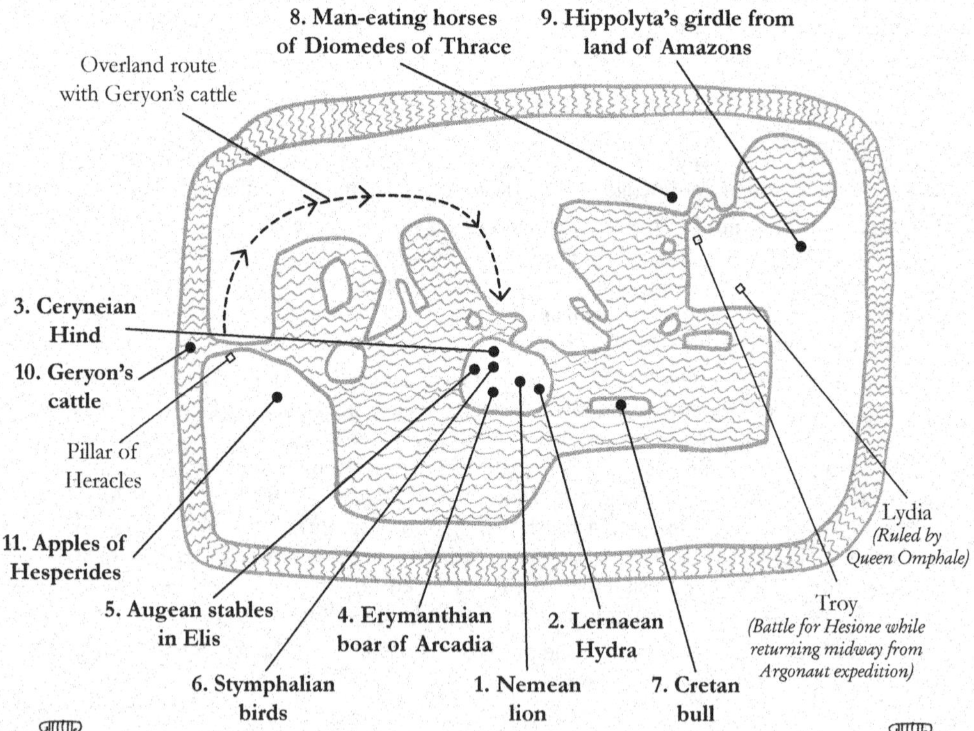

Tasks of Heracles, and other adventures (Representational, not drawn to scale)
Notice how with each task Heracles has to travel farther away from Greece.

BOOK FIVE

Jason

'Are all the heroes from your land the sons of gods?' asked the gymnosophist.

'Not all. Not Jason, who fetched the Golden Fleece from faraway Colchis in the east. But, unlike Heracles, he failed to win the admiration of the gods.'

'Because his father was not an Olympian?'

'No, because he owed his victory to an Eastern woman, a witch, whom he later betrayed.'

Pelias

Salmoneus, king of Elis, claimed that *he* was Zeus himself. That the torches burning on the sides of his chariot were lightning, and the noise of the kettledrums attached to and dragged by his chariot was thunder. Annoyed by this impertinence, Zeus hurled his thunderbolt at Salmoneus and reduced him, his chariot and his city to a pile of ash.

Salmoneus's daughter, Tyro, married Cretheus, king of Iolcus, and bore him a son whom they named Aeson.

Tyro was also in love with a river god, but he rejected her advances. So the sea god Poseidon, who desired Tyro, took the form of the river god, and ravished her. From this union was born a son. He was called Pelias.

Pelias grew up to be an ambitious man. He imprisoned his older brother, Aeson, and declared himself king of Iolcus. But he did not have Zeus's favour for he was a son of Poseidon, and the grandson of Salmoneus. Worse, Hera did not like him because he had once desecrated her temple by killing people who had taken refuge there.

The oracles warned Pelias that 'a man who wears only one sandal' would kill him. So all the guards in the palace and the city were told to look out for such a man. Little did he know that such a man was yet to be born, and it would be his own nephew, Jason, son of Aeson.

- Just as Zeus kills Salmoneus for imitating him, Krishna slays the king of Pundra for pretending to be the 'true' Vasudeva by wearing yellow silk and a crown with a peacock feather. In the end both pretenders are killed by real weapons wielded by the gods: Salmoneus by Zeus's thunderbolt, and the false Vasudeva by Krishna's Sudarshan-chakra.
- In the Greek world, the destiny of a man is bound by the Fates and the whims and rivalries of the Olympians. That Jason will eventually kill Pelias is pre-decided and has nothing to do with Jason's free will. This idea distinguishes Greek mythology from Abrahamic mythology where humans have the free will to choose God or submit to evil. The Hindu world is governed by kama, desire, as well as karma, destiny determined by past deeds. Additionally, in devotional schools, the possibility of God's intervention to realize desires or to change destiny exists.

Jason

Aeson's wife Alcimede was pregnant with Jason when Pelias became king. She was sure Pelias would kill her child as soon as he was born. So, at the birth, she told the midwives to cry as if the babe was stillborn, then smuggled the infant out of the palace and gave him to Chiron, the centaur, to be raised and educated in secret.

Years passed. When Jason came of age, Chiron told him the story of his birth, and advised him to participate in the games held in honour of Poseidon organized by the usurper of his father's throne, King Pelias of Iolcus.

On his way, Jason helped an old woman cross a river, and lost one of his sandals while doing so. The old woman was the goddess Hera and she blessed Jason with success and fortune.

When Jason arrived at the games, the guards announced him as 'the man wearing only one sandal'. The oracle's warning echoing in his mind, Pelias decided to send this man—his would-be killer—on a quest that would surely kill him.

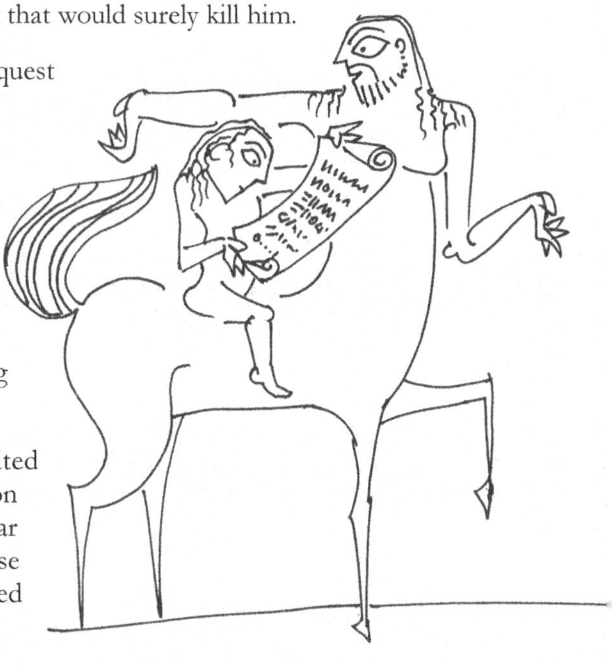

Pelias asked Jason, 'What is the most dangerous quest today for a man aspiring to be a hero?'

Jason replied, 'Fetching the Golden Fleece from Colchis.'

'Then be a hero and fetch me the Golden Fleece.'

Jason had no choice but to accept the challenge. He had been tricked by the man who was holding his parents prisoner.

Making the most of the situation, Jason invited young men from all over Greece to join him on this adventure. Few Greeks had travelled as far east as Colchis, the land where the sun rose. Those who had dared, had never returned. It was located beyond Hellespont, the sea that connects the Mediterranean Sea to the Black Sea.

- On recognizing his killer ('the man with one sandal'), Pelias protects himself by sending Jason on a dangerous quest from which he may never return. Similarly, Shishupala's mother tries to protect him from Krishna by extracting a promise from the lord (that he will forgive the first hundred of Shishupala's transgressions) when she recognizes him as the man destined to kill her son (when Krishna picks up her son, his birth defects disappear). But in both cases, destiny prevails.
- These stories reveal the geographical knowledge of ancient times when the eastern

edge of the Black Sea, where the country of Georgia is now located, was believed to be the land from where the sun rises.

- The story reveals the great discomfort of the Greeks with the unknown East, a fear that continues even today.

Helle

Hellespont was named after Helle, the daughter of King Athamas of Boeotia, and the cloud nymph Nephele. Helle had a brother called Phrixus. One day, Athamas fell in love with a woman called Ino, and cast his wife aside. So Nephele left Boeotia, while Ino became the queen.

Ino was determined to get rid of her stepchildren. She went to the city's granary and secretly roasted all the grain meant for sowing. When the seeds did not germinate despite the rains, the frustrated and anxious farmers consulted the oracle, who—having been bribed by Ino—told them that only a sacrifice of the king's children would appease the angry gods.

Athamas protested but his subjects rushed past him into the palace to grab the royal children. Luckily for the children, their celestial mother presented them with a flying ram, with fleece that was golden. 'Sit on this and escape east to Colchis across the sea. No one will follow you there and you will be safe,' Nephele told them. 'And remember, while you are flying over the sea, do not look down towards the earth, for you may lose your balance, and fall.'

During the flight, Phrixus followed his mother's instructions, but not Helle. She looked down, lost her balance, and fell into the sea. The spot where she fell came to be known as Hellespont, the eastern end of the Mediterranean Sea, beyond which no Greek had ever sailed.

On reaching Colchis, Phrixus sacrificed the flying ram, as his mother had advised, to Zeus, and gave its fleece to the local king, Aeetes, who gave him shelter.

- Tales of children whose lives are threatened by stepmothers is a common theme in mythologies around the world. In the Buddhist Dashrath Jataka, Dashrath sends his son Ram to exile in the forest as he fears Ram's stepmother, Kaikeyi, plans to kill him.
- Nephele is the cloud nymph created by Zeus in the very likeness of Hera. Ixion tries to rape this cloud nymph mistaking her to be Hera. For his audacity, Ixion is cast in Tartarus.
- The ram that carries Phrixus to Colchis is sacrificed to Zeus. It is turned by the Olympians into the constellation Aries of the zodiac.
- Aeetes is the son of the Titan Helios, the sun. Aeetes's brother, Phaeton, once wanted to ride their father's celestial chariot. Helios indulged him but Phaeton lost control, as a result of which the sun came so close to the earth that it scorched the ground and burned most of the trees, angering Zeus who killed Phaeton with a bolt of thunder.

Argonaut

Many Greek warriors joined Jason's quest: some because they were too famous to refuse, and others because they hoped the quest would make them famous.

Amongst those who came were the great hero Heracles, and his arms-bearer, Hylas; Calais and Zetes, the winged sons of the North Wind; the musician Orpheus, and the mighty Bellerophon; Telamon and Peleus, the sons of Aeacus; and the fierce

Spartan warriors Castor and Pollux, brothers of Helen. Jason was the designated captain, though many believed Heracles was more worthy of leading the men.

Jason got one Argus to design a sturdy ship for him, and in this task the shipwright was helped by the goddess Athena. Parts of the vessel were made using wood from the groves of Dodona. These groves were frequented by oracles who sought to decipher the will of the gods by listening to Zeus whispering through the rustle of oak trees. By using wood from these trees the ship itself was bestowed with prophetic powers. It often warned the sailors of dangers that they could face if they did not set sail, or go ashore, in time. Since it was built by Argus, the ship came to be known as the *Argo*, and sailors as the Argonauts.

The *Argo* was so heavy that the sailors could not drag it into the sea, but Orpheus played his music and the ship moved on its own, ready to sail and take the Argonauts on their adventure.

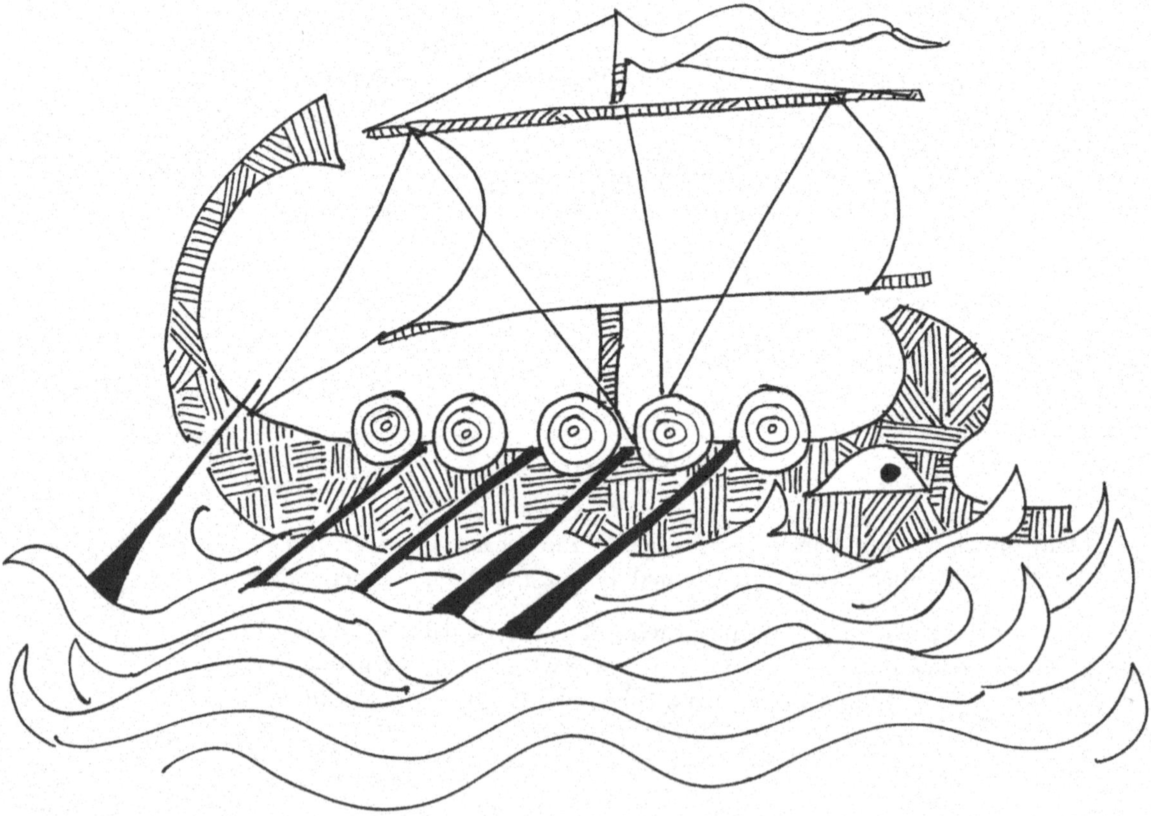

- The trope of unrelated men coming together for a mission appears frequently in Greek mythology, such as the hunt for the Calydonian boar, the quest for the Golden Fleece and, finally, the Trojan War. Such a collaboration is rare in Hindu mythology. In the Mahabharata, during the great war, kings take sides depending on family obligations and individual vendettas. In the Ramayana, it is the animals of the forest, monkeys and bears mainly, that come together to help Ram rescue Sita from the island of Lanka.
- The story of the *Argo* and its sailors is the theme of the Greek epic *Argonautica* by Apollonius Rhodius, composed 2300 years ago.
- Unlike most Greek heroes, Jason shows signs of brooding and depression, making him more human, a detail that earned him and his story much criticism.
- Ancient writers were of the opinion that the *Argo* was amongst the first ships to sail on the high seas. Earlier ships sailed along the coast.

Atlanta

Atlanta, a female warrior, wanted to join the Argonauts but Jason did not allow it, fearing the presence of a woman would distract the all-male crew.

Atlanta's father had abandoned her at birth because he wanted a son. She had been suckled by a she-bear and later raised by hunters. She could run at great speeds, so fast that she could even run on water.

Tales of the effect Atlanta had had on the men who were hunting the Calydonian boar were fresh in everyone's memory.

The fierce Calydonian boar had been sent by Artemis to torment King Oeneus who had insulted the goddess by denying her offerings he had promised her. Warriors from all over Greece were invited to hunt this creature but they had failed both individually and collectively. When Atlanta came, her presence was fiercely opposed by all. Only Meleager, son of Oeneus, supported her, for he fell in love with her, despite being married. Atlanta managed to strike the first blow on the boar, and Meleager eventually killed the beast. Meleager then offered the head and hide of the boar to Atlanta, angering his uncles who took this gift away from her by force. Enraged, Meleager killed his uncles, only to be slain by his mother, who then took her own life, unable to bear the loss of her brothers and her son. King Oeneus concluded that Atlanta, like the wild boar, had been sent by the goddess to destroy his family.

It was perhaps to forget Meleager that Atlanta wanted to join the Argonaut expedition. She even chased the ship by running on the waves behind it. But finally she gave up the chase and returned to land.

Many men wanted to marry Atlanta, but she claimed she would marry the man who could outrun her in a race. Hippomenes begged Aphrodite to help him win Atlanta's hand in marriage and so the goddess gave him a set of irresistible apples and a plan. During the race, every time Atlanta outran Hippomenes, he threw an apple in front of her. Unable to help herself, she would stop to pick up the apple and Hippomenes would run ahead, gaining lost ground. Thus Hippomenes won the race and Atlanta's hand in marriage.

But then the couple made the mistake of making love in a temple of Zeus, a crime for which they were turned into lions, which—according to folklore—cannot mate with each other. Thus they roamed the world together, but were never united in love.

- In the Mahabharata, Shikhandi is a woman who is trained to be a warrior. But unlike Atlanta, whose femininity and sexuality are acknowledged in the Greek myths, Shikhandi is raised as a man, allowed to enter the battlefield after she acquires male genitals from a yaksha.
- Powerful female characters in Greek mythology eschew sexual relationships with men, as if contact with men will drain them of their powers. Thus Athena, the goddess of wisdom, and Artemis, the goddess of the hunt, are virgins. Atlanta takes the oath of virginity and dedicates herself to Artemis, yet she falls in love with Meleager and Hippomenes. In both instances, the relationship remains unfulfilled.
- In many versions, Atlanta does join the Argonaut expedition to be with Meleager who proved his love by abandoning his wife. She chases him by running on the sea. But they were forbidden to mate for the loss of her virginity would affect the voyage. Eventually she gives up and lets him go onward while she returns to land.
- A recurring theme in Greek mythology is the punishment Olympians mete out to those who desecrate temples by having sex in them. Though the Greek gods have intense sex lives, celibacy is valued. This idea had a huge impact on Christianity as well.

Lemnos

After the Argonauts set sail, the first island they came upon was Lemnos, where there were no men. The women were so happy to see the Argonauts that they took care of all their needs. So wonderful was the hospitality that the men forgot all about their mission. Jason married the leader of the women, and encouraged his fellow sailors to marry the other women. The women bore children and a new race known as the Minyans came into being.

But Heracles was not so easily fooled. He investigated and found out that the women had murdered their husbands.

These women had once angered Aphrodite who had then caused their bodies to emit a foul odour. Repulsed by them, their husbands sought the company of other women, who eventually became their secret wives. When the women discovered this, they murdered their husbands.

Heracles pressured Jason and the Argonauts to leave the island, reminding them of the mission, which they did, albeit grudgingly.

- The fear of women's sexuality and their trapping the hero is a consistent theme in Greek as well as Hindu mythology. In the Nath-yogi tradition, celibate yogis are constantly fighting the pull of the sensual yoginis.
- The phrase 'Lemnian deeds' refers to the vengeful slaughter of a group of people, often of the same gender. In the story of the Argonauts, women slaughter their unfaithful husbands. Herodotus tells the story of Pelasgian men who kidnapped Athenian women and took them to the island of Lemnos, determined to make them their wives. However, the women refused to submit and insisted on teaching their children Athenian, not Pelasgian, ways, angering their husbands, who killed the children first and then the defiant mothers. The Danaids were sisters who killed their husbands on their wedding night and so were cast into Tartarus, trying forever to fill a bucket of water using broken pots.
- Lemnos is also the island where Philoctetes is abandoned at the start of the Trojan War after he is bitten by a serpent that causes his foot to rot and smell foul. After ten years, the Greeks come to fetch him as it is foretold that Troy will not fall without Heracles' bow, which is in Philoctetes' possession.

Doliones

After it passed Hellespont, the *Argo* reached a peninsula which was home to a civilized and friendly race called the Doliones and the barbaric and hostile race of the six-armed Gegeines. The Doliones welcomed the Argonauts and told them where they could find food and how they should avoid the wild Gegeines.

While the other Argonauts went off in search of food, Heracles decided to stay back and guard the ship; a good decision, as it turned out, for the Gegeines did attack the ship, but Heracles was able to fend them off.

When it was time to leave, the Doliones bade the Argonauts farewell. The *Argo* set sail, but at night, a storm pushed the ship back towards the peninsula. In the darkness, the Doliones mistook the

Argonauts for raiders. The Argonauts too did not realize they had returned to the same shore whence a few hours earlier they had set sail. In the skirmish that followed, many were slain, including Cyzicus, the young king of the Doliones.

In the morning light, when the truth was discovered, there was great sorrow. The queen of the Doliones was so upset that she killed herself. A great funeral was organized in honour of the dead on both sides, but it did not assuage their grief.

- The queen of the Doliones kills herself on her husband's funeral pyre. Greek mythology occasionally refers to women killing themselves to share the death of their husbands. Was this practice—what is known as sati in Hinduism—a custom of the Indo-European or Aryan race that spread both to Greece and India?
- Cyzicus had killed one of the lions of Cybele and the goddess arranged for the 'accidental' slaughter of his people by the Argonauts.

Hylas

When the *Argo* was ready to set sail again, Heracles did not join the ship. His manservant and arms-bearer, Hylas, who had gone inland foraging for food, had not returned, and Heracles refused to leave without him. Although Jason insisted that the quest could not wait for just one man, Heracles was resolute. Telamon and Peleus, sons of Aeacus, also joined him, abandoning the Argonaut mission.

Hylas was the son of Theiodamas, whose wife had had an affair with Heracles. When the relationship was discovered it led to a duel in which Theiodamas was killed. Perhaps out of guilt, or genuine affection for the beautiful boy, Heracles took Theiodamas's son under his wing as his arms-bearer.

Hylas was never found. While fetching water from a stream for his master, he had caught the eye of a group of water nymphs who were so enamoured by his beauty that they abducted him.

Heracles, after a long but fruitless search, decided to return home to Greece, via the famed city of Troy.

- The idea of man–boy love is conspicuous by its absence in Hindu mythology. This form of homoerotic expression was common in Greek mythology. In Hindu mythology, homoerotic expression takes the form of gender transformation: a man becomes a woman as in the case of Ila and Narada, or a woman becomes a man as in the folklore of Bahucharji mata in Gujarat, each time after they fall into a waterbody or enter an enchanted forest.
- The love Heracles bore for Hylas is parental according to the Greek poet Theocritus who wrote 2300 years ago, though Christopher Marlowe refers to it as homoerotic in his play *Edward II* (1593), similar to the relationship between Zeus and Ganymede.
- Heracles chooses Hylas over the Argonaut expedition. Some scholars claim that he does this in a spirit of generosity, to avoid overshadowing Jason's leadership.
- The similarity of the Greek word *melon* for both apple and sheep has led people to see parallels between Heracles' quest for the golden apples at Hesperides in the north and Jason's search for the Golden Fleece at Colchis in the east.

Castor and Pollux

The next stop on the *Argo*'s voyage was the land of the Bebryces, whose ruler, Amycus, welcomed the Argonauts and after offering them refreshments, invited them to a game of boxing. Only, this was no game, as the Argonauts soon discovered; Amycus fought to kill. And no one was allowed to leave his kingdom until they played the game.

The first of the Argonauts to rise to Amycus's challenge was Castor. He and his twin, Pollux were born of the same mother but had been sired by different fathers: Castor by the mortal Tyndareus and Pollux by the immortal Zeus. When Castor lost to Amycus, Pollux took up the challenge. Unlike his twin, Pollux was immortal, and he managed to avenge his brother and box Amycus to death.

Watching Pollux grieve over Castor, Zeus offered him a place on Mount Olympus where he could drink ambrosia and find happiness. But the thought of life without his twin was unbearable, so Pollux begged his father to grant half his immortality to Castor. Zeus agreed, and the two brothers lived half their days on Olympus and half their days in Hades, alternating their places with each other. He also cast the two brothers in the sky where they continue to live as stars in the constellation Gemini, sharing immortality.

- Hindu mythology has stories of two inseparable and invincible asura brothers, Sunda and Upasunda, who cannot be killed unless they quarrel with each other. And so the devas send the beautiful Tilottama who makes the brothers compete for her love, and they end up killing each other.
- Pollux is the Roman name for the Greek Polydeuces.
- The twins Castor and Pollux, also known as the Discouri, were popular deities in Greece and Rome and were associated with pear trees, war dances and with the constellation Gemini. As helmeted horsemen who carry spears, the twins are often compared with the Ashwini twins of Hindu mythology.
- Amycus is a son of the sea god Poseidon by a nymph. That he is killed by a son of Zeus, Pollux, reflects the rivalry of the two Olympians for control over earth.
- Castor and Pollux share the same mother as Helen and her twin sister, Clytemnestra. According to Homer, Castor and Pollux fight and die while trying to bring Helen back from Troy. In this version, Amycus is a Trojan.

Harpies

After Bebryces, the Argonauts beached on an island that was home to Phineus, king of Thrace, who had the gift of foresight. In exchange for the ability to tell humans the future, the gods had deprived Phineus of eyesight and they sent the Harpies to torment him.

When the Argonauts asked Phineus the way to Colchis, he said, 'I can only answer if I eat and I cannot eat because of the dreaded Harpies. Every time food is served to me, they come and eat a third of it, carry off another third, and excrete upon what is left so that it cannot be consumed. Thus the gods punish me, slowly starving me to death, preventing me from sharing my knowledge of the future with humankind.'

Amongst the Argonauts were the brothers Calais and Zetes, two winged youths often addressed as the Boreads as they were sons of the wind god Boreas. They kept guard while the Argonauts laid out food before Phineus. Just as Phineus was about to eat, the Harpies appeared to ruin his meal. Only, this time the flying twins stopped them. Not just that, the Boreads decided to capture the Harpies and chased after them as they flew out into the sea. Iris, the rainbow goddess, told the flying twins to stop pursuing the Harpies, as the Olympians did not want the creatures to die, but she promised that the Harpies would no longer bother Phineus. So the Boreads agreed to let the Harpies go.

Unfortunately, it was foretold that the Boreads, children of Boreas, would die if they failed to catch whatever they pursued. And so they could not return to the Argonauts and forewarn them about the dangers that they would encounter on the sea route to Colchis. They simply fell into the sea and drowned.

- Harpies are depicted as having the heads of women and the bodies of birds. They are imagined as forms of wind, violent storms like tornadoes that carry everything away.
- Greek storytellers speak of two Harpies. Virgil, the Roman, refers to a third in his epic *Aeneid*.
- In some versions, the Harpies fly so far out into the sea that they fall into the sea from exhaustion and drown, as do Calais and Zetes. In other versions, Heracles kills the twins for it is they who convince the Argonauts to set sail, leaving Heracles behind while he is searching for Hylas.
- The 'floating rocks' (Symplegades) came to be known as the 'turning rocks' (Strophades) to mark the spot where the sons of the wind god Boreas 'turned away' from their pursuit of the Harpies.

Symplegades

With the Harpies finally gone, Phineus ate to his heart's content and then told the Argonauts how to reach Colchis.

'You will have to go past the Symplegades,' he said, 'two floating rocks that mark the entrance to the Black Sea. They crush all things that pass between them, which is why no sailor from the west has ever been able to travel so far east. Only the ram of Phrixus, flying high above in the sky, succeeded in getting past them. But there is a way to outsmart the Symplegades.'

As advised by Phineus, on reaching the floating rocks Jason released a dove that flew between the rocks. The floating rocks rushed forward to crush the bird, but it managed to escape, losing only the tip of its tail in the process. The Argonauts now knew how fast the floating rocks moved and could calculate the speed at which they would have to row if they wished to pass through unharmed. Sure enough, the Argonauts, rowing faster than they ever had, managed to clear the floating rocks, with only slight damage to the rear end of the ship.

- While ships play a major role in Greek mythology, in Hindu mythology one finds references to flying chariots and small river boats. In the vrata-kathas there are tales of Indian sailors whose wives pray for the well-being of their husbands who are seafaring merchants. About 1500 years ago, for some mysterious reasons, Hindus were forbidden to travel across the sea. Sea trade was then outsourced to the Arabs who were later replaced by Europeans.
- The Symplegades or 'floating rocks' are located in the present-day Bosphorus Strait that connects the Mediterranean Sea and the Black Sea.
- The floating rocks are a popular metaphor. For example, in *Practical Criticism: A Study of Literary Judgement*, published in 1929, I.A. Richards describes excessive intuitive reading and excessive literal reading of poetry as the Symplegades or the floating rocks that wreck understanding of poetry.

Aeetes

Aeetes, king of Colchis, welcomed Jason and on learning of his mission said, 'You can have the Fleece, but you must prove you are worthy of it. First, you must plough a field with the help of fire-breathing bulls. Then sow the teeth of a dragon in the field. And finally, defeat the never-sleeping serpent that guards the tree on which the Golden Fleece rests.'

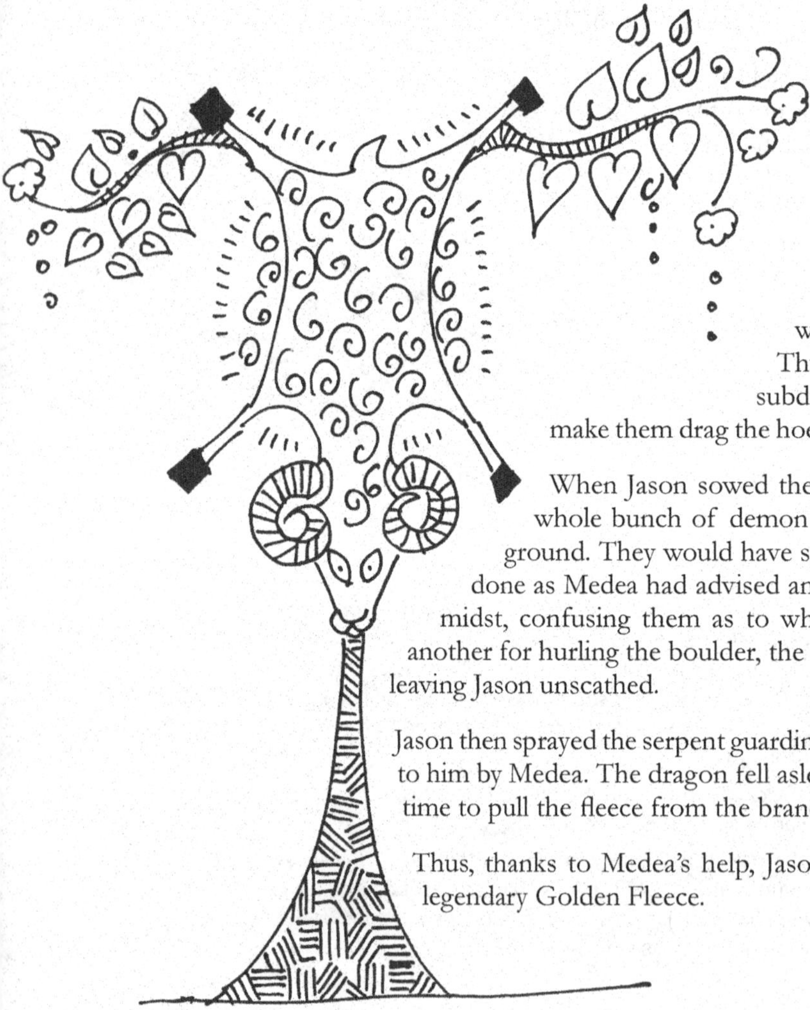

As Jason wondered how he would achieve these feats, help came from an unexpected quarter: the daughter of Aeetes, a sorceress called Medea, who had fallen in love with him.

Medea gave him a special ointment to apply on his body that would allow him to withstand the fire of the bulls. Thus anointed, Jason was able to subdue the beasts, yoke them and make them drag the hoe across the field to plough it.

When Jason sowed the dragon teeth in the field, a whole bunch of demon warriors sprouted from the ground. They would have surely killed Jason had he not done as Medea had advised and thrown a boulder in their midst, confusing them as to whom to attack. Blaming one another for hurling the boulder, the demons attacked each other, leaving Jason unscathed.

Jason then sprayed the serpent guarding the tree with a potion given to him by Medea. The dragon fell asleep, giving Jason just enough time to pull the fleece from the branches of the tree.

Thus, thanks to Medea's help, Jason succeeded in fetching the legendary Golden Fleece.

- The Sanskrit Adbhuta Ramayana, composed 500 years ago, tells the story of the many adventures of the monkey-god Hanuman in Patala, the subterranean world, as he tries to rescue Ram who has been abducted by the sorcerer Mahiravana. In this story, which follows a rather linear structure like most Greek myths, Hanuman encounters and overpowers many demons and monsters. Like most Greek heroes, Hanuman is the son of a god, Vayu, the Vedic god of wind, and a mortal mother, Anjana, who raises him with her mortal husband, Kesari.
- As Ariadne helps Theseus out of love, so does Medea help Jason. Is the victory of Jason then the work of Aphrodite?
- As for many Greek myths, the source of this story is not just written works but also artwork found on vases. Many of these illustrations show Jason emerging from the mouth of the never-sleeping serpent of Colchis, which does not match the description found in the written sources. Also, in these, he is helped by Athena, not Medea.
- The tale of seeds giving birth to warriors mirrors the story of Cadmus sowing dragon teeth. In Greek mythology, humans are born of clay. That is how Prometheus created mankind. However, they can also be created by sowing dragon teeth. Deucalion and Pyrrha created a new line of humanity after Zeus's great flood by throwing rocks over their shoulders.
- Poseidon ravished a nymph taking the form of a ram to sire the flying ram with Golden Fleece given by Nephele to her children.
- Rationalists, who see myth as proto-history, interpret the myth of the Argonaut expedition as indicative of bringing animal husbandry or grain cultivation from the East to Greece. Or it might have been about 'washing gold' from streams using sheepskin.

Apsyrtus

Aeetes, who was convinced that Jason would fail in his mission, was furious when the lad triumphed. He was angrier still when he learned that his own daughter had helped Jason succeed. He ordered his soldiers to stop Jason from escaping from Colchis by any means. Unfortunately, by the time the soldiers reached the port, the *Argo* had already set sail, with Jason aboard and Medea by his side.

Aeetes decided to pursue the *Argo* and bring back both the Fleece and his treacherous daughter. His ships were the fastest in the sea and caught up with the *Argo* in no time. But as his ship approached the *Argo*, he found pieces of flesh floating on the sea: they were parts of a human body that Aeetes recognized as his dear son, Apsyrtus.

Apsyrtus had been lured aboard the *Argo* by his elder sister, Medea, who then cold-bloodedly killed him, chopped his body to pieces and threw them in the sea, knowing that the shock and horror of the act would stop Aeetes from pursuing them. Her plan worked—Aeetes gave up the chase. But as he turned back, he cursed that his daughter would never find happiness with the man for whom she had betrayed her father and killed her brother.

The *Argo* arrived in Greece after a long and complex journey. Guided by Medea, instead of going through the Bosphorus, the ship sailed via a route known only to witches.

Grateful for Medea's help and moved by her unconditional love, Jason agreed to marry her, thus returning to Greece, not just with the Fleece, but also with a witch for a wife.

- In other versions of the tale, Apsyrtus pursues his sister and Jason on a ship and is killed in a fight with Jason. Atlanta is wounded in this fight and healed by Medea.
- Having murdered her brother, Medea goes to her aunt, the witch Circe, who performs rituals to cleanse her of the violent act.

Medea

On returning to Iolcus, Jason gave Pelias the Golden Fleece, which the king accepted grudgingly.

The people of the city were fascinated by Medea. They watched how, with her magical herbs, she cured the sick, and made beautiful the ugly.

Pelias's daughters saw how she cut up an old and sick goat, threw the pieces of its flesh in a cauldron full of herbs and brought it back to life as a young and healthy lamb. They watched her kill and restore to life Jason's old father, Aeson.

'I can do the same for your father,' she whispered in their ears.

The daughters believed the witch and while their old father slept, they murdered him, cut his body into many pieces and threw them in Medea's cauldron of herbs. Only this time, the meat cooked itself with the herbs and there was no sign of resurrection. Thus did Medea fool the girls and kill Pelias, the man who had sent her husband on a dangerous mission.

Medea had hoped that by killing Pelias she would make her husband king. But the people of Iolcus were not so forgiving. They drove the witch and her husband out of the city, and the couple took refuge in the city of Corinth.

- In the medieval mythology of Nath yogis, the wandering hermits of India, there is the story of how Goraksha-nath uses his yogic powers to kill and bring back to life the son of his guru Matsyendra-nath by the Amazon queen Pramila. He does this to prove that life and death are delusions and to liberate his guru from the sexual snare of his wife.
- In Hesiod's *Theogony*, the marriage of Jason and Medea is listed as one of the marriages between mortals and immortals, suggesting that Medea is divine.
- Medea is often linked to Hecate, the goddess of magic.
- Medea embodies a woman who is both powerful and frightening. She is representative of the exotic Eastern woman for the Greeks who preferred their women more submissive.

Creusa

Medea was deliriously happy with Jason in Corinth, where she gave birth to two children. Jason, however, was not happy being a householder when he could have been a king. He felt frustrated and angry, until the king of Corinth made a proposal: 'Marry my daughter, Creusa, and rule this land with her as your queen.'

Jason wondered what would happen to Medea, but the king told him that no one in Greece considered the eastern witch his wife; she could stay in Corinth as his concubine. This thought appealed to Jason but when he told Medea she was heartbroken. But witch that she was, she cold-bloodedly plotted her revenge.

She gifted Creusa a beautiful robe to wear on her wedding night. As soon as Jason's new bride wore it she burst into flames. A horrified Jason and the king of Corinth rushed to Medea's chambers to seize and punish her, only to find that she had killed her own children, and was flying away towards the sun on a chariot drawn by flying serpents.

An angry Jason chased after her, but he could only make it as far as the sea while Medea flew beyond the horizon. Frustrated, angry and miserable, a homeless, wifeless, childless Jason walked along the beach till he came upon the ruins of the *Argo*, decaying beside the sea. Jason rested in its shadow, recollecting his great adventures, and his tryst with Medea. As melancholy consumed him, the prow of the old rotting ship broke and fell on him, crushing him to death.

- Like Jason, Ram of the Hindu epic Ramayana abandons his wife. But while Ram does it to uphold the family reputation, Jason does it for personal ambition. Ram never remarries while it is Jason's desire to remarry that sparks the crisis. Both Jason and Ram die heartbroken: Jason for betraying his wife, and Ram for being unable to hold on to her.
- In older versions of the story, the Corinthians kill Medea's children after her escape. The wilful killing of her children seems to be the invention of the playwright Euripides in the fifth century BCE.

- In some tales, after leaving Corinth, Medea goes to Thebes, cures Heracles of his madness that made him kill Iphitus, and is given refuge until the residents drive her away, Heracles' protests notwithstanding. She then takes refuge in Athens where she marries Aegeus. Unfortunately for her, Aegeus's son Theseus comes back and claims the throne she hoped would go to her children. Thus rejected by the Greeks, she returns to Colchis.
- Medea's story makes us wonder about justice and revenge in an unjust society. It also reveals the tension and discomfort that follow powerful foreign women.
- Eventually the *Argo* was turned by the Olympians into the constellation of Argo Navis found in the southern hemisphere. In the eighteenth century, this rather large constellation identified by the ancient Greeks was split into three: the keel, the deck and the sails.

Orpheus

Amongst the Argonauts who accompanied Jason to Colchis was Orpheus, the son of Apollo and a Muse. He could play the lyre and sing songs that could move

rocks, and make animals weep and trees dance. After his return from Colchis, he fell in love with and married Eurydice.

Orpheus and Eurydice lived together happily until a satyr tried to rape Eurydice and she died during the attack. Heartbroken, Orpheus sang tragic songs that filled the Olympians with such melancholy that they begged him to stop. They told him to go to the land of the dead and convince Hades to let Eurydice return to the land of the living.

Moved by his music, Hades granted Orpheus's wish, but had one condition: 'Her ghost will follow you but you must not turn back to look upon it until you reach the land of the living.'

Orpheus agreed but in his anxiety, just before they reached the land of the living, he turned around to check if Eurydice was truly following him or if Hades was fooling him. Instantly, the ghost of Eurydice disappeared, returning to the land of the dead, and Orpheus came back alone.

Orpheus lost all interest in love after this. The Maenads, worshippers of Dionysus, invited him to join them, but he refused. Angry that he preferred music and men to them, they attacked him with sticks and stones, but the sticks and stones, enchanted by his music, refused to hurt him. So the women tore at him with their bare hands and ripped him to shreds. His head floated downstream, singing songs of his beloved Eurydice.

- The theme of not looking back is found in other mythologies as well: the Biblical story of Lot's wife turning back to see the burning Sodom and thus turning into a pillar of salt, and the Odia folk tale of Sakshi Gopal where Krishna turns into stone when a young devotee turns around to check if Krishna, who is supposed to act as witness in a case against him, is still following him.
- Orphism believed in the divinity and immortality of the soul and the mortality of the flesh that had to suffer the material world. It promoted asceticism and is said to have been inspired by Indic monastic traditions such as Jainism that possibly reached Greece 2500 years ago. This belief in rebirth, known as metempsychosis, was very different from traditional Greek beliefs. In time it came to be closely associated with

Dionysian mysteries, for Orpheus, like Dionysus, did encounter the dead and come back to the land of the living.

- According to the Greek poet Phanocles, who lived in the third century BCE, Orpheus joined the Argonauts as he was in love with Calais, the son of the wind god Boreas.
- The River Helicon sank underground when the women who had killed Orpheus tried to wash their bloodstained hands in its waters.
- Orpheus's lyre was turned into a constellation.

Bellerophon

Like Orpheus and Jason, most Argonauts lived unhappy lives on their return, perhaps suffering on account of Medea's rage. So it was with Bellerophon.

Soon after his return, Bellerophon accidentally killed his brother and so turned to Proteus, king of Tiryns, to cleanse him of the crime. Proteus did so and invited the Argonaut to stay in his palace and tell him tales of his adventures.

Unfortunately, the king's wife fell in love with Bellerophon and invited him to her bed. When Bellerophon refused, she accused him of rape. Proteus could not hurt the man who was a guest in his house, so he sent Bellerophon to his father-in-law, King Iobates, with a sealed letter containing orders to kill him.

Iobates put aside the letter and invited Bellerophon to dine with him and tell him tales of the Argonaut expedition. When he opened the sealed letter nine days later he was shocked. He too could not kill a guest as per the laws of hospitality. But he came up with a clever plan. He challenged Bellerophon to overpower the Chimera, a fire-breathing monster with the head of a goat, the body of a lion and the tail of a serpent.

The oracles told Bellerophon that he would not be able to kill the Chimera until he rode above it on the flying horse, Pegasus. Athena gave Bellerophon a golden bridle with which he could capture Pegasus when he came to drink water from a mountain spring.

Riding Pegasus, Bellerophon travelled through the sky and reached the countryside ravaged by the Chimera. He threw a block of lead into the monster's mouth. The fire that the Chimera breathed out melted the lead, and the monster choked to death. A triumphant Bellerophon returned to a hero's welcome. Iobates gave him his daughter as his wife and half his kingdom.

But Bellerophon was consumed by pride and decided, after his many adventures, that, like Heracles, he too deserved a place with the gods. And so he rode towards Olympus on Pegasus, angering Zeus who hurled his thunderbolt, causing Pegasus to bolt; Bellerophon tumbled towards the earth. He spent the rest of his life as a blind, crippled hermit, shunning human contact: another Argonaut with a miserable end.

- In Hindu mythology, the monstrous are not to be killed but to be venerated. The Odia Mahabharata speaks of how the archer Arjuna is at first frightened but then awestruck by Navagunjara, a creature that is a composite of nine beasts: rooster, peacock, lion, serpent, bull, tiger, deer, elephant and human. What in Greek mythology is chaotic becomes a mystery in Hindu mythology, an order beyond the comprehension of the human mind.
- In Hindu mythology, the flying horse is called Ucchaishrava. It emerges from the ocean of milk. In Greek mythology, Pegasus is created from the blood of Medusa.
- Taking care of guests is a key virtue in the eyes of Zeus. Those who treat guests poorly suffer his wrath.
- Bellerophon's desire to rise to Olympus is a case of hubris, excessive pride that makes a hero forget his place in the cosmos, forcing Zeus to act against him.
- Chimera today means a fantastic idea that can be imagined but not realized.
- In the Middle Ages, especially after the Rennaissance, it was Perseus, and not Bellerophon, who was depicted riding Pegasus and attacking the sea monster who threatens Andromeda. This image later metamorphosed into that of St George killing the dragon (the Devil) to save the damsel in distress (the Church). It symbolized the concept of Chaoskampf or the conquest of chaos by the colonizer, the scientist and the missionary in order to bring order to the newly discovered savage worlds of America, Africa and Asia.

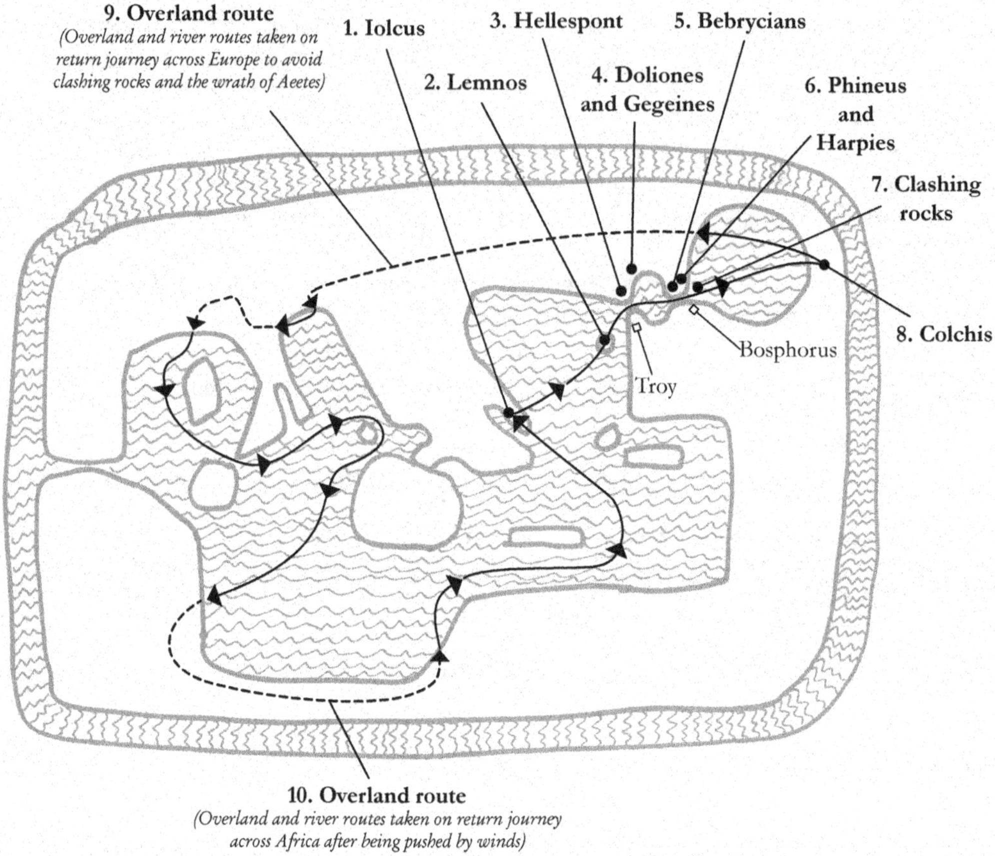

Argonaut Expedition

(Probable route: representational, not drawn to scale)

On overland routes across Europe and Africa, the *Argo* was carried on shoulders over mountains or made to sail on plains using Oedipus's music.

BOOK SIX

Helen

'Did Zeus ever father a mortal daughter?' asked the gymnosophist.

'Only one, Helen, born when Zeus took the form of a swan and seduced Leda, princess of Sparta. But maybe her real mother was Nemesis, the goddess of retribution, who bore this child to show humans their place in the world. She caused the first war between Europe and Asia.'

'A fight that you carry forward.'

'I will end all fights. I will bring peace.'

The gymnosophist did not argue. He was more eager to hear the story of Helen and the war she sparked.

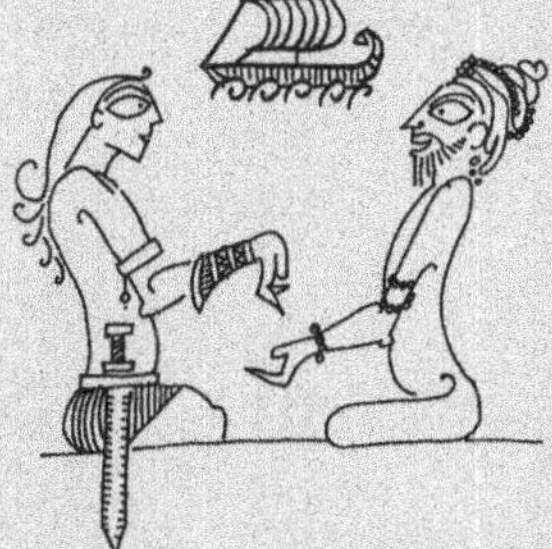

Tantalus

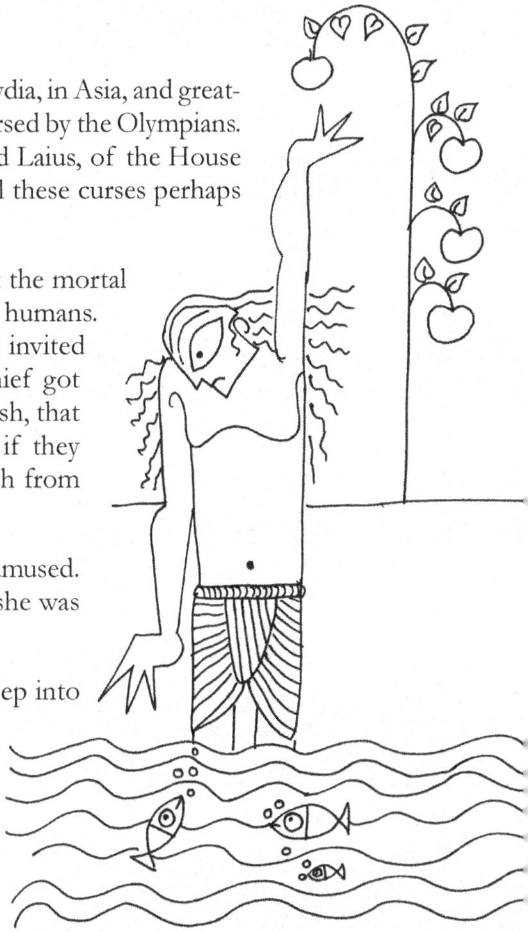

The story of Helen must begin with Tantalus, king of Lydia, in Asia, and great-grandfather of her husband, Menelaus. Tantalus was cursed by the Olympians. His son, Pelops, was cursed by a mortal. Pelops cursed Laius, of the House of Thebes, which resulted in the Theban tragedies. All these curses perhaps planted the seed of the terrible Trojan War.

Once, Zeus invited Tantalus to eat with the gods. But the mortal misbehaved and stole ambrosia to distribute it amongst humans. To make amends with the angry Olympians, Tantalus invited them to his house for a meal. But his desire for mischief got the better of him. He served the Olympians human flesh, that of his own son, Pelops, because he wanted to check if they were really gods: if they could distinguish human flesh from animal flesh and bring the dead back to life.

The gods smelt the food and turned away in disgust, unamused. Only Demeter ate what she was served, distracted as she was by the loss of her daughter Persephone in winter.

For his audacity, Tantalus was condemned and cast deep into Tartarus, where Zeus made him stand waist-deep in a freshwater lake, under a tree branch laden with succulent fruits. Every time a thirsty Tantalus bent down to drink the water, it receded from him. Every time a hungry Tantalus stretched his arms to eat the fruit, the branch withdrew from him. Thus he suffered eternal thirst and hunger for killing his own son, and worse, for daring to test the gods.

The gods resurrected Pelops, the son of Tantalus. His missing shoulder bone, eaten by Demeter, was replaced by one made of ivory.

- The Buddha said, 'Desire is the cause of suffering.' Tantalus embodies desire that is never fulfilled, an eternal hunger. The word 'tantalizing' comes from Tantalus's story. As long as we are *tantalized*, we are spellbound and heartbroken by the material world.
- Tantalus's punishment indicates the Greek disgust with the practice of cannibalism. Human sacrifice was why Zeus caused the flood that wiped out humanity. The story also shows the Olympian rage at being doubted, and not being recognized by mortals.
- Lydia, like Troy, is located in Asia, in the region now known as Turkey.

Pelops

Pelops, son of Tantalus, grew up to be a handsome youth, and Poseidon claimed him as his lover, as Zeus had claimed Ganymede of Troy long ago.

However, as Zeus would not let any son of Tantalus into Olympus, Poseidon had to let the lad return home. As a sign of his love, the sea god gave Pelops horses that could run on water as well as on land.

Pelops learned that King Oenomaus of Pisa had organized a chariot race. The winner would marry the king's beautiful daughter, Hippodamia, and inherit his throne; the losers would be beheaded. The contestants had to race Oenomaus himself, but it was an unfair race, for the king's horses were a gift from the war god Ares and assured him victory. Oenomaus did not want his daughter to marry anyone because he himself was in love with her, and because it had been foretold that he would perish at the hands of his son-in-law.

When Pelops came to Pisa, he found the severed heads of the princess's previous suitors hanging on the gate and suddenly became insecure, despite having the horses of Poseidon. But then Hippodamia fell in love with him as soon as she saw him and was eager to assure his victory. Together, the two hatched a plan: they spoke to the royal stable-keeper, Myrtilus, and offered him Hippodamia's virginity if he helped Pelops win.

Myrtilus, a son of Hermes, who had always loved the princess secretly, could not believe his luck and agreed. He replaced the bronze pins in the wheels of the royal chariot with ones made of beeswax. As a result, the royal chariot fell apart in the middle of the race; Oenomaus fell to the ground, and his head dashed against rocks by the roadside, causing his death.

On the day of their wedding, Myrtilus reminded Pelops and Hippodamia of their promise. In response, Pelops caught hold of Myrtilus and hurled him off a cliff.

As he was falling to his death, a betrayed Myrtilus invoked the Olympians and cursed Pelops that all his descendants would have unfaithful spouses. It was this curse that caused Helen to leave her husband, grandson of Pelops, and elope to Troy with Paris.

To purify himself from the pollution that followed the killings of Oenomaus and Myrtilus, and to honour the memory of the dead suitors of Hippodamia so cruelly killed by Oenomaus, Pelops revived the chariot games that had long ago been established by the Olympians to mark their victory over the Titans. These were the Olympic Games. After the re-establishment of the games, Pisa came to be known as Olympia, and the island on which it stood came to be known as Peloponnese, the island of Pelops.

- Many Hindus take tales of Hindu mythology literally and so believe that ancient Indians could transplant human heads for animal ones. Likewise, if one takes Greek mythology literally, the story of a shoulder bone being created out of ivory to replace Pelops's lost body part suggests a knowledge of implant surgery. In the tale of the Trojan War, victory eludes the Greeks until they fetch the bones of Pelops—probably this ivory implant—from Pisa.
- The land controlled by Pisa was called Pisatis which included Olympia where the Olympic Games were held. Pelops renamed the old games as the 'Olympic' Games. Heracles introduced new sports like boxing and wrestling. Ancient written sources record the year 776 BC as the year when the Games began, or at least the year

when records of Olympic victors began to be kept.

- During the Olympic Games held to mark the victory of Olympians, Apollo, the sun god, beat Hermes, the messenger god, in the footrace, and Ares, the war god, in boxing. As a result Apollo, the embodiment of Greek male beauty, became the patron of all sports and the Olympic Games in particular. A laurel wreath, sacred to Apollo, has therefore been the victory trophy of the Games since.
- Greek mythology is full of stories of athletic games organized to mark the death of a warrior in battle. They also served as a ritual of cleansing for those who had killed someone. This was the hallmark of a masculine warrior society. Usually the weapons of the dead were distributed amongst the winners.
- Greek society was aristocratic and hierarchical as indicated by the treatment of the charioteer Myrtilus.

Chrysippus

Hippodamia bore Pelops two sons: Thyestes and Atreus. He had another son, Chrysippus, from his affair with the nymph Axioche. Chrysippus was extremely beautiful and talented and Pelops's favourite, and thus resented by Hippodamia's sons.

Laius, prince of Thebes, whom Pelops had given shelter, fell in love with the beautiful Chrysippus. When he tried to make love to the boy, the boy resisted, so Laius took him by force. For this abuse of hospitality, Pelops banished Laius from Pisa and cursed that Laius's own son would kill him.

Soon after, Chrysippus was found dead. Some said it was suicide. Others said it was murder. Pelops held Hippodamia and her sons responsible. Had they not hated Chrysippus? Had they not shamed him after his rape?

Pelops exiled Thyestes and Atreus and died soon after. Ashamed, Hippodamia killed herself.

- Unlike in Hindu mythology, where one has to spend one's accumulated karma to be able to curse another, cursing in Greek mythology has nothing to do with karma; it is simply a manifestation of rage. Anyone—the gods, the wronged or the oppressed—can curse those who disrupt the cosmic order.
- Like gods, even humans can curse cities through their rulers. Myrtilus curses Pelops, hence Pisa, for not keeping his word. Pelops curses Laius, and by extension Thebes, for breaching the rules of hospitality.
- One reason for the Roman disdain for Greece was the love of older Greek philosophers and kings for young boys. Though the Romans absorbed much of Greek mythology and made it their own, they did not appreciate the frequent man–boy love stories, preferring instead a much more hetero-normative lifestyle. Many attribute the popularity of man–boy love found in medieval Persia and even in modern Afghanistan (a practice called bachcha-bazi) to the spread of Greek culture following Alexander's invasion.

Thyestes

Thyestes and Atreus, exiled from Olympia, found refuge in the city of Mycenae, which, coincidentally, needed a new ruler since the sons of Heracles had slain their old king, Eurystheus.

Now, the two sons of Pelops were fiercely competitive—neither brother wanted the other to sit on the throne.

'Maybe it should be whoever can present a golden fleece to the people of Mycenae,' suggested Thyestes. Atreus liked the idea because he already had a golden fleece in his possession. He had promised to offer this to the goddess Artemis but had later changed his mind.

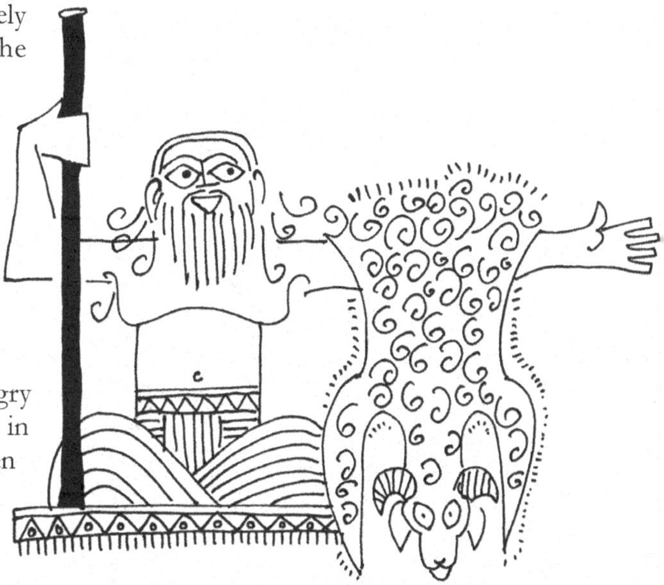

What Atreus did not know was that an angry Artemis had made his wife, Aerope, fall in love with Thyestes and she had already given her lover the golden fleece. This betrayal of Atreus by his wife Aerope was yet another outcome of Myrtilus's curse on Pelops's descendants.

And so it was that Thyestes, and not Atreus, presented the people of Mycenae with a golden fleece, and was made king of the city.

- The story of brothers fighting over property is a recurring theme in Hindu epics as well. In the Ramayana, Vali fights Sugriva over the throne of Kishkinda, and Ravana challenges Kubera for the throne of Lanka. In the Mahabharata, the Kauravas and the Pandavas fight over Hastinapur.
- The golden fleece of Atreus is different from the Golden Fleece recovered by Jason from Colchis.
- Like Minos who has to secure a bull from the sea, Atreus has to present a golden fleece to show that he is favoured by the gods, and is therefore a legitimate king. As in many cultures, in the Greek world too, royal power is derived from the gods.
- A royal sceptre, which is essentially a shepherd's staff, is created by Hephaestus, who gives it to Zeus. It then passes from Zeus to Hermes, to Pelops, to Atreus, who then gives it to Thyestes when the latter becomes king, a shepherd of sheep and humans. Sheep rearing was a popular economic activity in ancient Greece just as cattle rearing was in India. In Hindu mythology, a king is often called 'go-pala' or cowherd, protector of the cow, the cow being the primary source of livelihood of the people. The cow was also a metaphor for the earth. The sheep was more a metaphor for people, who were supposed to follow the shepherd-king.

Atreus

Atreus was furious at being betrayed by his wife. But he found an ally in Zeus who sent Hermes with a message. After hearing this message Atreus told the people of Mycenae, 'Would you want as king a son of Pelops who gives you a golden fleece or a son of Pelops who makes the sun travel eastwards?'

Then, to the surprise of all, Atreus was able to make the sun travel backwards.

The people immediately rejected the kingship of Thyestes, and made Atreus king.

As the first step in his revenge, Atreus killed his unfaithful wife. He then invited Thyestes to a feast in which he served the flesh of Thyestes's sons, which he unknowingly devoured. Having thus hurt and humiliated his brother, Atreus exiled him.

- Unfaithful wives are a recurring theme in Greek mythology. By contrast, faithfulness is a recurring theme in Hindu mythology. Faithfulness grants magical powers to a woman, makes her a sati, enabling her to withstand fire and protect her husband from weapons.
- Tales of cannibalism frequently appear in Greek mythology, as in the stories of Lycaon, Tantalus and Thyestes. In Hindu mythology too, there are tales involving rakshasas and asuras who feed human flesh to humans. Asuras feed Shukra the flesh of Kacha, who is actually a spy of the devas. Shukra is then forced by his daughter to save Kacha by imparting to him the secret of resurrection, the sanjivani vidya. In another story, Ilavila feeds the sage Agastya the flesh of his own brother, Vatapi, who has the power to resurrect himself in a man's stomach and burst out of his body. Unfortunately for Ilavila, Agastya digests Vatapi before he can resurrect himself.
- The story of the rivalry between Atreus and Thyestes tells us how the will of the Olympians overpowers all human strategies. Thyestes may seduce his brother's wife to gain the throne of Mycenae, but Zeus ensures that only Atreus will rule Mycenae.
- The theme of killing a child and feeding it to a parent as punishment for the parent's crime recurs in Greek mythology. In Ovid's *Metamorphosis*, Procne's husband, Tereus, rapes Philomela and then cuts out her tongue to silence her. Philomela then weaves a tapestry to tell her sister of her tragic situation. Enraged, Procne kills the son she bore Tereus, and serves him the child's flesh. When he has finished the meal, she presents him with his son's head. A disgusted Tereus runs after the sisters with a knife but the sisters appeal to the Olympians and are turned into birds: Procne into a swallow and Philomela into a nightingale, whose song communicates her lamentation.

Pelopia

The oracles told Thyestes that he could have his revenge if he fathered a son on his own daughter. A vengeful Thyestes did not think twice and raped his daughter, Pelopia.

Pelopia kept her pregnancy secret when her uncle, Atreus, sought her hand in marriage. When she delivered Thyestes's child, Atreus assumed it was his firstborn and named him Aegisthus. Later, Pelopia gave birth to two more sons, Agamemnon and Menelaus.

In time, Atreus pardoned Thyestes and let him return to Mycenae. But Thyestes had not forgiven Atreus. He revealed to Aegisthus the truth about his birth, and motivated him to kill his stepfather.

After Aegisthus murdered Atreus, Pelopia took her own life, for she was unable to decide what was worse: the death of her husband at her son's hands, or public knowledge that her firstborn was a product of incest.

Thyestes, now king of Mycenae, did not have the heart to kill his daughter's sons, his grandsons who were also his nephews. So he sent Agamemnon and Menelaus into exile. The brothers went to Sparta, where King Tyndareus had invited suitors to marry his daughters, Helen and Clytemnestra.

- Incest is a common theme in Greek epics and plays. This is conspicuous by its absence in Hindu, Buddhist and Jain epics and plays. The only place where incest seems to appear in Indic works is when speaking of primordial twins, as in the story of Yama and Yami in the Rig Veda, or in Jain mythology where the Golden Age is described as a time when husbands and wives were born as twin pairs and so were also brothers and sisters.
- Perseus of Argos takes refuge in Mycenae. Laius of Thebes takes refuge in Pisa. Atreus and Thyestes of Pisa take refuge in Mycenae. Agamemnon and Menelaus of Mycenae take refuge in Sparta. Thus we find the interlinking of Greek cities through their heroes. There is also an interlinking of Europe and Asia—Pelops moves from

Lydia to Pisa, and before that Io moves from Europe to Asia, and Europa moves from Asia to Europe, followed by her brother Cadmus who establishes Thebes. These are tales of migration.

- The adultery and incest and cannibalism are signs of the collapse of order and the rise of chaos. Things are spinning out of control and eventually lead to the Trojan War.

Tyndareus

Tyndareus of Sparta was married to Leda whose beauty so enchanted Zeus that he took the form of a swan and made love to her.

Leda delivered two eggs. In each egg there were two children: one by her mortal husband and the other by her divine lover. From one egg emerged a pair of boys: the mortal Castor and the immortal Pollux. From the other egg emerged a pair of girls: the plain Clytemnestra and the enchanting Helen.

Helen was so great a beauty that Theseus of Athens abducted her when she was still a child. Her brothers, Castor and Pollux, attacked Athens and brought her back. The people of Athens were so ashamed of what their king had done that they used their newly found democratic power to vote him out of kingship.

Word spread across the Greek world of Helen's beauty, of how she had effortlessly enchanted Theseus of Athens, and caused his fall. She became the subject of fascination and fear, inspiring many ballads.

When Castor and Pollux did not return from Jason's expedition to fetch the Golden Fleece, Tyndareus sought able sons-in-law who would inherit his kingdom. And so he invited the kings of Greece to come to his city so that he could choose husbands for his daughters. He who married Helen would also become king of Sparta.

Every king of Greece arrived in Sparta bearing expensive gifts for Helen's hand and the Spartan throne. On seeing Helen, they all fell so madly in love with her that each one was willing to kill all his rivals in order to win

her hand. Fearing the dreadful violence of rejected suitors, Tyndareus turned to Odysseus of Ithaca for help. Odysseus, who was known for his cunning, agreed to help if he was given the hand of Penelope, Tyndareus's niece, in marriage. When Tyndareus consented, Odysseus came up with an elegant solution.

All suitors were asked to swear an oath to protect the body and honour of the man who would eventually marry Helen. When everyone agreed, straws were drawn and the choice of groom was left to the Fates. Thus did Menelaus win the hand of Helen in marriage.

So as not to displease the powerful Agamemnon, Tyndareus gave him the hand of his other daughter, Clytemnestra, and his army to retake Mycenae by killing the pretender Thyestes.

Thus the two grandsons of Pelops became rulers of Sparta and Mycenae. In time, both their wives would be unfaithful to them, for the curse of Myrtilus still clung to the House of Pelops.

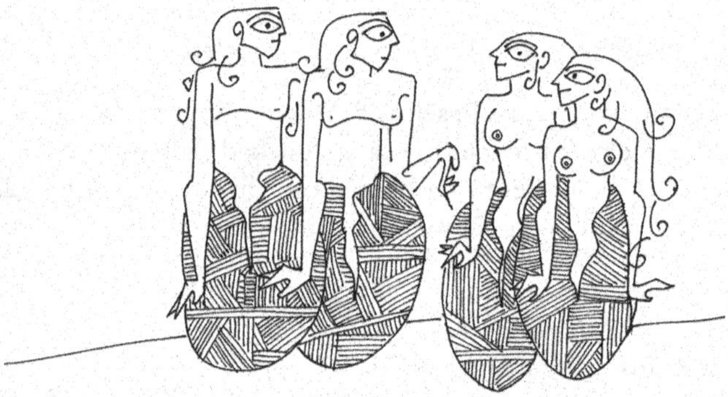

- As in Greek stories, Hindu epics also speak of destitute men (the Pandavas, for example) who become powerful when they marry powerful women (Draupadi, princess of Panchala).
- A study of Krishna lore reveals many Greek influences. In Hindu stories, typically a man carries his own karmic burden and does not inherit the karma of his parents. But in Krishna's story, he cannot be king as he is a Yadava, and all the Yadavas are cursed because their originator, Yadu, was cursed by his father, Yayati, that if he or his descendants assumed the crown they would find no peace. So the Yadava city of Mathura functioned democratically as a republic, rather than as a monarchy. The curse of Yayati, like the curse of Myrtilus, extends over generations.

- In one version of the birth of Helen, Nemesis, the goddess of retribution, took the form of a goose and was raped by Zeus who took her in the guise of a gander. From that union was born Helen, who was raised by Leda in Sparta. This alternate story suggests that Helen was a tool used by the gods to crush the hubris of the Greeks and the Trojans.
- Another story speaks of the rivalry of Castor and Pollux with their cousins, Lynceus and Idas. The two sets of brothers fought over women, food and cattle and eventually killed each other.
- Not much is known about the character of Menelaus. Different authors present him differently—some as a simpleton under the shadow of Agamemnon who adores his indifferent wife; others depict him as a brute.

Thetis

Helen's marriage to Menelaus did not matter to the Olympians, especially not to Aphrodite, who had actually offered her as a prize to another man: Paris, prince of Troy, also known as Alexander.

It all started when Zeus fell in love with two nymphs: Aegina, whom he could seduce, and Thetis, whom he could not.

Zeus took Aegina to a deserted island to protect her from the wrath of her father. He turned the ants on the island into its inhabitants, who came to be known as Myrmidons. They served Aegina, protected her, and followed her son, Aeacus, with the discipline and loyalty seen in ants.

Meanwhile, Zeus approached Thetis, intent on seducing her, until he learned from Heracles and Prometheus that she would bear a child greater than the father. So he withdrew and ordered Aeacus's son, Peleus, to take her as his wife.

Aeacus had two sons: Peleus and Telamon, who had joined the Calydonian hunt, the Argonaut expedition, and accompanied Heracles when he attacked Troy. During the Calydonian hunt they had accidentally killed their half-brother, Phocus, and so had to leave the island of Aegina. Telamon moved to the island of Salamis, and Peleus north to faraway Phthia, where the Myrmidons followed him.

Thetis did not appreciate being given away to a mortal man without her permission, and resisted the idea of marriage, refusing to even meet Peleus. But then, one day, Peleus—directed by Zeus—caught her off guard on the beach while she was dancing naked with other sea nymphs. He grabbed her tight and did not let her go though she tried to escape, wriggling furiously, and even changing her form. Finally, she submitted and accepted him as her husband. From this union would be born Achilles, the greatest hero known to the Greek world.

- Thetis is a sea nymph or Nereid. In Hindu mythology, the damsels who dance in paradise are called apsaras, which means born of water (apsa, in Sanskrit). The Greeks classified nymphs according to their origin. There were tree nymphs, water nymphs, mountain nymphs and cloud nymphs. Such a classification is not found in Hindu mythology.
- Thetis is one of the fifty daughters of the ancient sea god Nereus, who ruled the sea before Poseidon. Nereus is the son of Pontus, the oldest sea god, and husband of Gaia. Nereus is often confused with Triton, son of Poseidon, a man with a fish tail instead of feet, who blows conch shells.
- In her ability to shape-shift, Thetis is like Proteus, the 'old man of the sea' according to Homer, an old sea god who keeps changing forms, giving rise to the adjective 'protean'. Fabulous shape-shifting creatures inhabit Hindu mythology too. Durga fights an asura who assumes multiple forms: from elephant to lion before being killed as a buffalo.
- According to Plato, when Aeacus died, he became a judge of the dead, responsible for the spirits that came from the West (Europe), complementing Rhadamanthus who judged the dead who came from the East (Asia), and Minos, who had the casting vote.
- Alexander the Great traced his ancestry, on his mother's side, to Aeacus.

Eris

All the Olympians were invited to the wedding of Peleus and Thetis except Eris, the goddess of discord. An angry Eris decided to teach all the assembled gods a lesson. She threw amongst them a golden apple, known as the Apple of Discord, on which were engraved the words 'For the most beautiful'.

Hera, Athena and Aphrodite, all claimed the apple and fought over it. Their bickering worsened as no god, not even Zeus, dared judge which of the three goddesses was the most beautiful, and hence worthy of the apple. Finally, the goddesses were told to go to Paris, prince of Troy, known for his understanding of female beauty and his fair judgement.

The three goddesses presented themselves to Paris and tried to impress him with their beauty. When he could not decide, each one of the goddesses tried to bribe him secretly. Hera promised to make him the ruler of the greatest kingdom in the world. Athena promised to make him the most admired warrior in the world. Aphrodite promised him the hand of the most beautiful woman in the world—Helen of Sparta.

Paris accepted Aphrodite's offer, and judged her to be worthy of the apple, but in doing so he and the land of Troy earned the enmity of Hera and Athena forever.

- The Hindu goddess of discord is called Kalaha. She is also known as Alakshmi, goddess of misfortune. While the Greek goddess of discord has Ares, the god of war, as a brother, the Hindu goddess of discord has Lakshmi, the goddess of wealth, as a sister. In Roman mythology, Eris was called Discordia.
- Paris was famous for organizing bullfights. He had a bull that had defeated all other bulls in the land. He offered a golden crown to anyone who could defeat his bull. Ares, the god of war, took the form of a bull and defeated Paris's bull. Without hesitation, the Trojan prince gave the promised golden crown to Ares. This fairness of the judgement of Paris earned him the respect of the Olympians, who therefore asked him to choose the most beautiful of the three goddesses.
- Eris's apple results in the world's first beauty contest. Troy is located in Asia while Greece is in Europe. While Asia succumbs to the passion embodied in Aphrodite, Europe chooses Athena and Hera, who embody skill and domestication.

Priam

Troy was named after its king, Tros. It was Tros's son Ganymede whom Zeus claimed as a lover, and in lieu of whom gifted many magnificent horses to the city.

Tros had another son, Ilus, after whom Troy was also known as Ilium. Ilus had a son called Laomedon who, unwittingly, became an employer of the gods. Poseidon, to be precise.

The sea god had once dared to raise his voice against Zeus, and an angry Zeus had stripped Poseidon of his divine powers and cast him down to earth to serve as Laomedon's servant.

Unaware that he was addressing a god, Laomedon, observing his prodigious strength, asked Poseidon to build great walls around Troy. Since walls built by gods can never be breached, Zeus sent his son Aeacus, father of Telamon and Peleus, to assist Poseidon. While the portion of the wall built by Aeacus could be breached, the Fates decreed that only the sons of Aeacus would be able to do so, none other.

After the stipulated duration of punishment, when it was time to return, Poseidon refused to leave without collecting wages due to him. Laomedon, in keeping with habit, always looking for an excuse to pay less or not pay at all, argued that the walls around Troy were not entirely built by Poseidon; he had had Aeacus's help. He did not realize he was bargaining with a god, who expected full payment. Troy would pay a terrible price for their king's cupidity.

A furious Poseidon sent a sea monster to torment Troy. It would not go away until the king offered as sacrifice his favourite child, his daughter Hesione.

That was the time when Heracles was passing by Troy. He was returning home after the *Argo* had sailed on without him while he was looking for Hylas. With him were Telamon and Peleus, sons of Aeacus.

Laomedon begged the mighty Heracles to rescue his daughter. In exchange, Heracles demanded the celestial horses that Zeus had given Troy as payment for Ganymede. Laomedon agreed, but once Poseidon's sea monster had been defeated and Hesione had been rescued, he went back on his word.

So Heracles attacked Troy and with Telamon's help breached the great walls around the city. Heracles then proceeded to kill Laomedon and all his sons. Only one son, Laomedon's youngest, Podarces, was spared, for whom Hesione paid a huge ransom. Later he came to be known as Priam, the ransomed one.

Telamon claimed Hesione as his prize for breaching the walls of Troy and took her with him to Greece, where she lived as his concubine.

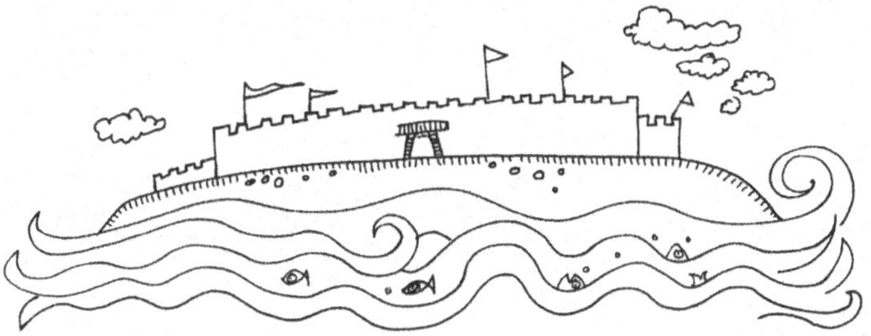

- Zeus sends Aeacus to build part of the Trojan wall so that it is not eternally impregnable. Thus he introduces a flaw in perfection. This idea is found in Hindu mythology too: since no one is granted the boon of immortality, the asuras who invoke Brahma always ask for boons that make them near-invincible. But there is always a loophole that the devas then exploit and kill the asura.
- Non-payment of dues inevitably results in the wrath of the gods. Similar themes are found in Hindu mythology. Harischandra angers Varuna when he refuses to sacrifice his son even though Varuna has cured him of dropsy. Repaying deva-rina, or debt to the gods, is a key theme in Hindu rituals.
- Zeus makes Ganymede immortal by casting him in the sky as the constellation Aquarius, the cup-bearer of the zodiac. Ganymede is also the name of one of Jupiter's moons, alongside Io, Europa and Leda.
- The story of the building of the Trojan wall by two Olympians (Apollo joins Poseidon in many versions of the tale) and a mortal (Aeacus) comes from the Greek poet Pindar who lived 2500 years ago.
- The story of Heracles saving Hesione from a sea monster mirrors the story of Perseus saving Andromeda from another sea monster. Hesione's father offends Poseidon, the sea god, while Andromeda's mother upsets the Nereids, the sea nymphs.

- In his many adventures, Heracles often demands payment for his services, diminishing his stature as a hero. That he fails to get his due in many cases contributes to his frustration.
- Heracles wanted to breach the famous Trojan walls himself but could not. When he learned that Telamon had done so, he became angry and wanted to kill Telamon. But Telamon, anticipating Heracles' insecurity, built an altar using stones from the broken wall to honour Heracles, pleasing the hero immensely; thus Heracles forgot all about his desire to hurt Telamon.

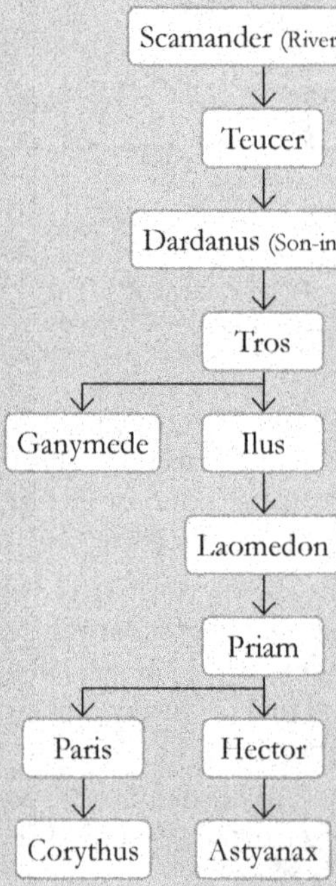

House of Priam

Paris

Priam married Hecabe and she bore him fifty children, amongst them Hector, Paris, Deiphobus, Helenus, Troilus, Polyxena, Laodice and Polydorus.

At the time of Paris's birth, it had been foretold that he would cause the fall of Troy. And so his father Priam ordered his men to leave him in the forest at the mercy of the wild animals. But a shepherd took pity on the infant and took him home and raised him as his own.

Paris grew up to be a very handsome and talented young man, so much so that when he participated in the Trojan games, he earned the love of the king, who was overjoyed to learn that the lad was actually his own son.

Soon after this, Priam ordered an expedition to Greece to bring back his sister Hesione, who was being forced to serve Telamon as his concubine in Salamis. Telamon, however, refused to let her go. This Greek refusal to let the Trojan princess go would eventually play a key role in igniting the Trojan War.

Paris, who was part of this expedition, decided to take a detour to Sparta, eager to meet the woman described to him by Aphrodite. There he learned that she was married to another. But neither that, nor the existence of his own wife, Oenone, a nymph whom he had married when he lived as a shepherd, unaware of his royal origins, mattered at that moment. For Helen truly was the most beautiful woman he had ever seen. Helen too fell in love with the handsome Trojan prince as soon as she saw him and agreed to elope with him to Troy, leaving her husband behind.

At first the news of their elopement upset the Trojans for they feared a war with the Greeks. But when they saw Helen, the people adored her and agreed that her place was in Troy.

- In some versions of the tale, Hera and Athena hide the real Helen and replace her with a phantom Helen. Thus, the Helen who leaves with Paris is a pseudo-Helen. A similar theme is found in a version of the Ramayana where the Sita whom Ravana kidnaps is a pseudo-Sita, a phantom, while the real Sita is protected by Agni, the fire god. However, where Ravana forcibly abducts Sita, Helen willingly elopes with Paris. And so equating Helen with Sita is a false equivalence.
- Priam, king of Troy, and his queen, Hecabe, have fifty children, of whom twelve are daughters. Dhritarashtra, king of Hastinapur, and his queen, Gandhari, have a hundred sons, and one daughter. In both epics, the father of the enemy is seen as highly fertile.
- Paris is also known as Alexander. Unlike his ancestors who went back on their word in matters of wages, Paris is known to be fair in his judgement and true to his word. But all his integrity vanishes when he succumbs to Aphrodite's enchantment.
- Gigantic male statues used as columns are often called telamons.
- Telamon fathers Ajax on his Greek wife Periboea and Teucer on his Trojan concubine, Hesione. The two half-brothers fight on the Greek side.

Menelaus

On learning of Helen's elopement, every Greek king rushed to Sparta, determined to help Menelaus retrieve his wife from Troy. They came because they were all in love with Helen, and also because they were bound by an oath sworn long ago at the time of Helen's marriage.

For the Greeks, Helen had not eloped. She had been abducted, and so had to be rescued. Bound by their oath to her husband, and love for her, the kings of Greece rallied around Menelaus.

Menelaus was a simple man who knew that he was no leader. So he appointed his more capable and more ambitious brother, Agamemnon, as the commander of this Greek enterprise.

- Hindu mythology speaks of the swayamvara, or a girl's groom-selection ritual, which was popular in warrior communities. Men would gather in the girl's father's house, show their skill in archery and then let her choose her husband. Later, the power of choice was taken away from the daughters and given to the fathers. This is how Ram wins the hand of Sita in the Ramayana and Arjuna wins the hand of Draupadi in the Mahabharata. Helen's groom-selection ritual has led to speculation that this was an ancient Indo-European, or Aryan, practice that spread from Eurasia to Europe in the west and India in the east.
- Zeus orchestrates wars such as the Theban and Trojan wars to rid the world of its excessive population. A similar theme is found in Hindu mythology where Vishnu, the preserver of the world, promises to cause war between humans to reduce the burden on the earth.
- In Homer's *Iliad*, Menelaus is presented as a brave warrior, braver than Paris, who defeats Paris in a duel and helps recover the body of Patroclus, the male companion and lover of Achilles.
- In Homer's version, Helen regrets her decision and wants to reunite with Menelaus eventually. But other authors disagree and see her as enjoying the carnage that follows her abduction. Many authors believed that Helen never loved Menelaus, and even manipulated him till the very end. In Euripides's play *Helen* husband and wife are united after death in the Isle of the Blessed.
- In Homeric epics, the Greeks are referred to as Argives, as they all have roots that can be traced to Argos, the city of the original mother, Io. Later, the Argives came to be known as Hellenes, descendants of Hellene, son of Deucalion. The Hellenes were renamed Greeks by Aristotle.

Laodice

Agamemnon sent a delegation of Greek soldiers to Troy to fetch Helen back through diplomatic means. Acamas of Athens, son of Theseus, was also part of this mission.

Priam, however, refused to let Helen go. 'The Greeks took my sister Hesione and forced her to be Telamon's concubine,' he said. 'Why then should my son, a Trojan prince, not keep Helen as his wife? The exchange is fair.'

During his stay at Troy, Acamas fell in love with Laodice, Priam's most beautiful daughter, who was wedded to a Trojan nobleman. But it was a love that remained unfulfilled, ripped apart by the winds of war. Unlike Helen, Laodice felt that an elopement would be inappropriate.

- In the Mahabharata, before the war at Kurukshetra, there are intense negotiations for peace. There is an entire chapter called Udyoga Parva devoted to the negotiations.
- Laodice's husband, Telephus, king of Mysia, was a son of Heracles, and therefore Greek, but related to the Trojans by marriage. He was torn between fighting the Greeks and helping them. In some tales, he fights the Greeks when they stop at Mysia on their way to Troy. But Achilles injures him and he can only be healed if touched by Achilles' spear. When cured, he helps the Greeks find their way to Troy. Thus he supports both sides.
- That Troy is continuously associated with payment, fair and unfair, suggests that the Trojans were traders. Zeus takes Ganymede and in exchange gives horses to his father, the Trojan king; Laomedon promises but does not pay Poseidon and Heracles for their services; and Helen is seen as fair trade for Hesione.

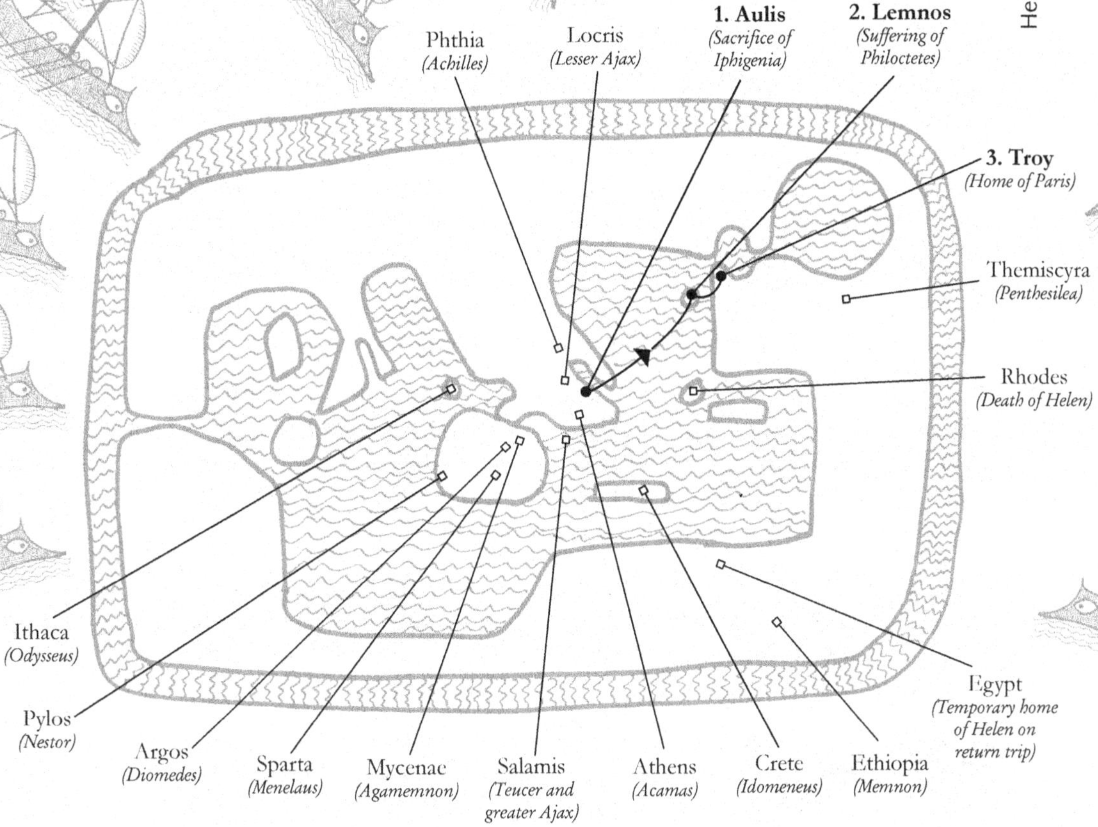

Trojan War: City of major warriors
(Representational, not drawn to scale)

Achilles

With the failure of diplomacy, war was inevitable. So Agamemnon ordered the Greek kings to gather with their ships in the port of Aulis. He knew that only a descendant of Aeacus could breach the walls of Troy; just as Telamon had breached it for Heracles, he would need the help of Peleus, or maybe his son, Achilles.

Soon after his birth, Achilles' mother, the sea nymph Thetis, tried to make him invulnerable by dipping him in the River Styx. Every part of his body touched by the waters of that river, which separates the land of the living from the land of dead, became impervious to weapons. However, the heel by which Thetis held her son was untouched by the Styx, and hence remained vulnerable.

Thetis then sent Achilles to train as a warrior under the centaur Chiron, where he matured into a gifted and exceptional warrior. It was during his training that he met a young man called Patroclus and fell passionately in love with him. The two became inseparable.

Patroclus, a prince of Opus, had accidentally killed a child during a game, and so had been exiled from his father's house. He had no home to go back to. When news came that the Greeks had declared war against the Trojans, he decided to accompany Achilles and his Myrmidons to Troy.

But Thetis did not want Achilles to go to Troy, for it had been foretold that he would die there. Determined to save her son, she took him from his father's house to the island of Scyros where she hid him in the women's quarters, dressed in women's clothes.

Spies found out that Aeacus's grandson was probably hiding amongst the women in Scyros. So Odysseus came to the island disguised as a merchant and presented his wares to the women there: jewellery, cosmetics, cloth, perfumes and a sword! At a prearranged signal, a trumpet was sounded giving the impression that the island was being attacked. The girls screamed and ran for cover. All except one—Achilles!

The moment Achilles grabbed the sword, his identity was revealed, and despite Thetis's protests, he was taken to Aulis.

- In the Mahabharata, the archer Arjuna disguises himself as a eunuch-dancer and lives in the women's quarters of the palace of Virata, the king of Matsya. But he rides into battle to protect the city when it is threatened by the Kauravas, thus revealing his true identity. The tale mirrors the story of Achilles who pretends to be a girl and hides in the women's quarters until there is a crisis and a call to arms.
- Chiron, the centaur, who lives on Mount Pelion, is the teacher of many Greek heroes: Achilles, Jason, Perseus, Heracles, Theseus, Peleus, Telamon and even, some say, Dionysus. Unlike other centaurs who are unruly and lascivious, Chiron is restrained, noble and wise.
- While on the island of Scyros, Achilles befriends the daughters of King Lycomedes, and fathers a child on one of them, Deidamia. The son born thus is Pyrrhus, who plays a key role in the Trojan War. Pyrrhus is also known by another popular name, Neoptolemus.
- The asteroids around the planet Jupiter are classified as belonging to the Greek camp and the Trojan camp. Patroclus is the only asteroid named after a Greek in the Trojan camp and Hector is the only asteroid named after a Trojan in the Greek camp.

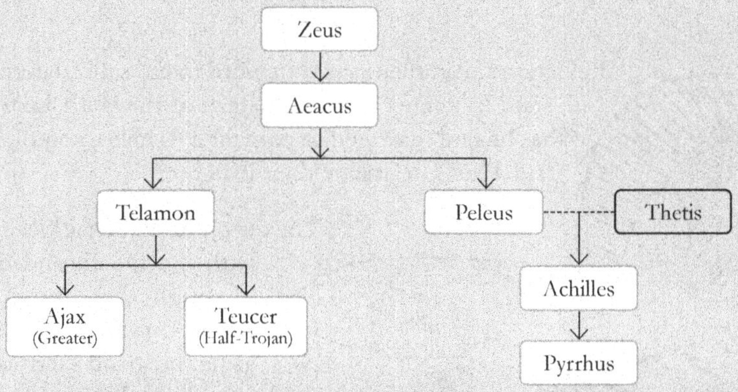

House of Aeacus

Iphigenia

It was a gathering of kings and warriors and ships like no other. There was Menelaus of Sparta and his brother Agamemnon of Mycenae. Achilles came with his lover Patroclus, and his cousins Ajax and Teucer, sons of Telamon, and a group of the finest Myrmidon warriors, renowned for their ant-like discipline. There was another Ajax from Locris, known as Ajax, the lesser, as he was not as big and strong as Telamon's son who was popularly addressed as Ajax, the greater. The cunning Odysseus came from Ithaca. Palamedes, who had outwitted Odysseus and ensured his recruitment, joined as well. There was old King Nestor from Pylos. And Philoctetes who had lit Heracles' funeral pyre; he came bearing weapons gifted to him by Heracles himself. Then there were Idomeneus of Crete, Protesilaus of Phylace, and Diomedes of Argos, and from Athens, the sons of Theseus, Demophon and Acamas. Agamemnon specially invited the oracle Calchas.

But the ships could not set sail. A huge storm prevented them from leaving the port, raging on as it did for months. At last Calchas revealed that Artemis was furious with Agamemnon for he had once boasted that he could throw a spear further than her. The only way to appease the goddess and end the storm was by offering her as sacrifice what Agamemnon loved most in the world: his daughter Iphigenia.

Reluctantly, Agamemnon sent word to his wife Clytemnestra to send Iphigenia to Aulis. Instead of the truth, he told her that he had managed to convince Achilles, son of Peleus and Thetis, to marry their daughter.

The queen of Mycenae was thrilled with the match and quickly brought her daughter to Aulis, only to watch in horror as her husband sacrificed her to Artemis with his own hands.

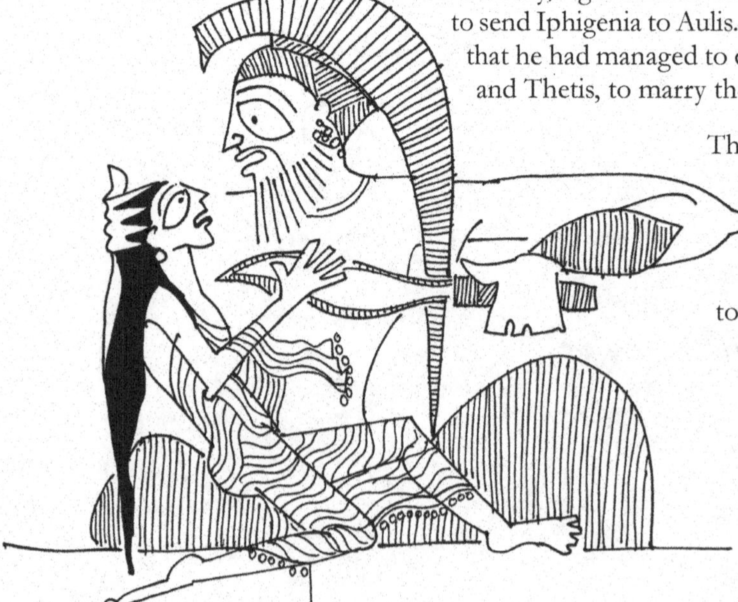

- In Tamil retellings of the Mahabharata, the sacrifice of a perfect youth is necessary to enable the victory of the Pandavas over the Kauravas and so Arjuna's son, Aravan, is offered to the goddess of the battlefield.
- It seems odd that while Zeus punishes Tantalus for sacrificing his son and offering his flesh as food for the god, Artemis would demand from Agamemnon the sacrifice of his daughter. Clearly, classical Greeks were ambiguous about human sacrifice, indicating it was an old practice, perhaps related to the Goddess, that was on the wane.
- In some versions of the tale, Artemis saves Iphigenia and takes her to Tauris where she serves as the goddess's priestess.
- The idea of a god demanding the sacrifice of a child is found in Abrahamic mythologies too, as in the story of the prophet Abraham who is asked by God to sacrifice his dear son, only to be stopped at the last minute.
- The killing of Iphigenia fractures the relationship between Agamemnon and Clytemnestra forever; this unfolds after the Trojan War.

Philoctetes

Moments after the sacrifice, the storm died down and the Greek fleet that had been waiting for several months finally set sail. They were guided by a mysterious sailor known as Corythus, the son of Paris by his first wife Oenone, whom the Trojan prince had abandoned after the arrival of Helen in Troy.

On the way, the Greeks stopped at the island of Lemnos to offer sacrifices to the gods. Here Philoctetes was bitten by a snake sent by the goddess Hera, whose loathing for Heracles—which extended to his friend as well—trumped her hatred for the Trojans. Although the poison did not kill him, Philoctetes' foot began to swell and rot, emitting a horrible odour.

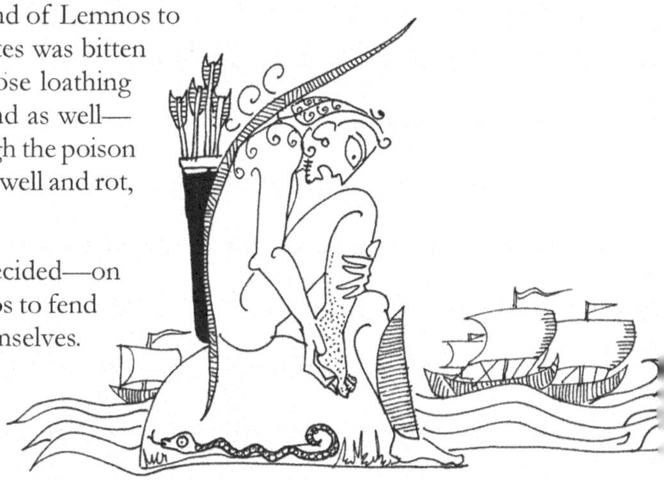

Though everyone liked Philoctetes, they decided—on Odysseus's advice—to leave him on Lemnos to fend for himself and sail onwards to Troy themselves. What the Greeks did not realize was that as long as Philoctetes did not fight by their side, victory would elude them.

- The story of Philoctetes is found in the *Little Iliad*, which forms part of the Epic Cycle of stories, dating to the seventh century BCE.
- All the great Greek tragedians, including Sophocles, Euripides and Aeschylus, wrote plays on Philoctetes, but only one, *Philoctetes* by Sophocles, survives.
- Philoctetes is one of the warriors inside the Trojan Horse.

Protesilaus

It was foretold that the first Greek soldier to step on Troy would surely die. And so when the Greek ships reached the shores of Troy, not a single soldier was willing to jump on to the land.

Finally, Odysseus leapt out of his ship, but cleverly landed on his own shield which he had thrown on the ground first, thus technically not stepping on Trojan soil. The next to follow was Protesilaus, under the impression that the first Greek had already landed on Trojan soil. Thus tricked by Odysseus, he was killed, as had been foretold, by Hector, the eldest Trojan prince and a fine warrior.

The gods felt sorry for Laodamia, Protesilaus's wife, who had watched her husband set sail for Troy shortly after their wedding. They had not even consummated their marriage. Taking pity on her, the gods decided to let his ghost visit her for a few hours. However, this brief time spent with the ghost of her husband only intensified Laodamia's misery. She commissioned a statue of him, and spent every waking hour serving it as if it was truly her husband. Fearing for her sanity, her father ordered that the statue be burned. Laodamia protested and finally threw herself into the fire, choosing death over life as a widow.

A tree grew on the spot where Laodamia died. It grew so high that its topmost branches could see across the sea. But they would wither as soon as they were tall enough to catch sight of the Trojan shores, indicating the rage and bitterness of a husband and wife separated by the tragic war.

- Yearning for a lover from whom one is separated, or viraha, is a common theme in Hindu mythology. Radha yearns for Krishna who leaves Gokul for Mathura. Urmila mourns for Lakshman who goes to the forest with his brother Ram.
- In an alternative version by the Latin writer Conon who lived in the age of the Roman emperor Augustus, Protesilaus survives the Trojan War and wants to set sail for Greece with Priam's sister, Aethilla, but she and other Trojan women burn the ship and force him and his men to start a new city with them—the city of Scione.
- In the first century CE, the Latin writer Hyginus put together the *Fabulae*, a collection of mythological narratives from his time. Though not a great work of literature, it does give us an idea of the stories that were current at the time. The story of Laodamia's tragic love for the statue of her husband is one such tale.

Briseis

The Greeks had thought that they would breach the walls of Troy, raid the city, kill Paris and bring back Helen to Greece within a year. But the walls, built by Poseidon, proved formidable. And the part built by the mortal Aeacus was too well fortified.

So the Greeks had no choice but to camp on the beaches of Troy and lay siege to the city—a siege that stretched for years. Ten long years!

During this time, the soldiers survived by sacking the settlements around Troy for

provisions. In these raids, men were killed and women were captured and turned into concubines who cooked for the Greeks in the day and satisfied their lust at night.

Amongst these concubines were Chryseis who belonged to Agamemnon, and Briseis, who belonged to Achilles. Chryseis's father, a priest of Apollo, invoked the god and begged him to strike the Greek soldiers with sickness until they let his daughter go. Apollo shot the arrow of disease amidst the Greeks, until at last, tired of sickness, and having consulted the oracles, the men begged Agamemnon to let his concubine go. 'Only if she is replaced by Briseis, who is as beautiful as her,' he said. The Greeks agreed without consulting Achilles.

When Agamemnon forcibly claimed Briseis, Achilles was so angry that he declared he would not fight in the war until his concubine was returned to him and Agamemnon had apologized.

- Many European Orientalists believed there was much in common between the Greek war epic of Troy and the Hindu war epics, the Ramayana and the Mahabharata. However, they failed to notice that in the Hindu epics, women are not treated with disrespect or captured to serve as concubines.
- The story of the concubines that eventually leads to Achilles withdrawing from the battlefield of Troy forms the theme of Homer's most celebrated work, the *Iliad*.
- Briseis is described as a princess, the daughter of a local king, who is captured during the Greek raids and turned into a concubine to serve the Greek warriors.
- In medieval times, Briseis becomes Briseida, or Cressida, daughter of Calchas, the Trojan oracle who defects to the Greek camp. She is in love with the Trojan prince Troilus, but when she is allowed to go over to the Greek camp on her father's request, she meets and falls in love with the Greek warrior Diomedes, thus breaking Troilus's heart.

Patroclus

Briseis was not returned, and Agamemnon refused to apologize. So Achilles would not fight. As a result, after nine years of continuously winning battles against the Trojans on the beaches, the Greek army started facing defeat. More and more Greeks began to die in battle, or return injured. The formidable army that had once been offensive now became defensive and afraid.

Achilles, however, did not care. He would not take up arms, not until his conditions were met and his humiliation by Agamemnon avenged. Patroclus tried to convince his lover, but Achilles refused to budge, like a petulant child.

Finally, to motivate the disheartened Greeks, Patroclus entered the battlefield wearing Achilles' helmet. Mistaking him for Achilles, the Greeks were revitalized, fighting with a renewed vigour, and the terrorized Trojans became defensive.

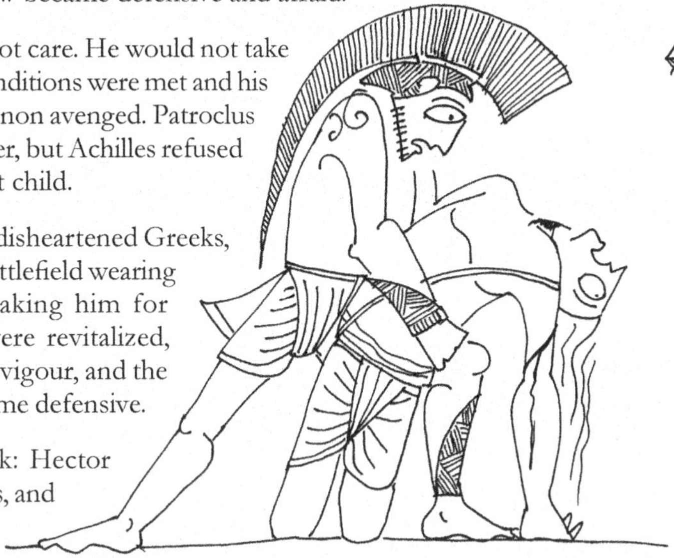

But then tragedy struck: Hector caught hold of Patroclus, and assuming that he was Achilles, killed him with a spear.

- Mistaken identity is a common theme in mythological stories. In the Mahabharata, Ashwatthama kills five youths he finds sleeping in the Pandava camp at night, mistaking them to be the five Pandavas.
- In his childhood, Patroclus had accidentally killed his friend Clysonymus following a fight over a game of dice. Forced into exile as punishment for his crime, he found shelter in Peleus's home. Shortly after his arrival, Achilles and he were sent to study under Chiron.
- Patroclus kills Sarpedon, the son of Zeus and king of Lycia, who fights on the side of Troy as an ally though he has nothing against the Greeks and feels the Trojans are wrong. Sarpedon is sometimes identified as the brother of Minos of Crete, who was gifted with a very long life.
- In Classical Greece, Plato, the philosopher, describes the relationship between Achilles and Patroclus as a model of romantic love while Xenophon disagrees. In the twentieth century, the Hollywood movie *Troy* shows the relationship between the two men as asexual, while in the contemporary novel *Song of Achilles*, author Madeline Miller makes the relationship romantic as well as sexual. People have seen the relationship of Achilles and Patroclus differently depending on their comfort with homosexuality.

- Alexander the Great's love for his male friend Hephaeston was probably inspired by the story of Achilles' love for Patroclus. Alexander loved the epic the *Iliad* and Achilles was his hero. It is reported that both he and Hephaeston visited the tomb of Achilles and that when Hephaeston died, Alexander was plagued by dreams of his own death, just as Achilles could not bear to live without Patroclus.

Hector

When news of his lover's death reached Achilles, his rage knew no bounds. He blamed Hector, not his own intransigence, for Patroclus's death and challenged the Trojan prince to a duel. His mother tried to stop him but he refused to listen to reason, so she gifted him with a divine armour made by Hephaestus himself to protect him from harm. Hephaestus owed Thetis a favour for she had raised

him by the sea when he had been cast out of Olympus by his own mother, Hera, who found him ugly.

The fight between Achilles and Hector was witnessed by all. Priam, Hecabe, Andromache, Paris and Helen watched from above the city walls. Agamemnon, Diomedes, Odysseus and Menelaus watched from their camp by the sea. After a long and gruelling duel, Achilles triumphed. He plunged his spear in Hector's chest and let out a cry of victory whose rage disturbed even the gods.

Not content with merely killing Hector, Achilles tied the corpse by the ankles to his chariot and rode around Troy three times, thus defiling the body. All those who saw this—the Greeks, the Trojans, even the Olympians—were disgusted. But Achilles was beyond caring. He was angry and heartbroken and wanted nothing else in the world now but to die.

That night, while everyone slept, Priam slipped into the Greek camp and fell at Achilles' feet, begging him to return the body of his beloved eldest son so that he might be cremated as befitted a royal warrior. 'I will give you a cartful of gold in exchange,' said the sad king.

Achilles did not care for the gold for in his heart he knew he had crossed the lines of propriety in rage and the gods were upset with him. A broken man, this greatest of Greek warriors let the weeping king take the body of his eldest son back to Troy.

- The killing of the good Hector who fights for his family, despite all its faults, inspired Michael Madhusudan Dutt to write the Bengali epic *Meghnad-vadh Kavya* in the nineteenth century on similar lines: Meghnad, son of Ravana who had remained true to his family despite their many flaws, is killed by Ram's brother Lakshman, unfairly. In oral tales based on the Ramayana, Sulochana, Meghnad's widow, goes alone to Ram's battle camp to fetch the body of her husband, just as Priam goes to Achilles to retrieve the body of his son, Hector.
- During the course of the war, Hector once challenges the Greeks to a duel. Ajax, son of Telamon, is chosen by lots. In the long clash that follows, both warriors are equally matched and the fight ends in a stalemate. The duellists express admiration for each other; Hector gifts Ajax a sword and Ajax gives Hector a girdle.
- In Dante's thirteenth-century work *Inferno*, Hector and his family are located in Limbo, the space reserved for virtuous non-Christians.
- Hector is the only asteroid named after a Trojan in the Greek cluster of asteroids around Jupiter.

Penthesilea

As the war continued, the Trojans called upon their allies to help; they begged the Amazons to come to their rescue.

Penthesilea, the Amazon queen, came to fight but she came with a death wish. She had accidentally slain her Amazon sister with a spear during a deer hunt and wanted to punish herself. But suicide was not a noble option. She wanted to die in battle and so readily accepted Priam's invitation to war.

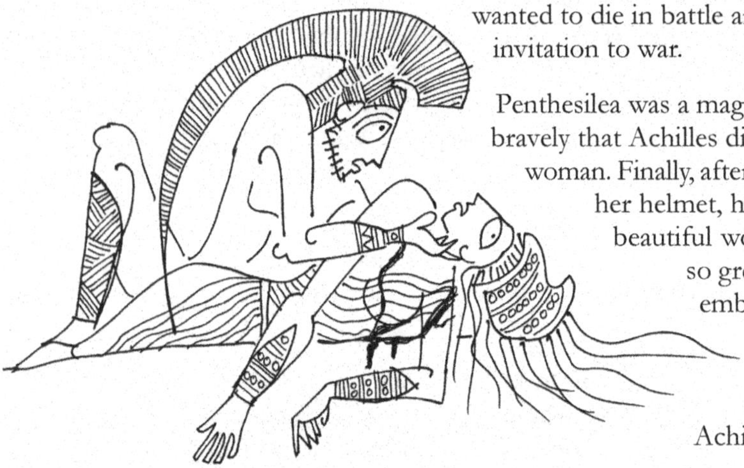

Penthesilea was a magnificent warrior and fought so bravely that Achilles did not realize he was fighting a woman. Finally, after he had killed her and removed her helmet, he realized she was a woman, a beautiful woman. In fact, her beauty was so great that, enamoured of her, he embraced her passionately, causing the soldiers around him, especially one Thersites, to jeer. Angry and humiliated, Achilles killed Thersites.

- In the Mahabharata, Bhishma refuses to fight a warrior called Shikhandi as he was born with a female body and acquired a male body only later in life; women were not allowed on the battlefield. Yet the Puranas, composed centuries after the Mahabharata, speak of the Goddess and her army of female warriors, the Matrikas.
- All Greek heroes are connected in one way or the other with the Amazons. Theseus meets, fights, falls in love and is responsible for the death of Antiope. As it is with Heracles and Hippolyta, and Achilles and Penthesilea.
- The story of Achilles' battle with the Amazons is found in *Aethiopis*, which forms part of the Epic Cycle of stories, dating to 700 BCE.
- The reason why Penthesilea wants to fight the Trojan War comes from *Posthomerica*, written by Quintus Smyrnaeus, a Greek poet who lived around the fourth century CE.

Memnon

After the Amazons came the Ethiopians, led by Memnon.

Memnon was the son of Eos, the goddess of dawn, and a Trojan prince called Tithonus. Eos had asked the Olympians to grant Tithonus immortality but forgot to ask for eternal youth. So as time passed, he grew weaker and older, shrinking with age. Taking pity on him, the goddess turned him into a cicada, or tree cricket, whose mating chirp is the cry of Tithonus who belongs neither to the world of mortals nor to that of the immortals.

Family ties compelled Memnon to help the Trojans. In the course of battle he killed young Antilochus, who tried to save his old father Nestor of Pylos. Nestor then challenged Memnon to a duel, but Memnon refused to fight him as he was too old. Nestor then asked Achilles to fight the Ethiopian on his behalf, and the duel that followed lasted for days, for both warriors were equally matched. In the end Achilles was able to defeat and kill him.

As soon as Memnon was cremated, his entire army turned into birds and flew away to the west. Since his death, his mother Eos weeps for him at dawn every day, her tears taking the form of dewdrops.

- In Hindu mythology, dawn is both a god called Aruna and a goddess called Usha. In art, the dawn god is depicted as the charioteer of the sun god whose body is perfectly formed only till the waist, not below, which makes him a deity of uncertain gender.
- The story of Achilles' battles with the Ethiopians is also found in *Aethiopis*, as well as *Posthomerica*, composed a thousand years later.
- The killing of Memnon follows the pattern of the killing of Hector. Achilles was provoked to fight Hector after he killed young Patroclus, and Achilles is provoked to kill Memnon after he slays Antilochus.
- In Egypt there are two tall statues built in honour of Amenhotep, the pharaoh who ruled the Nile civilization 3400 years ago. They were considered in Graeco-Roman worlds as the 'colossi of Memnon' that made sounds as the ancient warrior spoke to his celestial mother. Oracles interpreted these sounds for many ancient travellers.
- In Roman mythology, Eos is known as Aurora.

Troilus

Patroclus's death had driven Achilles mad, and so perhaps he was looking for love everywhere. First, it was the corpse of the Amazon queen Penthesilea. Then it would be the Trojan prince Troilus. And then, Troilus's twin sister, Polyxena.

He saw the Trojan prince and his sister riding secretly out of Troy one night, and making their way to a mountain spring. Troilus, with his long hair, was beautiful and reminded Achilles of Patroclus, so Achilles approached him and offered him his love but the boy rejected it as one rejects the attentions of a lunatic, especially one who was clearly Greek, not Trojan. When he tried to leave on his horse, Achilles grabbed him by the hair and dashed his head on the ground.

It had been foretold that if Troilus lived till the age of twenty, the walls of Troy would never be breached. His death at Achilles' hands before he turned twenty sealed the fate of Troy.

Achilles then turned his attention to the girl who had accompanied the boy. She looked just like him. Her name was Polyxena and instead of fearing or resisting the Greek warrior, she charmed him with her manners and words and spent time talking to him. Achilles liked her and in the course of the conversation revealed, as a gesture of his true love for her, that he could not be killed unless he was injured in his heel.

- Greek mythology is replete with tales of twin brother–sister pairs such as Helle and Phrixus, Polyxena and Troilus, Artemis and Apollo, Eris and Ares. Similar twin brother–sister pairings are found in Hindu mythology as well: Yama and Yami in the Vedas, and Kripa and Kripi, Hidimba and Hidimbi in the Mahabharata.
- Ancient Greek writers described Troilus as a Trojan prince with a love for horses who was killed brutally by the lustful Achilles. However, in medieval times, writers, including Shakespeare, spoke of Troilus as a Trojan prince who is infatuated with Cressida, the daughter of a man who defected to the Greek side. When she is exchanged for hostages, Troilus is heartbroken to learn that she has switched affections and chosen the Greek Diomedes instead.
- The name Troilus can be interpreted in many ways: as a combination of 'Tros' and 'Ilus', the founders of Troy; as 'little Troy'; as 'about-to-be-destroyed Troy'.
- Images found on ancient Greek pottery suggest that Athena directs Achilles to kill Troilus. The images show Achilles pulling Troilus by the hair as he attempts to ride away on his horse. Achilles then mutilates the body of Troilus at the mountain spring that is sacred to Apollo, thus earning the god's wrath.

Polyxena

Polyxena told her father about Achilles' love for her and his desire to marry her. Priam liked this idea and believed that it might put an end to the wretched siege. So he organized a secret meeting with Achilles in good faith.

Paris, however, opposed the idea for he feared that a truce between the Trojans and the Greeks would mean that he would have to give up Helen. When he learned from his sister about Achilles' vulnerable heel, he planned an ambush.

As the secret meeting between Achilles and Priam was taking place, Paris climbed the high walls of Troy and shot a poisoned arrow that struck Achilles in the heel.

A dying Achilles accused Polyxena of treachery and refused to listen to her pleas of innocence. 'From the land of the dead I shall have my vengeance,' he swore, breathing his last.

- The tale of Achilles' vulnerable heel was not known to Homer. It comes to us much later, from the Latin work *Achilleid* by the Roman poet Statius, who lived in the first century CE. Just as Thetis tries to protect her son Achilles, in the folk versions of the Mahabharata, Gandhari tries to protect her son Duryodhana. The Kaurava queen, who has kept herself blindfolded for years, knows that when she removes her blindfold, whatever she lays eyes on first will become invulnerable to weapons. She tells her son to come naked before her so that she can make him invincible. But Duryodhana, in shame, covers his loins. So like Achilles' heel, his loins remain vulnerable to injury, and eventually become the cause of his death.
- Although the proposed marriage of Achilles and Polyxena is an attempt to make peace, the Greeks see it as a betrayal on the part of Achilles and a trap laid by the Trojans to take down their most powerful warrior. On being struck by Paris, Achilles blames Polyxena for his misery and even as a ghost demands that the Greeks punish her for betraying him.
- Paris is imagined mostly as a coward and weakling who is favoured by Aphrodite and Apollo. Once he is almost killed by Menelaus in a duel, but Apollo saves him.

Teucer

Ajax, the greater, son of Telamon, was sent to retrieve the body of Achilles from the Trojans. Ajax was a powerful defensive warrior, skilled in the use of shield and

spear. During his duel with Hector both warriors impressed each other so much that they exchanged gifts after the fight ended.

Most of the time, Ajax defended the Greek ships and in this he was helped by his half-brother Teucer the archer, son of Telamon's Trojan concubine, Hesione. While Ajax protected Teucer with his shield, Teucer shot arrows that kept the Trojans at bay.

Odysseus joined Ajax on the mission to retrieve Achilles' body, fighting off the Trojans while Ajax carried the corpse on his massive shoulders. When they returned to the Greek camp both claimed Achilles' divine armour, forged by Hephaestus. Agamemnon gave the prized armour to Odysseus who argued his case with clever words that simple Ajax could not counter.

Feeling cheated, Ajax got drunk and spent the night attacking and killing the sheep penned in the Greek camp, thinking he was slaughtering the Greeks who had insulted him. In the morning, when his senses returned, he saw the dead sheep and heard the soldiers' laughter, and realized what he had done. Embarrassed, he fell upon his own sword and killed himself.

Despite opposition from Agamemnon and Menelaus, who were angry that Ajax had killed their sheep, Teucer demanded that he be given a decent burial. However, the Greeks ignored him for he was half-Trojan, the son of Hesione, Priam's sister.

After burying his brother, Teucer refused to fight and returned to Greece; but his father denied him entry inside their home in Salamis. 'My son, born of a Greek wife, is dead. I have no use for my son born of a Trojan concubine,' Telamon said, slamming the gates on Teucer's face.

- There are no tales of fighting for a fallen body, or over a fallen warrior's weapons and armour, in the wars described in the Ramayana and the Mahabharata.
- There are two warriors named Ajax in the Trojan War: 'greater' Ajax and 'lesser' Ajax. Greater Ajax is the son of Telamon, grandson of Aeacus, who built part of the Trojan wall. Lesser Ajax, son of Oileus, king of Locris, is said to have raped the Trojan princess Cassandra in the temple of Athena, thus incurring the wrath of the goddess, who created storms preventing the Greek ships from returning home.
- Teucer, son of Hesione and Telamon, is famous for his archery and the only reason his arrows don't strike Hector is because Apollo protects him.

Oenone

Tired of war, the Greeks consulted their oracle Calchas who saw a vision that revealed to him that winning Troy would be impossible without the weapons of Heracles. These could only be wielded by Philoctetes, who had inherited them, and who had been abandoned on the island of Lemnos before the war began by the Greeks who could not bear the stench of his rotting injured leg.

Odysseus and Diomedes were dispatched to fetch the injured warrior. 'Let's just bring back his weapons, not him,' said Odysseus, disgusted by the sight and smell of Philoctetes' leg. The upright Diomedes disagreed and insisted the warrior be taken to Troy along with his weapons.

As soon as they landed, Philoctetes raised Heracles's bow and shot an arrow at the walls of Troy. It struck a warrior standing on the walls. Paris!

The arrow hurt Paris but did not kill him. He realized he could survive if he was given the right medication. That is when he thought of his first wife, Oenone, the mountain nymph, whom he had forgotten after meeting Helen.

Paris begged Oenone to use her knowledge of herbs to save his life, but she refused; she had never forgiven his betrayal. 'Do you remember we had a son whom we named Corythus?' she asked. 'It was he who showed the Greek ships the shortest sea route to Troy. He looked just like you and when you saw Helen gazing at him with eyes of desire, you killed him yourself. Paris, you abandoned your wife for Helen. You killed your own son for her. You do not deserve to live.'

Paris died in Oenone's arms. Soon after, Oenone took her own life, for she could not bear the thought of living without Paris.

- While Hindu epics speak of kings with many wives as well as many concubines, Greek epics tend to speak of one wife and many concubines. So while Arjuna has many wives besides Draupadi, Paris abandons Oenone to make room for Helen.
- When Philoctetes is finally taken to Troy, ten years later, his wound is finally healed by the sons of Asclepius: the surgeon Machaon and the physician Podalirius.

- In some versions, Oenone burns herself on Paris's funeral pyre, suggesting that roots of the practice of widow-burning or sati that was glamorized in many Hindu tales may have been found in Indo-European tribes.
- The story of Oenone and Paris comes from *Posthomerica*.
- Oenone was a nymph on Mount Ida and a priestess of the Mother Goddess Cybele.

Helenus

Following the death of Paris, two sons of Priam, Helenus and Deiphobus, fought to claim Helen. When Priam gave her to Deiphobus, an angry Helenus left the city and went over to the Greek side. He revealed that he was an oracle and he knew what needed to be done for the Greeks to breach Troy. They would have to fetch the bones of Agamemnon's grandfather, Pelops; secure the services of Pyrrhus, the son of Achilles sired on a woman on the island of Scyros when Achilles was hiding in the women's quarters disguised as a girl; and steal the Palladium, a sacred image of Athena, located within Troy.

The first two tasks were easy. For the third, Odysseus and Diomedes slipped into the city disguised as beggars and stole the image of Athena under the cover of darkness. As they were escaping, they were spotted by Helen but she did not raise an alarm. Instead she said, 'Tell my husband that I stay true to the Greeks and pray for his success. That I do not betray you to the Trojans is proof of where my loyalties lie.'

- A palladium is similar to the 'grama-devata' or village deity of Hindu mythology that holds the power of the kingdom, and hence must be guarded by the king. Conquest of other kingdoms meant seizing these devatas and bringing these images to the capital city temple.
- The original Trojan Palladium was an image of Pallas created by Athena. Pallas was Athena's childhood friend whom she accidentally killed during a friendly duel. To keep her alive in memory, she created the statue and also took on the name Pallas Athena.

The image was given by Zeus to the Trojan kings for safekeeping. After Odysseus and Diomedes stole it, it eventually made its way into the hands of Aeneas, the Trojan, who took it to Italy where it was enshrined in Rome in the temple of Vesta.

- Oracles play a key role in the Trojan War. Calchas is a Greek and Helenus is a Trojan. In medieval times, Calchas was believed to be a Trojan who had defected to the side of the Greeks.
- In some tales, Pelops was driven out of Lydia by Ilus of Troy and so the return of his bones (or specifically the shoulder bone of ivory) marked his symbolic return home. Many of the Greeks who fought at Troy were descendants of Pelops.
- Odysseus and Diomedes contrast each other. Odysseus is cunning and manipulative, while Diomedes displays patience, maturity and nobility.
- In the *Little Iliad* of the Epic Cycle, Odysseus tries to stab Diomedes in the back so that he can take the credit for stealing the Palladium, but Diomedes catches him in time. Instead of killing Odysseus, Diomedes simply binds his hands and makes him walk ahead, hitting him with the flat of his sword, humiliating him. He does not kill the Ithacan as he knows Odysseus's cunning is needed if the Trojan War has to be won. The phrase 'Diomedian necessity'—for a job that needs to be done under compulsion—comes from here.

Trojan Horse

Finally, Odysseus managed to come up with an audacious plan to breach the city of Troy. He got the Greeks to build a hollow horse out of wood taken from old crumbling ships. Then Diomedes, Menelaus, a few other Greek soldiers and Odysseus himself hid within it. The rest, led by Agamemnon, pretended to set sail towards Greece. They stopped when they were beyond the horizon, ready to turn back and return to Troy in the darkness.

When the sun rose, the Trojans were surprised to find that the Greek camps were empty, and the enemy ships were sailing away. All that was left on the beach was a giant wooden horse, and Sinon the Greek, who explained what had happened.

'My fellow Greeks packed up. In their haste, or maybe in malice, for Odysseus never liked me, they forgot to take me. They have returned home having concluded that Troy is impregnable. This horse is a votary offering to Athena to ensure their safe journey home.' He then added, 'It has been built tall so that you Trojans cannot take it inside the walls and claim favour from Athena.'

This information intrigued the Trojans who wanted to claim Athena's favour for themselves. They decided to take the wooden horse inside their city walls. They opened the gates of their city, dug up the base and broke the top to ensure the horse would pass through; they then prepared to drag it into the city square.

Cassandra, Priam's daughter, who could see the future, warned the Trojans not to bring the wooden horse into the city, for she sensed it would bring bad luck. But no one believed her.

Laocoon, a Trojan priest, also declared the wooden horse was dangerous and should not be taken into the city, but even as he spoke a serpent came from the sea and attacked and killed Laocoon and his sons. This was seen as a sign that the wooden horse had the protection of the Olympians and so was not only safe but also a bearer of good luck. So the Trojans dragged the horse into the city and decorated it with flowers and danced around it all day until it was time to go to sleep.

In the dead of the night, Odysseus and the other Greek warriors slipped out the wooden horse and unlocked the gates of Troy. The Greek ships had returned by then and the soldiers quietly entered the city. With all the enemy guards asleep after the celebrations, the Greeks faced no resistance as they spread across the city, waiting for the signal to begin the rape and plunder of Troy.

- Jainism is an ancient monastic order based on rebirth, plurality and non-violence that emerged in the Indian subcontinent. The Jain Tirthankara Mahavira is believed to have been a contemporary of the Buddha. In Jain chronicles we find a story where a strategy similar to the Trojan Horse was used to prevent a war. Six princes who wanted to marry the princess Malli threatened to attack her kingdom if she did not agree. So Malli invited them to her palace and showed them a beautiful statue, the very likeness of her. But when the princes came near the statue, they encountered a foul stench. The princess explained, 'Ever since you threatened war, I have stopped eating and been putting all my food inside this hollow statue. Over time, it has started rotting, hence the foul odour. This body of mine that you find so beautiful is made of this garbage. In your lust, you do not realize it and are willing to kill for it. Is it worth it?' Hearing the words of the princess, the princes withdrew their army. Ashamed, they became hermits. Malli became the Tirthankara called Malli-nath, the one who shows the path to those lost in materialism.
- Cassandra can see the future but no one believes her. A similar character is found in the Mahabharata: Sahadeva can see the future, but he cannot give any information unless someone asks for it. If he speaks without being questioned, no one will believe him.
- The story of the Trojan Horse comes to us from Homer's *Odyssey*, Euripides's play *The Trojan Women* and Virgil's *Aeneid*.
- The builder of the horse was one Epeius, inspired by Athena.
- The number of soldiers who hid inside the horse vary from twenty to fifty across different accounts.
- The common list of Greeks who hid in the horse includes Odysseus, Diomedes, Teucer, Menelaus, Protesilaus, Epeius, Pyrrhus and Idomeneus. Agamemnon is conspicuous by his absence as he is with the ships waiting by an island beyond the Trojan horizon.
- The Trojan Horse has become a metaphor for the safe-looking container of a lethal consignment. The metaphor is even used for malicious computer programs that contain a virus.
- In one story, Helen goes around the Trojan Horse and mimics the voices of the wives of the Greek warriors who hide inside, hoping that they will reveal themselves. Is she then helping the Trojans, or simply testing the will of the Greeks? Her loyalty remains ambiguous throughout.

Astyanax

At the sound of the war trumpets, the Greeks began their pillage. Houses were set aflame, men killed, and women raped.

Hector's infant son, Astyanax, was thrown from the high walls of Troy. His widow, Andromache, was raped, as were his sister Cassandra and his mother, Hecabe. Priam, king of Troy, who witnessed the abuse of his city, and his family, wept and begged to be killed. The Greeks obliged.

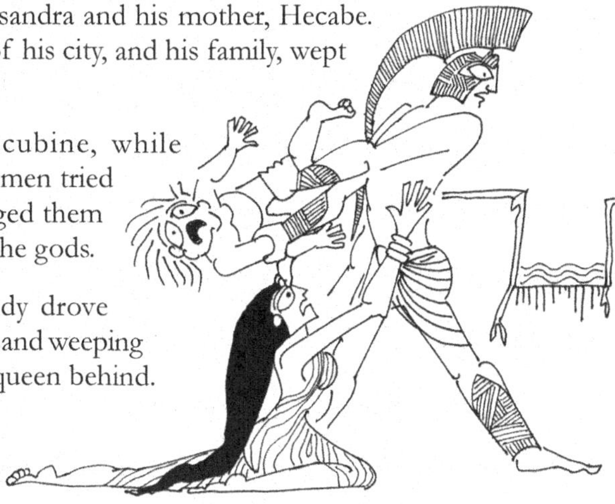

Pyrrhus claimed Andromache as his concubine, while Agamemnon claimed Cassandra as his. The women tried to take shelter in temples, but the Greeks dragged them out, or even raped them within, unmindful of the gods.

The horror and grief of the unfolding tragedy drove Hecabe mad and she started barking and whining and weeping like a dog. It was decided to leave the old mad queen behind.

Menelaus rushed through the palace looking for Helen, and found her in bed with Deiphobus. He killed the Trojan prince and was about to kill Helen when she bared her breasts. The sight of such beauty dissolved all his rage, and he led her back to his ship as his lawfully wedded wife.

- In the Ramayana, Ram storms Lanka with an army of monkeys to rescue his wife, Sita, who has been abducted by the rakshasa-king Ravana. After Ravana's defeat, his kingdom is not plundered and the Lankan women are not mistreated. The treatment of the conquered land and women in the Greek epics is remarkably different, and quite barbaric, angering even the Olympians.
- Euripides' play *The Trojan Women* was a commentary on the fate of the Greek island of Milos that was laid waste by the Athenians during the Peloponnesian wars of the fifth century BCE. Conquered after a long siege, the resident men of the island were butchered and the women and children sold into slavery.
- The Trojan War is seen as historical by some scholars as there are Hittite cuneiform texts dated to around 1300 BCE, which mention an unruly Anatolian warlord named Piyama-Radu (possibly Priam) and his successor Alaksandu (possibly Alexander, the nickname of Paris) both based in Wilusa (possibly Ilios), as well as the god Apaliunas (possibly Apollo).

Aethra

With Helen was an old woman, Aethra, the mother of Theseus, who had been enslaved and forced to serve as Helen's maid, first in Sparta, then in Troy.

When Acamas, son of Theseus, came to rescue her, she presented a young boy to him. 'This is your son, Munitus, borne by the Trojan princess Laodice,' she said. 'Do you remember her? You met when you came to Troy before the war, to negotiate peace, and take Helen back to her husband. Your mission failed, but your brief affair with the Trojan princess has borne this delightful fruit. Take care of it. In his veins flows the blood of Greeks and Trojans. Of love. Not hate.'

'Where is Laodice?' asked Acamas.

'That most beautiful of Priam's daughters prayed to the gods that she not be raped or killed or taken away in concubinage. For her the earth opened, and she descended with Persephone to Hades.'

Aethra then climbed aboard her grandson's ship, ready to sail to Greece along with her great-grandson, Munitus.

Demophon, brother of Acamas and son of Theseus, joined his grandmother and returned home to learn that his beloved wife Phyllis had died while he was away. In death, she had transformed into a lifeless almond tree. Demophon hugged it and wept; the tree bloomed.

- The story of Laodice's descent to Hades comes from *Bibliotheca*. It reminds us of Sita's descent to earth in the final episode of the Ramayana. In fact, many scholars have tried to link the story of Sita's birth from the earth and eventual return to the earth with the story of Persephone, daughter of Demeter, who is abducted and taken by Hades to the underworld. Persephone is responsible for Laodice's descent too.

Return

With the plunder of Troy satisfying their pent up rage and bloodlust, the Greeks prepared to return home. But before they could leave, the ghost of Achilles demanded that they sacrifice Polyxena over his grave, for it was her betrayal that had caused his death. Until that was done, he warned that the winds would not let the Greek ships leave Trojan shores. So Polyxena was brought to his grave and her throat slit.

The gods demanded that the Greeks also sacrifice the lesser Ajax for he had raped Cassandra inside Athena's temple. When the Greeks refused, Athena caused the winds and storms to further delay the return of the Greeks. Ajax the lesser was shipwrecked but he managed to find shelter on a rock. Then, consumed by hubris, he said, 'I will survive despite the Olympians.' Hearing this, Poseidon hurled his trident and broke the rock that had given Ajax shelter, causing him to drown.

Calchas, the oracle, decided not to travel by ship as he could foresee that most of the ships would crash against rocks and sink in the sea. He chose to travel by land instead, but still did not reach home. He met another oracle who foretold the day of his death. When the day passed and death did not come, Calchas started to laugh, and could not stop laughing until he died of laughter.

Idomeneus of Crete was caught in a storm and promised the gods that he would sacrifice the first human who greeted him on shore if he survived. When the ship reached Crete, the first person to greet Idomeneus was his firstborn son. Idomeneus had no choice but to sacrifice the youth and keep his promise to the gods. Idomeneus then discovered that his wife had taken a lover, Leucus, in his absence. Heartbroken at having lost both his son and his wife, he decided to leave his city that was no longer home, and live the rest of his days in exile.

- The Stri Parva, or the women's chapter, in the Mahabharata speaks of the horrors of war: how the fighting between men makes widows and orphans.
- The story of the Greek warlords returning comes from *Nostoi*, which forms part of the Epic Cycle of stories, dating back to 700 BCE.
- The Greeks sacrifice Iphigenia before leaving Greece and they sacrifice Polyxena before leaving Troy. In each case, Achilles is involved. Iphigenia is brought to Aulis on the false promise that she will be married to Achilles and the ghost of Achilles demands the sacrifice of Polyxena at his grave.
- In Mozart's eighteenth century opera *Idomeneo*, Poseidon stops the sacrifice of the prince Idamante but demands that old Idomeneus abdicate his throne and let the next generation take over.
- Dictys Cretensis was the legendary companion of Idomeneus who, as per lore, compiled a diary of the events during the Trojan War. A Latin version of this Greek work was made popular in the fourth century CE and was seen as the 'authentic' source of stories from the ancient Greek world.

Nauplius

During the Trojan War, Palamedes was falsely accused of accepting a bribe of gold from the Trojans and killed without a fair trial. His father, Nauplius, came to Troy and demanded justice for his son, but Agamemnon ignored him.

Enraged, Nauplius came up with a deadly plan. He lit beacons on rocky shores all along the sea route from Troy to Greece. As a result, many of the Greek ships that sailed from Troy crashed against the rocks and never reached home. Those men who did reach home found that their wives had taken second husbands because Nauplius, on his return to Greece, had told all these women that their husbands had abandoned them and settled in Troy with Trojan wives.

Diomedes was one of the unfortunate men whose wives had taken other lovers. She and her lover refused to let Diomedes enter his own city. So he took to the sea once again, determined to find a new home. But wherever he went, he was chased by birds. These birds were the ghosts of warriors who had fallen at Troy, who would cry all the time of their sorrow, driving Diomedes mad, until he sailed and made himself a home in faraway Italy. There he waited for a Trojan to whom he could return the Palladium stolen from Troy, for it had brought him nothing but bad luck.

- The Trojan War lasts for ten years. This is considered a long time in Greek mythology. Hindu mythology also mentions forest exiles of fourteen years, or a drought of twelve years, but these are contrasted with much longer timelines of hundreds and thousands, even millions, of years. The Vedas are full of huge numbers denoting time that are of no practical value, and certainly not part of human experience. They are calculated in imagination. These epochs align with the Indian obsession with vastness and infinity (ananta, in Sanskrit), compared to which human mortal life, with its finite lifespan, is insignificant. Thus, there are stories of kings visiting gods for a day and returning to find that a thousand years have passed on earth, for a day in the divine realm is a thousand years in the mortal realm. Such concepts are not found in Greek mythology.
- Nauplius descends from his namesake Nauplius, son of Poseidon, a great seafarer, who was part of the Argonaut expedition. Poseidon saved a maiden named Amymone from a satyr who was trying to rape her; he made love to her and she gave birth to Nauplius.
- There are many tales of the fate of Diomedes, who was worshipped as a god by many in post-Homeric times. The Roman poet Virgil connects him with many Italian cities.
- The Greek heroes all live within a few generations of each other. Minos, born of Europa, is a contemporary of Theseus, who is a contemporary of Oedipus. Cadmus is Minos's uncle. Perseus, born of Io, is an ancestor of Heracles, who is a contemporary of Jason. Heracles's follower, Philoctetes, who witnesses the hero's death, plays a key role in the Trojan War. This was called the Heroic Age.
- The Heroic Age of the Greeks (when the Trojan War was fought) and the Epic Age of the Hindus (the time of the Mahabharata) are located in the Bronze Age by rationalists who think of mythology as proto-history.
- Palamedes invented dice games to help Greek soldiers pass the time during the war.

Clytemnestra

Agamemnon, unaware of the fates of many of his companions, returned home to Mycenae in triumph. He was welcomed by his wife Clytemnestra, who was relieved to learn of Helen's rescue.

But all was not well.

While Agamemnon was away, Clytemnestra had had an affair with Aegisthus, son of Thyestes. She was angry with her husband for sacrificing her daughter, Iphigenia. She was angrier still when she learned that Agamemnon had brought back with him a Trojan concubine, Cassandra.

She welcomed the victorious Agamemnon and even Cassandra. But then, when they were bathing and refreshing themselves, she had them both killed. Thus the great conqueror of Troy, who had spent ten years away fighting, died at home, in his own bath, killed by his unfaithful wife.

- Unfaithful wives are a common theme in Hindu mythology as well. Jamadagni orders the beheading of his wife, Renuka, because she desires another man momentarily. Ahalya is turned to stone by her husband, rishi Gautama. Ram sends his wife, Sita, to the forest as her reputation is soiled following her abduction by Ravana.
- Hittite sources dating back to 1400 BCE mention an Akagamunas, ruler of Ahhiyawa (land of the Achaeans, or ancient Greeks).
- The earliest reference of the killing of Agamemnon by his wife comes to us from Homer's *Odyssey*, written in 800 BCE. Here, Odysseus encounters the shade (ghost) of Agamemnon who warns him against trusting women.

Orestes

Electra, another daughter of Agamemnon and Clytemnestra, was heartbroken when she learned that her mother had killed her father. She goaded her brother, Orestes, to kill their mother and her lover Aegisthus. With Apollo's support, Orestes did as his sister asked, for he was furious too.

For the crime of killing his own mother, the deadly Furies chased Orestes around the world. No king of Greece was willing to give shelter to the son of Agamemnon. The only one to share his suffering was his dear friend, Pylades of Phocis.

The Furies, however, did not punish Electra. She begged the gods to save her brother and end the family curse. Moved by her entreaties, Zeus agreed that the curse on the House of Pelops had to end. And so Athena was sent to argue with the Furies, saying that the killing of Clytemnestra by her son was no blood crime. 'A son is a father's child, not a mother's child. A woman is just the oven in which a man bakes his bread like a baker,' she said. The argument made sense to the Furies who stopped chasing Orestes.

- The concept of avenging angels like the Furies and Nemesis is not found in Hindu mythology. In righteous anger, the Hindu gods may assume fierce forms, like Shiva turning into Bhairava or Virabhadra, but there is no tale of punishment embodying itself into a being.
- In Hesiod's *Theogony*, the Furies are created from the blood of Uranus after Cronus castrated him. They are imagined as three vengeful goddesses. The Furies are referred to in the works of Aeschylus, Sophocles and Euripides, famous playwrights who lived around 500–400 BCE. The Furies are also called Erinyes. After the trial of Orestes, Athena renames them as Eumenides, or good spirits. In Roman mythology, they are called Dirae.
- Aeschylus's Oresteia trilogy has three plays which tell the story of the tragedy in the House of Pelops. The theme of *Agamemnon*, the first play, is the murder of the Greek king by his unfaithful wife. In the second play, *The Libation Bearers*, Orestes murders his mother and her lover on Apollo's orders. And in the final play, *Eumenides*, Orestes is troubled by the Furies until the intervention of Athena.
- The story marks the end of Greek matriarchy. Athena, the defender of Orestes, is born from the head of Zeus, thus distancing herself from the female body. That Apollo, defender of his own mother Leto, tells Orestes to kill his mother is also indicative of that shift.

Hermione

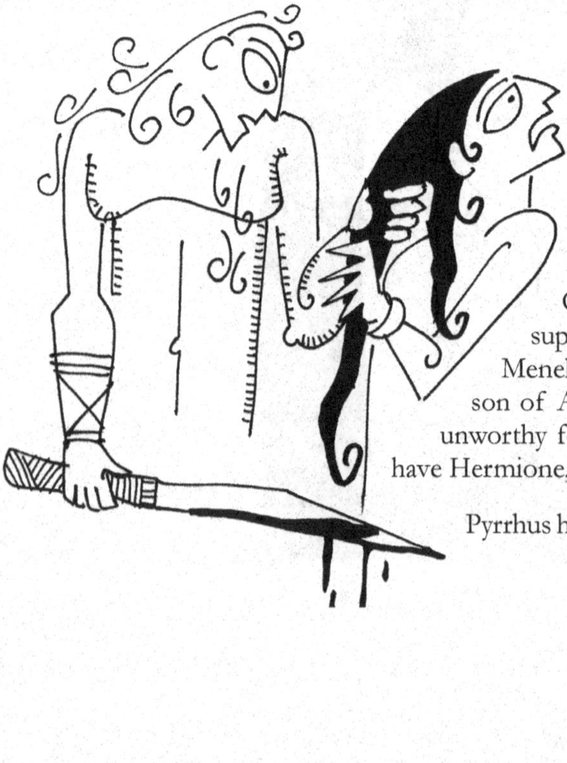

When Orestes returned to Mycenae after his ordeal with the Furies, he found Aletes, son of Clytemnestra and Aegisthus, sitting on the throne, with his sister, Erigone, by his side. Orestes proceeded to kill his half-brother and rape his half-sister, who then took her own life.

Orestes then learned that the woman he was supposed to marry, his cousin Hermione, daughter of Menelaus and Helen, had been given instead to Pyrrhus, son of Achilles and Deidamia, for he had been deemed unworthy following his crime of matricide. Determined to have Hermione, Orestes challenged Pyrrhus to a duel.

Pyrrhus had returned home from Troy with Hector's widow,

Andromache, as his concubine. His wife, Hermione, hated her, accusing her of being a Trojan witch who cast spells that prevented her from conceiving a child. To keep peace, he had given Andromache away to Helenus, son of Priam, also brought back to Greece as a slave. But Hermione kept grumbling.

Whether it was to escape the household quarrels, or because he enjoyed fighting, or because he felt the House of Agamemnon had wronged the House of Achilles at Troy, Pyrrhus accepted Orestes's challenge. Like their fathers who had fought over a concubine in Troy, the sons now fought over a wife in Greece. But in the duel that followed, Pyrrhus was killed; the House of Agamemnon thus prevailed over the House of Achilles.

Orestes married Hermione and eventually became king of all of Peloponnese. His sister, Electra, married his beloved friend, Pylades.

- Marriage often challenges the rivalries and friendships of war. In the Mahabharata, Arjuna, the Pandava, and Duryodhana, the Kaurava, are bitter enemies, but the two are related through marriage. Arjuna's son, Abhimanyu, marries Vatsala, Balarama's daughter, while Duryodhana's daughter, Lakshmana, marries Shamba, Balarama's nephew, and Krishna's son.
- Euripides wrote a play in which Apollo tells Orestes to go to Tauris and bring to Athens the image of Artemis that had fallen there from the heavens. Pylades accompanies Orestes to Tauris where they are captured by locals who are intent on sacrificing them to Artemis. The priestess of Artemis promises to let one of the two live if they deliver a letter to Athens for her. Both friends want the other to take the letter and survive. This story of each friend trying to save the other indicates a deep bond, emotional if not physical, between the two. However, the story takes a dramatic turn when the contents of the letter reveal that the priestess of Artemis is none other than Iphigenia, Orestes's sister, who had allegedly been sacrificed to Artemis by their father Agamemnon just before the Greek ships sailed to Troy. She had been saved by the goddess and taken to Tauris. Brother and sister have a joyous reunion, and all of them escape from Tauris and return to Athens, carrying the image of Artemis with them.
- Pylades of Phocis was the son of Agamemnon's sister. That made him Orestes's cousin. They were the best of friends, and many writers assumed they were lovers, such is the intensity of their relationship. When Orestes, chased by the Furies, was denied shelter by Pylades' father, Pylades left his home and accompanied his friend, sharing his misery, until the intervention of Athena. In *Erotes* (Affairs of the Heart), Lucian presents the relationship of Orestes and Pylades as the principal representative of homoerotic friendship.

Helen

The ship carrying Menelaus and Helen was caught in storms, forcing them to take refuge in Egypt for years. Finally, Menelaus managed to overpower Proteus, the shape-shifting old man from the sea, who revealed to him the safest and shortest passage to Sparta.

On returning home Menelaus lived out the rest of his days rather unremarkably with Helen by his side. It was not a happy life, for he was haunted by the death of the Greeks at Troy and those who never made it home. He regretted that Helen could not give him a son, and preferred the company of his son Megapenthes, born of his Trojan concubine. When Menelaus died, Megapenthes became king and he exiled Helen, considered the cause of so much misery.

Helen found shelter at Rhodes, where lived her friend Polyxo, who had lost her husband Tlepolemus at Troy. People expected Helen to give a lock of her hair at the shrine for their fallen king, a common practice of mourning among Greeks. But when Helen failed to do so and remained seemingly distant, indifferent to the tragedy she was responsible for, Polyxo had her hanged from a tree.

- The famous line 'the face that launched a thousand ships and burnt the topless towers of Ilium' comes from Christopher Marlowe's play *Doctor Faustus*, published in 1604.
- In Homer's *Odyssey*, Telemachus, the son of Odysseus, visits Sparta and finds Menelaus and Helen there.
- In Euripides's play *Helen*, written around 400 BCE, the real Helen is whisked away to Egypt by Hera and Athena, while the Greeks and Trojans fight over a phantom Helen. After the war, when Menelaus passes through Egypt, he is reunited with the real Helen.
- In the second century CE, Pausanias the Greek traveller and geographer wrote of how Helen was killed in Rhodes and how she shared her afterlife with Achilles.
- As a daughter of Zeus, Helen's character is mysterious and unfathomable. All men fall in love with her, but she does not seem to love them back. She seems manipulative at times, and indifferent at other times. One is never sure if she cares more for her lover or her husband, the Trojans or the Greeks. That is why perhaps it was concluded that she was also the daughter of Nemesis, created to destroy arrogant mortals.

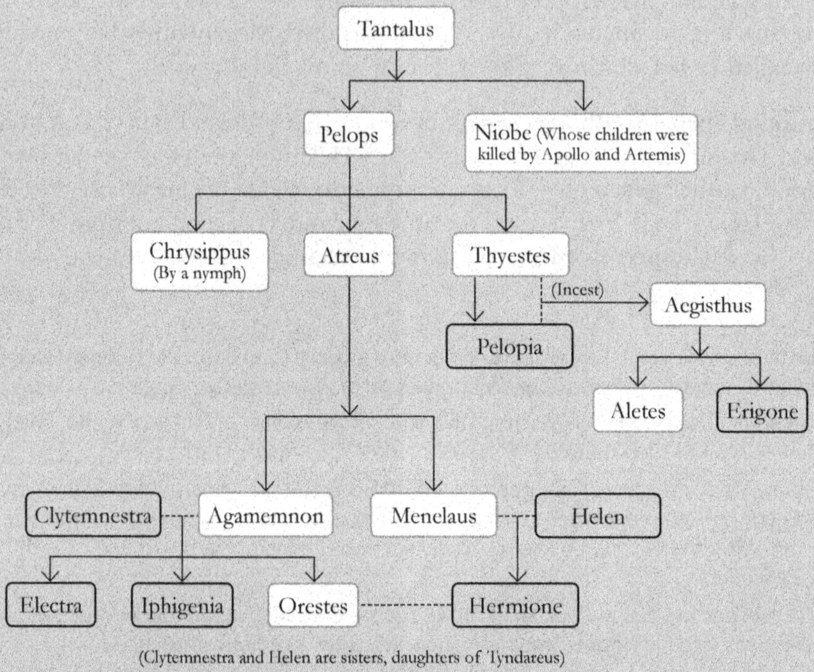

House of Tantalus

BOOK SEVEN

Odysseus

'What terrible retribution! Victors who never return home, or return to broken homes with unfaithful wives,' said the gymnosophist, shaken by the tales of Achilles and Agamemnon. 'Did no one return to a happy life?'

'Odysseus did, but after twenty years, ten of those spent battling Trojans, and ten surviving the sea.'

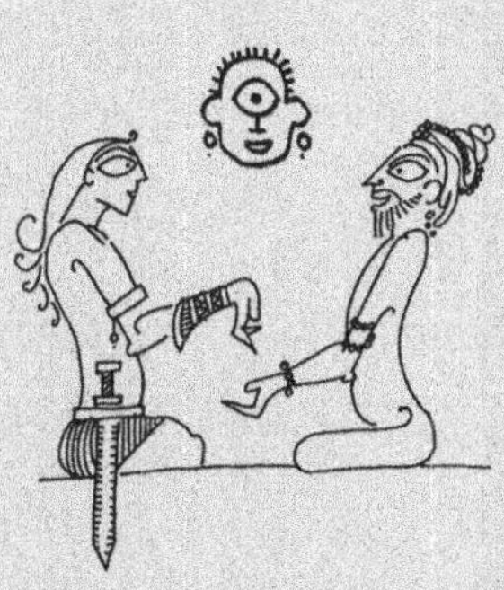

Recruitment

Odysseus, king of Ithaca, had descended from Hermes. In his veins flowed the blood of the master thief Autolycus and the trickster Sisyphus, who had exasperated even the Olympians.

Although he was obligated to help Menelaus in his quest to bring Helen back from Troy, he did not want to go because it had been foretold that if he left his home, he

would not return for twenty years. The thought of not seeing his wife, Penelope, and their son, Telemachus, for so long was unbearable. Thus when Palamedes came to recruit him on behalf of the Greeks, Odysseus pretended to be mad, tilling the land with a plough yoked to an ass and a bullock, sowing salt in the field. Suspecting trickery, Palamedes snatched Telemachus from Penelope's arms and placed him in the field before the plough. The 'mad' Odysseus immediately reined in the plough, revealing his deception.

Thus recruited, Odysseus sailed grudgingly with the Greeks to Troy, serving Agamemnon well with his cunning. He hoped that he would succeed in ending the war soon and return earlier than prophesied. But that was not to be.

When the Trojan War stretched on for ten years, Odysseus blamed Palamedes, his recruiter, for his misfortune. Frustrated, he wrongfully accused Palamedes of accepting Trojan gold as a bribe and encouraging the Greeks to end the siege of Troy and return home. Without a fair trial, Palamedes was stoned to death, a crime for which the Greeks suffered greatly later, at the hands of Palamedes' father, Nauplius.

- The contrast between the straightforward Achilles and the cunning Odysseus, who are central characters of the *Iliad* and the *Odyssey*, mirrors that between the rule-following Ram and rule-breaking Krishna of the Ramayana and the Mahabharata.
- The *Odyssey* is one of the earliest Greek epics written by Homer and dates back to around the seventh century BCE.
- Based on astronomical references found in the epic, it is assumed that the events that inspired the epic took place around 1200 BCE.
- The idea of leaving home, one's comfort zone, voluntarily or involuntarily, in order to experience new things and enlarge one's thoughts is a key theme in Greek mythology.
- While the Greeks admired Odysseus for his cunning, the Romans found him dishonourable, especially in the way he avoided being recruited and the way he avenged himself on Palamedes. The Romans knew him as Ulysses.
- Odysseus was jealous of Palamedes who was known for his intelligence. Besides games of dice, Palamedes invented counting, currency, a game like chess called 'pessoi' and even jokes.

Lotus-eaters

Thanks to the wooden horse that Odysseus designed, the Greeks were finally able to breach the mighty Trojan walls. And with that, at long last, the war came to an end and the Greeks sailed home. But as he and his crew set out for Ithaca, Odysseus did not know that another ten years of adventure awaited him.

Odysseus and his fellow sailors had got so used to war, of grabbing supplies rather than trading for them that in Cicona, their first port of call on their way to Ithaca, they plundered the city, killed the men, enslaved the women, and took what they wanted. The men felt no remorse as the Cicones were Trojan allies. This misdeed angered Zeus so much that he caused a storm to take Odysseus's ship completely off course to the land of the Lotus-eaters, where people did nothing but eat the lotus fruit, which filled them with so much tranquillity that they desired for nothing, not even home. Many sailors loved the idea and succumbed to the lotus fruit, offering it to Odysseus as well. But Odysseus was determined to go home, so he dragged his men back to the ship, bound their feet with chains to stop them from jumping off and swimming back to the island, and set out for Ithaca once again.

- The wandering mendicants of India who shun the householder's life and wander in the wilderness lost in the dull haze of the narcotic Indian hemp can be equated with the mild and harmless Lotus-eaters of Greek mythology.
- Odysseus is described as a man who is cunning, resourceful and naturally curious, eager to discover and learn, as we find in his many adventures. He is not merely a 'sacker of cities' despite what he does in Cicona.
- The land of the Lotus-eaters is sometimes identified with Libya and the blue lotus of the Nile is considered the source of the narcotic drug.
- The story of the Lotus-eaters is based on a recurring theme in the *Odyssey*: that of forgetting. Odysseus is being offered the chance to forget everything, the pain, the suffering, even the longing for home, and submit to a life of meaningless bliss. He refuses, as a hero should.

Cyclopes

Odysseus then reached the island of the Cyclopes, one-eyed giants who herded sheep. He did not realize the danger he was in until he found himself trapped in the cave of the Cyclops Polyphemus. He watched in horror as Polyphemus grabbed and ate his companions raw. Like sheep, he found himself being herded into a pen in the cave, awaiting his fate.

The clever Odysseus found grapes in the cave and turned them into wine. He then identified himself as Nemo, or Nobody, befriended the Cyclops, got him drunk and, while he slept, punctured his single eye with the trunk of a tree that he had spent all day sharpening to a point.

As Polyphemus howled in agony, the other Cyclopes of the island came to his cave. 'Who hurt you?' they asked. 'Nobody,' Polyphemus replied and so they left him alone and went away.

Polyphemus was determined not to let his attackers leave the cave alive. So when it was time to let the sheep out, he rubbed their back to make sure no one was riding them. But Odysseus was smarter and escaped by clinging to the underbelly of a sheep.

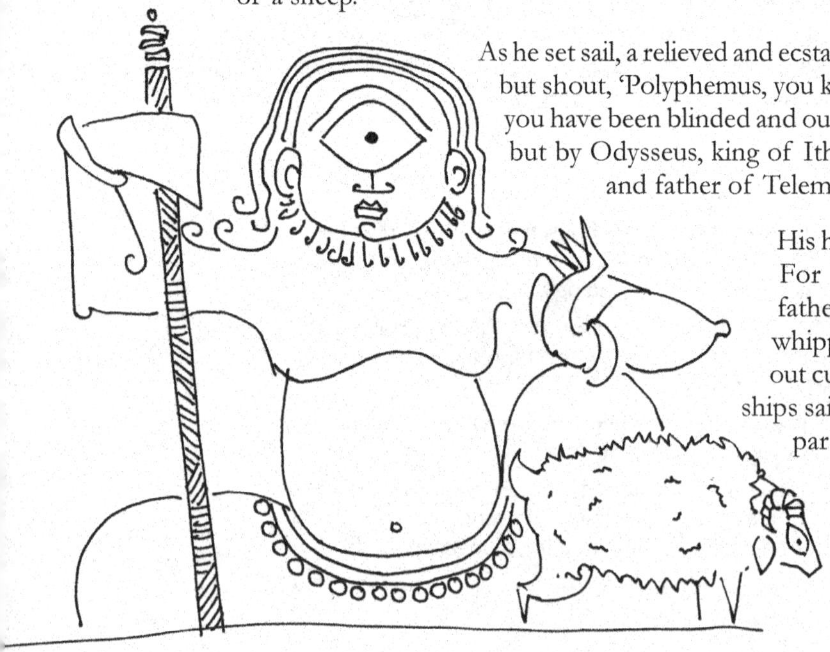

As he set sail, a relieved and ecstatic Odysseus could not help but shout, 'Polyphemus, you killer of my men, know that you have been blinded and outsmarted not by "Nobody" but by Odysseus, king of Ithaca, husband of Penelope and father of Telemachus.'

His hubris cost Odysseus dearly. For Polyphemus invoked his father Poseidon and the sea god whipped up storms and churned out currents ensuring Odysseus's ships sailed aimlessly for days in no particular direction.

- Homer describes the Cyclopes as simple one-eyed herdsmen, children of Poseidon. Hesiod's *Theogony*, written at the same time as Homer's epic, describes the Cyclopes as the children of Uranus and Gaia, which makes them the siblings of the Titans.
- The Cyclopes forged the thunderbolt for Zeus, the trident for Poseidon, bows and arrows for both Apollo and Artemis, and the helmet for Hades. Later, they came to be portrayed as assistants at Hephaestus's forge.
- Ovid's *Metamorphosis*, a Latin work dating back to first century CE, tells of how the Cyclops Polyphemus was in love with the sea nymph Galatea who preferred the shepherd Acis. Coming upon the lovers, the jealous and violent Polyphemus picked up a rock and crushed Acis.

Aeolus

Finally, Odysseus reached an island that was home to the wind god Aeolus. The wind god was kind and generous and, after taking care of him and his crew for a month, gave him a bag saying, 'It contains all the winds except the West Wind that will gently take you straight home to Ithaca.'

And sure enough, the gentle West Wind took Odysseus's ships straight towards Ithaca.

When the shores of Ithaca appeared on the horizon, Odysseus decided to take a nap. 'Wake me up after we beach the ship!' he told his companions. But when he shut his eyes and started snoring, his crew decided to investigate the contents of the mysterious bag, tied with a silver string, that Aeolus had given to Odysseus. Did it contain treasure?

As soon as the string was undone, all the winds were released and the ships were pushed back to the island of Aeolus. When Odysseus woke up and realized what his foolish crew had done, he begged the wind god to help with the West Wind once again.

'I will not help one who the gods so oppose,' said Aeolus, slamming the door to his house on Odysseus's face.

- Aeolus, the warden of winds, was a son of Poseidon who lived on a floating island.
- In some tales, Aeolus had six sons and six daughters. He got his sons married to his daughters and they lived happily according to Homer. But this tale of incest did not appeal to later writers such as Euripides, who told the tale of how Aeolus killed his son and his daughter and the child of their incestuous union.

Laestrygonians

Confused by the shifting currents that Poseidon continued to throw in their path, Odysseus, his sailors and his ships travelled for a long time and finally reached the land of the Laestrygonians where they were greeted by a rather tall girl who invited them all to her parents' house for dinner.

But when they reached the house, they realized that they *were* the dinner, for the Laestrygonians were cannibals, delighted at having a rich supply of food sail into their harbour. Odysseus and his crew—those who managed to escape the trap—ran back to the shore, but the Laestrygonians followed them over the nearby cliffs and hurled stones that smashed all the ships, save one. Odysseus and a handful of sailors managed to escape on the vessel. The others were trapped on the shores where the cannibals got to them, tearing them from limb to limb and eating them alive.

- When Odysseus leaves Troy he has twelve ships. He is left with only one after his encounter with the Laestrygonians.
- It is believed that the Laestrygonians lived in what is now called Sicily.

Circe

Odysseus's lone ship finally made its way to the island of Aiaia.

Odysseus waited on the shore while the sailors explored the island. Long hours passed until at last one sailor returned with horrifying news: the island was home to a sorceress named Circe who pretended to be kind and offered food and drink to strangers, only to turn them all into pigs.

Determined to release his men from the enchantress, Odysseus marched to her house. On the way, the god Hermes met him and gave him a herb to eat which would keep him safe from Circe's magical potions.

Circe was welcoming, charming and seductive and offered Odysseus a drink, but was surprised to find that it had no effect on him. Odysseus then drew his sword and threatened to kill Circe if she did not release his sailors from her spell. Circe released the soldiers but asked Odysseus to stay with her for a few days and share her bed, while his sailors ate, rested and recovered their strength. Odysseus, not wanting to upset the witch, and finding her rather enchanting, agreed.

A few weeks later, he decided it was time to go.

'You will reach home only after you consult Tiresias, the oracle, and ask him how your journey will end,' said Circe.

'Where is he?' asked Odysseus.

'Across the great ocean, beyond the River Styx, in the land of the dead. I will show you the way. Do not be afraid.'

- In the folklore associated with wandering Indian mendicants known as Nath yogis there is reference to yoginis, or sorceresses, who turn men into donkeys and pigs and goats for their pleasure, until they meet their match in the sage Jalandar-nath.
- Circe is the daughter of Helios, the sun. Her sister Pasiphae marries Minos. Her brother Aeetes is the keeper of the Golden Fleece in Colchis. This makes the witch Medea her niece.
- In 1955, Nirad C. Chaudhari published his book *The Continent of Circe* where he compares the transformation of a militaristic Indian society, from the times of the Aryans through the Maurya and Gupta periods, into a non-violent pacifist society by the Mughal and European rulers of India, to the transformation of Greek warriors into pigs by Circe.
- The *Odyssey* is strongly influenced by the Mesopotamian epic *Gilgamesh*, which tells the story of a king who goes in search of the herb of immortality and has many adventures on the journey. Like Odysseus's encounter with Circe, Gilgamesh encounters a power woman, the goddess Selene who is associated with fermentation, hence alcohol.
- The idea of a goddess or a witch who helps as well as distracts the hero is a common theme in mythologies around the world. In the Ramayana, a similar role is played by the ascetic lady Swayamprabha, who offers food to the starving monkeys who get lost in a dark cave. The monkeys do not want to leave until Hanuman insists they do and so Swayamprabha helps them go over to the other end of the cave and reach the southern tip of India.

The Underworld

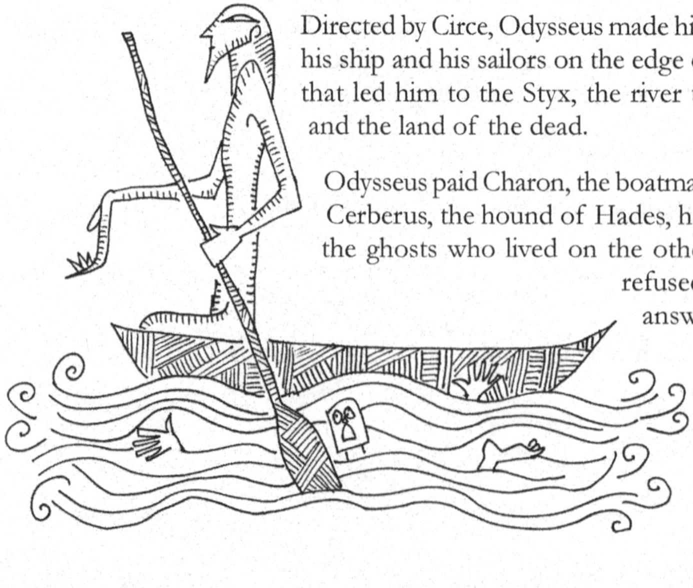

Directed by Circe, Odysseus made his way to the land of the dead. Leaving his ship and his sailors on the edge of the great ocean, he entered a cave that led him to the Styx, the river that separates the land of the living and the land of the dead.

Odysseus paid Charon, the boatman, the fee to ferry him across. He gave Cerberus, the hound of Hades, honeyed cakes. When he encountered the ghosts who lived on the other side, he offered them blood, but refused to let them drink it until Tiresias answered his question.

Tiresias came and said, 'I know your

question and I know the answer to your question: your journey will end not when you reach home, but when you journey with a rowing oar in your hand, beyond your house, so far inland where people have never seen the sea, and will mistake the oar in your hand for a winnowing fan. Fear not, Odysseus, you will not die *on* the sea but death will come to you *from* the sea.'

- In Hindu mythology, the journey to the land of the dead, the Pitr-loka, located beyond the River Vaitarni, is described in the Garuda Purana.
- Tiresias appears in many stories in Greek mythology. It is he who tells Amphitryon that the mystery lover of his wife Alcmene is none other than Zeus; who tells the mother of Narcissus that her son is safe as long as he does not know himself; who tells Oedipus that his wife is his mother and that he killed her first husband, his father.
- In Greek, the word *katabasis* is meant for an inward journey, such as one from the coast inland, or a descent from the world of the living to the world of the dead. The word *nekyia* refers to calling upon ghosts. Ghosts clearly play an important role in the adventures of Greek heroes. In the twentieth century, Jung used these words in the context of psychoanalysis.
- In Greek mythology, death is the loss of individuality, the transformation into a faceless ghost with no identity. When Odysseus makes the journey to the land of the dead, he hears their meaningless chatter, the complete depersonalization that follows the end of living. This gives more meaning to the life that one has, that one must experience to the fullest and whose wonders one must relish.

Sirens

After visiting the land of the dead, Odysseus returned to the island of Circe and she explained how he could journey home, warning him of the dangers that lay in his way. The very first hurdle in the way were the Sirens.

The Sirens were bird-like creatures that sang beautiful songs that enthralled sailors and made them sail their ship towards the rocky island inhabited by them. Here, their ships would get stuck between the rocks, and the Sirens would feast on them.

Circe had advised, 'Fill your ears with beeswax when you are sailing by their island so that you will not hear their irresistible song.' But Odysseus was curious about the Siren song, and he came up with a plan to hear it. He instructed his sailors to tie him to the mast of the ship and not untie him even if he ordered or begged them.

Thus with Odysseus tied to the mast, and the sailors' ears filled with beeswax, the ship sailed past the island of the Sirens. Unable to hear the song themselves, the sailors watched as Odysseus's eyes filled with longing upon hearing the song of those enchanting creatures. Later he would tell them how the song spoke of the glory of his days past and the wonders the future held for him.

'I wanted to hear more of it . . . to break free and swim towards them,' he confessed when the ship had moved into safe silent waters.

- On the southern edge of the west coast of India there are tales of seductive damsels known as yakshis who seduce young travellers, take them to their home, and then eat them alive.
- Traditionally, Sirens were imagined as bird-women with the head of a woman and the body of a bird. In modern writings, they are often confused with mermaids who seduce sailors.

- The Sirens lost a music competition to the Muses, who plucked their wings and used the feathers to make crowns for themselves. Rendered flightless, these women with claws for feet sat on the island in the middle of the sea and used their song to enchant sailors.
- In Christian times, Sirens were seen as metaphors for prostitutes who lured sailors away from their purpose.

Charybdis and Scylla

Then came the narrow strait between two monsters, Charybdis and Scylla, that Odysseus and his men had to navigate. Charybdis was a monstrous whirlpool that sucked in everything that came near her. Scylla was a six-headed dog-faced woman who grabbed and ate anything within reach.

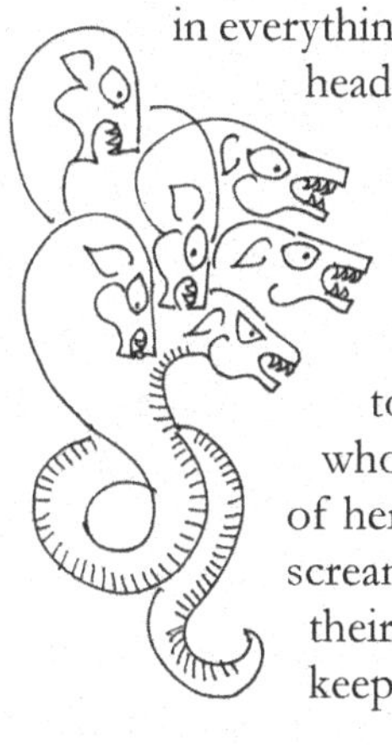

Navigation was not easy as the waters were restless. Circe had told Odysseus to steer the ship straight ahead. They managed to avoid Charybdis completely but not Scylla who was able to snatch six sailors, one with each of her six heads. The sailors begged Odysseus to stop, screaming as Scylla slowly ate them alive, tearing into their flesh. But Odysseus carried on; he had no choice but to keep moving if he wanted to escape. Sacrifices had to be made.

- In Hindu mythology, there are few, if any, tales of sea routes and entrances to seaways. But there are gateways protected by ferocious doorkeepers, often twins, such as Jaya and Vijaya who guard the gates of Vaikuntha, and Laya and Maya who watch over the entrance to the forest of Shiva and Shakti.
- Circe fell in love with the sea god Glaucus. But he preferred Scylla. Enraged, Circe turned Scylla into a dog-faced monster with six heads.
- Charybdis was the daughter of Poseidon who angered Zeus and so was turned into the bladder of a monster with an insatiable thirst for seawater. As she sucks in water,

she creates whirlpools. Aesop in his fables said that with her first sip, Charybdis exposed the mountains, with the second she exposed the islands, and with the final sip she would dry out the sea.

- The story of Charybdis and Scylla being on either side of a narrow strait through which ships had to pass gave rise to phrases about being trapped between two problems: between the Devil and the deep sea, between a rock and a hard place, out of the frying pan into the fire.
- The Strait of Messina is the narrow passage between the eastern tip of Sicily and the western tip of Calabria in the south of Italy, and is often identified as the strait across which stood the two monsters Charybdis and Scylla.

Helios

After many days of travelling over silent and safe waters, during which they exhausted all their supplies, the hungry, thirsty and miserable sailors reached an island where they saw cattle grazing.

'It is the island of Helios,' said Odysseus. 'Circe told me of this. We must not stop here, for we may upset him.'

But the sailors wanted to stop. They were tired and sick of the sea. A night's rest was all they desired. Odysseus gave in finally but warned them to leave the cattle alone. Yes, said the soldiers, but at night, while Odysseus slept, they slaughtered one of the sweet lowing cows and ate to their heart's content.

An angry Helios complained to Zeus and shortly after Odysseus's ship set sail, a bolt of lightning struck it. The ship broke, the mast sank, and the soldiers drowned. Only Odysseus survived, clinging to a piece of wreckage.

- In Hindu mythology, killing a cow is the greatest of crimes as cows give life-sustaining milk. This has led to a strict taboo against the inclusion of beef in Hindu dietary habits, though the tales say nothing about bulls or buffaloes. While the Greeks had no rules against killing or eating cows, harming animals sacred to the gods was strictly forbidden.
- Odysseus's fellow sailors do not listen to him. Despite clear instructions, they open Aeolus's bag and let loose the winds, and they kill cattle that belonged to Helios. Perhaps this suggests that Odysseus functioned better as a lone wolf than as a pack leader. His cunning won him the friendship of kings but not the loyalty of his people.
- Guarded by his daughters, Helios's cattle do not breed and do not reduce in number. In other words, they are immortal.
- Helios is sometimes identified with Apollo, just as Artemis is associated with Selene.

Calypso

The shipwrecked Odysseus washed up on an island that was the home of Calypso, a lonely nymph who fell in love with him.

For the next several years, she washed him, clothed him, fed him, entertained him, took care of his every need, but turned away every time he spoke of going

home. In other words, Odysseus lived in a beautiful, comfortable cage that he could never leave. Eventually he would forget, of that the nymph was sure. But Odysseus was determined not to.

At last a day came when the goddess Athena could bear the suffering of Odysseus no more. For years she had watched him spend hours staring at the sea, weeping for his home. Athena begged Zeus to order Calypso to let Odysseus leave. 'Let him go,' Zeus commanded. Calypso agreed, but she had one last trick. She offered her beloved Odysseus the unthinkable: immortality!

Odysseus refused, for he knew with immortality he would lose any memories of his home and family. He preferred the joy of living to an old age and dying surrounded by his loved ones. Calypso had no choice but to let Odysseus go. With a broken heart, she watched as her beloved made himself a raft, filled it with supplies and made his way towards Ithaca.

- In the Ramayana, when searching for Sita, Hanuman and his fellow monkeys are given food and shelter by the damsel Swayamprabha. She is lonely and desperate for companionship so she tries to make them forsake their mission and stay with her. But Hanuman insists on leaving. Unable to persuade Hanuman, impressed by his single-mindedness, she lets them go. In the tale, Swayamprabha functions like Calypso.
- Calypso is the daughter of the Titan Atlas. She hopes that Odysseus will forget his home and embrace immortality. But Odysseus resists. He yearns for home, his place in the world and society, and accepts his mortality. He knows that immortality, like death, means giving up the good life that only humans can experience even as they yearn for their place in the world and dread the inevitability of death.
- Unlike in his adventures with Polyphemus and Circe, Odysseus has neither the physical nor the psychological strength left now to break free from Calypso's island on his own. The gods have to intervene: and so Athena complains to Zeus who sends his messenger ordering Calypso to let Odysseus go.
- In the twentieth century, Captain Jacques Cousteau, the French mariner, became famous for his books and films on undersea research. His ship, the *Calypso*, became as famous as him. The *Odyssey* is structured as a flashback. It begins with Odysseus on the island of Calypso, ten years after the Trojan War, having spent three of those years wandering the seas on various adventures and seven imprisoned by the nymph.
- Homer's *Odyssey* is written in a Greek dialect which is often called Homeric Greek.

Phaeacians

While Zeus had forgiven Odysseus his many faults, Poseidon had not. He knew that he could not stop Odysseus from reaching home, but he refused to let it be easy. So he whipped up a storm that shattered Odysseus's raft, and watched as Odysseus tossed and tumbled on the waves, and was dragged naked to the island of the Phaeacians, covered in salt and filth.

Here, the local princess Nausicaa—who was playing ball on the beach while her maids were washing clothes—found him, gave him clothes and invited him to her father's house where he was made welcome, though not without some suspicion, by the king and his queen. 'Tell us your story,' said the queen Arete after Odysseus had been bathed and fed and made comfortable. So Odysseus told them his great adventure since he had left Troy, tales that involved monsters and gods and nymphs and cannibals. At the end of it, the king and queen were not sure if he was lying or telling the truth. They found it hard to believe that this was the legendary Odysseus.

'But the Trojan War ended ten years ago!' they remarked.

Odysseus started to weep for he realized his son would now be twenty, if alive, and his wife no longer the young maid he had left behind. Would his father still be alive? Feeling sorry for him, the king Alcinous decided to take him at his word. 'Our sailors will take you to Ithaca. They know where it is.'

Odysseus was in a deep sleep when the Phaeacian ship reached Ithaca. Not wanting to disturb his slumber, the sailors left him sleeping on the beach and returned home. When Odysseus awoke, he was not sure where he was. He asked a passing shepherd who said, 'Ithaca!'

- In Mohiniattam, a classical dance form that emerged in the state of Kerala, beautiful young women often play with balls to enchant men. They are often free to play in the midst of household chores like washing and collecting water, performed outside the house. A similar scene is played out on the beach on the island of the Phaeacians.
- It is suggested that there is unrequited love between Nausicaa and Odysseus as he never shares any information about Nausicaa with his wife, Penelope.
- Since Nausicaa is the first mythic character shown to be playing a game with a ball, she is considered an inventor of ball games.
- Scholars have speculated that Nausicaa may have been the real author of the *Odyssey* considering the realistic description of the washing scene.
- According to Aristotle, Odysseus's son Telemachus eventually marries Nausicaa.
- A common technique in ancient Greek epics is the use of narration by the hero of the tale. In the *Odyssey*, Odysseus narrates his adventures to the king of the Phaeacians. In the *Aeneid*, Aeneas narrates his adventures to Dido.

Penelope

Odysseus did not reveal his identity to anyone, for Tiresias had told him that there would be trouble when he arrived home.

As there had been no sign of Odysseus in the ten years since the Trojan War, his neighbours had assumed he was dead. They were eager to claim his beautiful wife and his lands and his sheep as their own, ignoring the protests of young Telemachus. The suitors came every evening to his house and ate all they could find in the kitchen and the larder, forcing the servants to serve them. 'You must select one of us as your husband,' they threatened Penelope when she protested, 'or we will rape you and your servants, kill your son and burn down your house.'

Penelope managed to keep the men at bay

by declaring that she would marry them after she finished weaving a shroud for her father-in-law, Laertes, who was old but still alive. All day she would weave the shroud, but at night, she would unravel it, removing the threads, so that the shroud was never finished.

Every day she hoped that Odysseus would return before her deception was caught, yet there was no sign of him, and now she had no choice but to choose a new husband from amongst the suitors, or risk rape and plunder.

- Chastity is a very important notion in Hindu mythology. The chastity of a wife grants protection to the husband, while her infidelities make him vulnerable. Chastity is admired in Roman and Christian mythology too, with Penelope being lauded as the epitome of wifely virtue and chastity. However, in these mythologies chastity is not associated with any mystical powers.
- Widow remarriage is rare in Hindu mythology, and limited mostly to vanara (monkey) and rakshasa (barbarian) women, not women of high status like epic heroines.
- Weaving is a feminine activity in Greek mythology. Penelope, like Circe and Calypso, is shown weaving by Homer. When Heracles is forced to cross-dress as a woman and serve Omphale, he too is portrayed holding a spindle.
- For three years, Penelope weaves by day and unravels by night the shroud meant for her father-in-law. This act resembles the meaningless, monotonous, repetitive suffering of those cast into Tartarus.

Suitors

When Odysseus entered his own house, he found that Penelope had organized a contest, the winner of which could claim her and her husband's house as his trophy. No one recognized him, except his old dog Argus, who wagged his tail before breathing his last. The servants were too distracted to notice him, as they were busy catering to Penelope's suitors.

Unable to ignore their attentions any further for fear that they would harm her son and her servants, Penelope declared to the suitors that she would marry the man who could perform a particular feat: string Odysseus's bow and shoot an arrow through the metal hoops of twelve axes placed in a single row. 'Odysseus could do it. So must my next husband,' said Penelope.

The suitors liked the idea and began to try one by one. But to their shock none could even string the bow. This made them angry: Was this yet another ploy by Penelope to keep them away?

Odysseus suddenly walked up and said, 'May I try?' The suitors scowled at the temerity of the stranger but Penelope said that no guest in the House of Odysseus would be turned away.

To everyone's astonishment, the stranger effortlessly strung the bow, and shot an arrow through the twelve hoops of the axes. This was no stranger—this was Odysseus! Before anyone could utter a word, Odysseus picked up another arrow and struck one of the men who had abused his wife. Then he shot another arrow, and another. Telemachus joined him, as did the servants of the household. Before long, every 'suitor' had been killed.

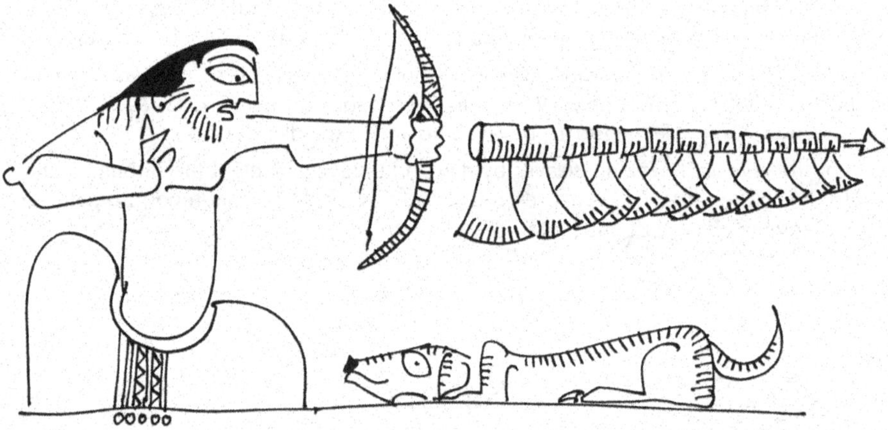

- Like the Ramayana and the Mahabharata, the *Odyssey* also speaks of an archery contest as a method to identify a suitable groom for a noble lady. This suggests a common Indo-European root, an ancient tribal custom according to which, in case of a conflict, the better warrior wins the woman.
- The primary purpose of the *Odyssey* is to record how Odysseus restores balance in his universe, reaffirms his place as head of his household, and destroys the suitors who display hubris when they forget their place in society.

Reunion

Penelope greeted her husband with tears in her eyes, and introduced her son to his father. All the servants hugged their master. An old maid checked his thigh and found an old hunting scar, thus confirming that this was indeed Odysseus. Odysseus's father, the old Laertes, who had refused to live in the house of his son after it had been invaded by the suitors, returned to embrace his son. Everyone was happy.

Still, Penelope was doubtful.

'Shall I ask the servants to move our bed to the courtyard so that we can spend this night of reunion beneath the stars?' she asked.

Odysseus smiled. 'My clever and faithful wife, you know that bed cannot be moved for it was carved out of the trunk of an old olive tree with roots still in the ground. Did we not build our house around this fixed bed?'

Penelope nodded in delight as her husband took her in his arms. Yes, her husband was finally home.

- Secrets that bind married couples is a theme we find in Hindu mythology too. In the Ramayana, Ram and Sita share tales with each other that they do not tell anyone else. When Hanuman comes to Sita, she narrates one such tale to him—of how Indra's son Revanta tried to attack her in the forest in the form of a crow and how Ram stopped him—so that Hanuman can prove to Ram that he indeed met Sita in Lanka.
- We would like to believe that the story of Odysseus ends with a happily-ever-after, but in keeping with Greek mythic structure, tragedy follows soon after the reunion.

Telegonus

Odysseus knew that lasting peace was impossible until he appeased Poseidon. And for that, as advised by Tiresias, he had to go inland and find a place where people had never seen the sea, had never eaten salt, and so would mistake a rowing oar which he carried over his shoulder to be a winnowing fan. Odysseus found such a place, and set up an altar and made oblations to Poseidon. Only then came peace.

But then fears of death enveloped him. Some oracles told him that his son would be his killer, and so he exiled his son Telemachus, paying no heed to Penelope's pleas. The words of Tiresias, that he would not die at sea but that death would come *from* the sea haunted him. So he kept watch on the sea, wary of strangers and pirates.

One day, Odysseus found a young man stealing his cattle. Without trying to find out who he was, Odysseus attacked him and in the fight that followed he was killed by a spear tipped with the poison of the stingray fish. This indeed was death *from* the sea. And the killer was his son, a son that Odysseus never knew he had: Telegonus, son of Circe, who had come to Ithaca looking for his father and had failed to identify the island as his father's.

Telegonus carried Odysseus's body to his house, met Penelope and then fetched Telemachus. He took mother and son to the enchanted island of Circe. There, he married his stepmother Penelope and Telemachus married Circe. Telegonus fathered Italus, whose name is given to the country Italy, and Telemachus fathered Latinus, whose name is given to the Latins.

- In the Mahabharata, Babruvahana attacks and kills Arjuna, failing to recognize the latter as his father. Later, Arjuna is brought back to life by a Naga-mani, the magical snake jewel, provided by Babruvahana's mother Uloopi, who informs him that he committed no crime and that this was the fulfilment of a curse. Arjuna had been cursed by Ganga that just as he had killed his grand-uncle Bhishma, he would suffer death at the hands of his own son. Thus the horror of patricide is explained using karma.
- The story of Telegonus comes from the now-lost epic *Telegony*.
- Information about Latinus and Italus comes to us from Hyginus's *Fabulae*.
- In Greek mythology, Latinus and Italus are described as both the children and grandchildren of Odysseus, since his sons Telegonus and Telemachus married their stepmothers, Penelope and Circe. But the timelines don't quite match.

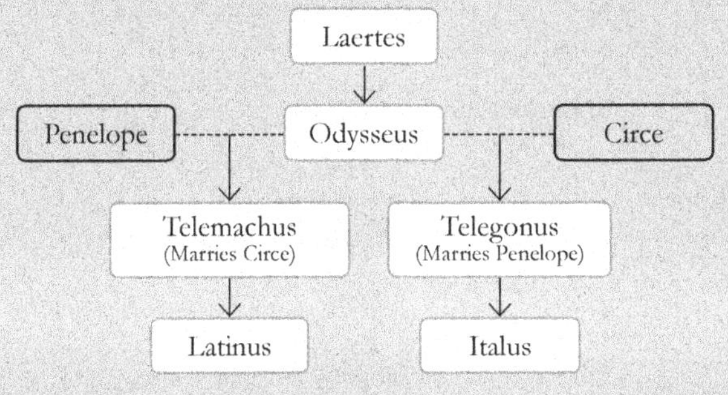

House of Odysseus

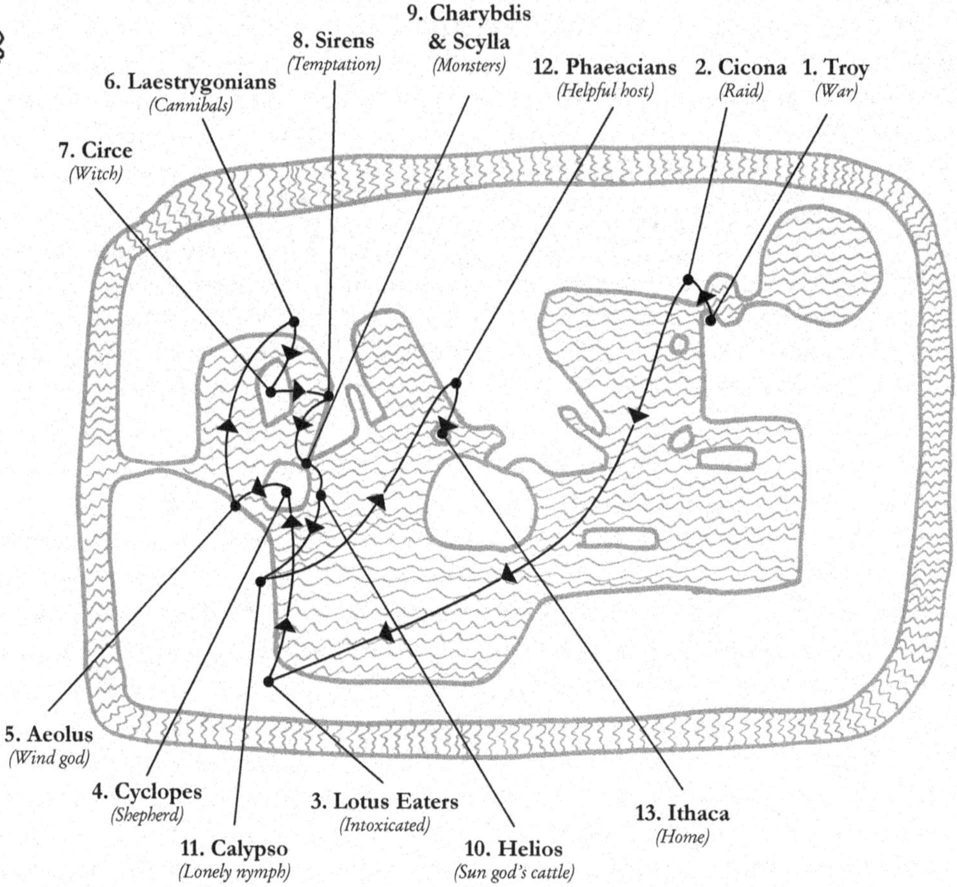

Odysseus' Expedition
(Probable route: representational, not drawn to scale)

BOOK EIGHT

Aeneas

'What a homecoming,' sighed the gymnosophist after listening to the tale of Odysseus. 'And what of those who lost their homes?'

'There is a reason why the Olympians let humans have hope. It sustains even the shattered,' said Alexander. 'Let me tell you the story of Aeneas, he who escaped the fires of Troy, and went on to establish a great new city.'

'And what was the price the Olympians demanded?'

'The rejection of love.'

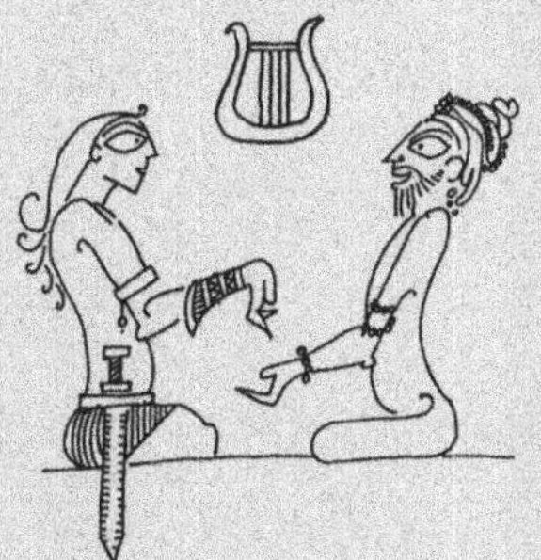

Anchises

Only three Olympians were immune to the powers of Aphrodite: Athena, Artemis and Hestia. Everyone else was made to fall in love with mortals. To prevent Aphrodite from bragging, Zeus decided to make her fall in love with a Trojan youth called Anchises.

Anchises, who was tending cattle on the hills near Mount Ida, had no clue that the beautiful woman who seduced and made love to him was a goddess. From this union was born Aeneas.

'Do not reveal this secret to anyone,' Aphrodite warned Anchises, when it was time for her to leave. 'Our son will be the father of a new line of kings, after the fall of Troy,' she prophesied.

Unfortunately, Anchises could not stop himself from boasting to his friends one evening after drinking a lot of wine. For his insolence, he was struck by Zeus's thunderbolt and lost the use of his legs, becoming forever dependent on his son Aeneas.

This happened long before the abduction of Helen, when Troy was at the height of its glory. All his life Anchises knew the dreadful fate that awaited his city and its residents, but he never told anyone. He was well aware of the terrible price one paid for revealing the secrets of the gods.

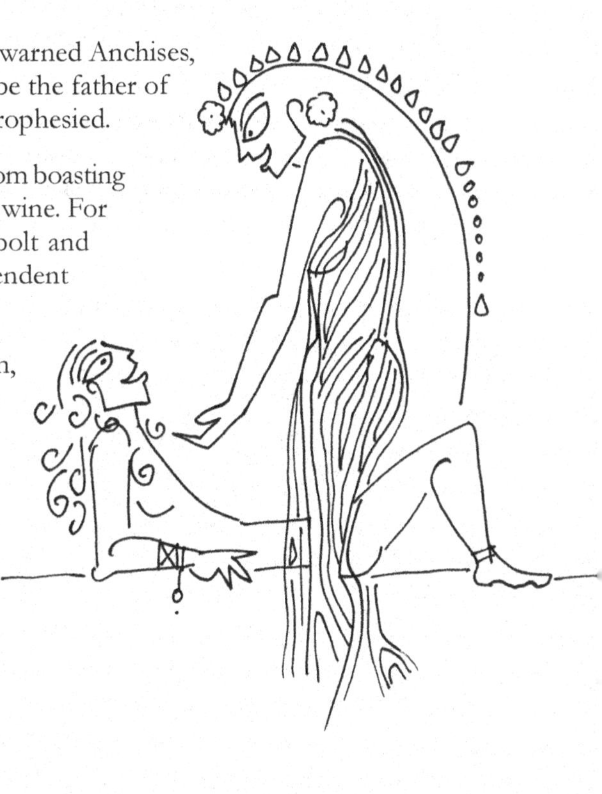

- How can Alexander tell the story of Aeneas when it is chronicled in the *Aeneid*, a Latin epic by Virgil, composed 300 years after Alexander? The tale was probably known even before. For example, the story of Aphrodite and Anchises is part of the Homeric Hymns, attributed to Homer but of unknown authorship, that were composed 400 years before Alexander.
- Like Anchises, who knows the fate of Troy but can do nothing to change it, in the Mahabharata, Sahadeva knows the fate of his clan but can do nothing to stop the war.
- It is curious why the Romans would associate their roots with the losing Trojan side rather than the winning Greek side. Perhaps it indicates the attitude of the Romans towards the Greeks. At one level the Romans envied and imitated the Greeks and adopted many things Greek, including their gods, their architecture and their philosophers; but at another level, they looked down upon the Greeks, viewing them as too talkative and fun-loving, lacking the respect for tradition that formed the cornerstone of the Roman Empire.
- Asteroids around the planet Jupiter are conventionally called Trojans and one of the larger asteroids is named Anchises.

Creusa

As Troy was being sacked, the men killed and women raped, Aeneas was warned in a vision by his mother Aphrodite to escape the city and sail to a land across the Mediterranean to the west.

So he gathered his things, picked up his father and fled. The Greek soldiers who saw him would surely have killed him had Agamemnon not stopped them, saying, 'Look how this youth risks his own life to save his old and frail father. He deserves to live. So few like him in the world any more.'

Aeneas then went back to fetch his wife Creusa, one of Priam's many daughters. But sadly, by then, she had been killed. Her ghost advised him to carry on, to find a new home and a new wife.

With his father and his young son Iulus by his side, Aeneas hid in a cave near the sea until the triumphant Greeks left. He then gathered around him the few Trojans who had managed to escape, mostly old and infirm, and set sail in the direction of the setting sun, hoping to find refuge and eventually a new home. They came to call themselves the Aeneads.

- Both Greek and Hindu mythologies reveal the human anxiety over the survival of the family tree. In the Mahabharata, the only survivor of the Pandava clan at the end of the Kurukshetra war is Arjuna's unborn grandchild.
- Virgil's *Aeneid* marks the end of the more democratic Roman republic, and the rise of Roman dictatorship under the Caesars. It became essential to connect the new rulers with the gods to justify their claim to rule. Through Aeneas, the Romans were connected with Aphrodite. Aeneas demonstrates the Roman idea of 'pietas' or piety and filial respect by taking care of his father at the risk of his own life. Iulus or Julus, also known as Ascanius, son of Aeneas, inspired the name Julia, the family to which Julius Caesar and Augustus Caesar belonged. Thus Iulus played an important role in Roman mythology.
- In some versions, Iulus was born in Italy, not Troy, to the Latin wife of Aeneas.
- Creusa, wife of Aeneas, must not be confused with Creusa, princess of Corinth, killed by Medusa.

Polydorus

The Aeneads first sailed to Thrace whose king was an ally of Troy. But next to the rocky beach were trees that oozed human blood. Aeneas took this as some kind of warning. Rather than proceed he stopped under the trees, where he encountered the ghost of Polydorus, Priam's youngest and Hecabe's favourite son.

The ghost whispered, 'My father, king of Troy, sent me to Thrace to ensure at least one member of the family would survive should Troy fall. I carried sacks of gold with me to pay for my upkeep. But as soon as Troy fell, Polymestor, the king of Thrace, realized it was more profitable to just kill me and keep the gold. And so, disregarding all rules of hospitality, he ordered that I be killed and my body be thrown into the sea, without a proper burial. The waves pushed me back to the shore, and the spears that impaled me took root on this rocky beach, growing into trees that ooze my blood. Do not come to Thrace, Aeneas. Make a home elsewhere, where people are more hospitable.'

- One of the stories in Hindu mythology that demonstrates the idea of how some people value wealth more than relationships is of Sunahshepa whose poor father, Ajigarta, sells him to King Harischandra. The king wants an adopted son whom he can sacrifice to the gods in the place of his real son, Rohit. The priests refuse to do human sacrifice and so Ajigarta offers to behead his own son if given more cattle. This story comes from the Aitreya Brahmana composed around the time of Homer's *Iliad*.
- Euripides's Greek tragedy *Hecuba*, written around 460 BCE, tells us the tragic story of Polydorus. Here, Hecuba (Hecabe) avenges her son's death by attacking and blinding Polymestor.
- In Hyginus's *Fabulae*, Polydorus is sent to his older sister, Iliona. Not trusting her husband, Polymestor, she raises her own son as her brother and her brother as her son. After the Trojan War, Agamemnon offers Polymestor the hand of his daughter Electra if he kills Priam's son and daughter. Polymestor does so, thus accidentally killing his own son.
- Polymestor denies Polydorus burial rites by throwing his corpse into the sea. Aeneas conducts the proper funeral rites so that the ghost of Polydorus can be at peace and travel to the land of the dead across the Styx.

Andromache

His journey in search of a homeland took Aeneas to Epirus in Greece, where he found a city that looked very much like Troy, a diminutive double with much diluted grandeur. On enquiry, he learned that Helenus, son of Priam, known for his prophetic ability, and his queen, Andromache, widow of Hector, were its king and queen.

Helenus explained, 'After my father gave Helen to my brother Deiphobus instead of me, I left Troy and went over to the Greeks and revealed all the secrets that would enable them to bring down Troy. For my favours, I was spared. I joined Achilles' son, Pyrrhus, and travelled with him to Epirus, for I divined that one day I would be master of all that was his.'

Andromache added, 'I was concubine to Pyrrhus. He was not interested in home or kingdom.

He loved conquest and felt he should claim the hand of Hermione, daughter of Menelaus and Helen, in marriage; but she was betrothed to wed her cousin, Orestes, son of Agamemnon. A duel took place between them in which Orestes prevailed. With Pyrrhus gone, the people chose Helenus as king, for he was of royal blood and an able ruler, and he chose me as his wife. So you see, the gods have ensured that at least some Trojans rule over some Greeks.'

Andromache provided Aeneas with supplies he would need for his voyage. And Helenus made a prediction: Aeneas would establish a new city in the land that was once home to those who built the city of Troy. At the destined spot, he would find a giant sow suckling thirty white piglets.

- These stories reveal how the consequences of war are blurred in the long run, for in some instances, the conquerors end up being ruled by the vanquished.
- In 280 BCE, Pyrrhus of Epirus won a war against the Romans in which his own 'victorious' army suffered so many losses that he feared another such victory would see him returning to Epirus alone. The phrase 'pyrrhic victory', a victory where the losses sustained makes it as good as defeat, comes from here.

Dardanus

Where did the people who built the city of Troy come from, Aeneas wondered. His father, the oldest Trojan on the ship, remembered the stories he had heard as a child and said, 'It must be Crete, for Teucer came from Crete.'

Teucer left Crete after it was struck by famine. He came to Asia and the oracles told him to settle down in a land where he would be attacked by creatures born of the earth. On his first night, mice, who are 'creatures born of the earth', attacked his tent. Thus, Teucer made his home there and established the worship of Apollo who helped him rid the region of the rats.

Aeneas sailed east to Crete, but his crew suffered great sickness on landing on its shores.

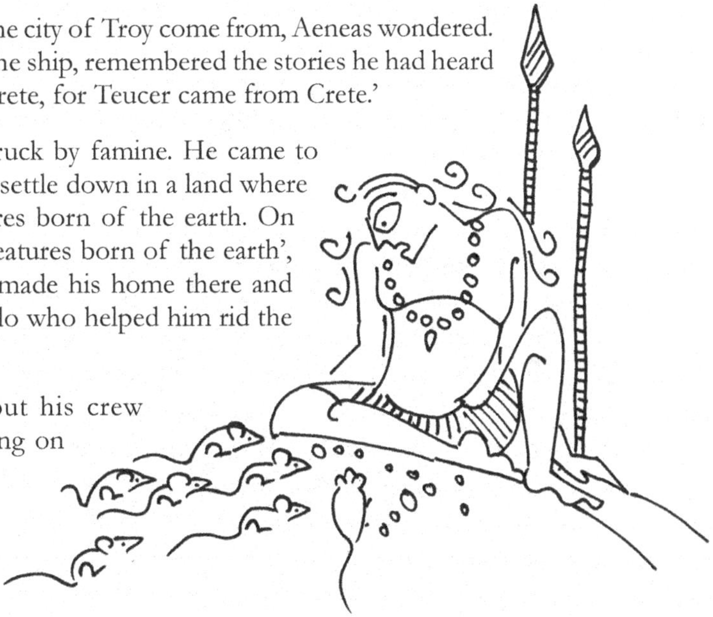

'Then it must be Italy, for Teucer's son-in-law Dardanus came from Italy,' said Anchises, regretting his earlier decision.

This westward journey meant travelling through unknown waters where he encountered the Cyclopes, Scylla and Charybdis, and the Harpies who told Aeneas, 'When you and your sailors eat your plates along with the food on it, know that you have found your home.'

These adventures proved too much for Anchises, and he died before the ship reached Italy.

- The theme of heroes and kings establishing cities is a common theme in Greek mythology, but not so much in Hindu mythology. The great cities of mythology such as Ayodhya and Hastinapur seem to have always existed. Kubera does establish Lanka and after being cast out by Ravana, moves north and founds Alaka. Krishna too establishes the city of Dwarka after Jarasandha burns down Mathura. But these are exceptions rather than the rule.
- Virgil clearly wants the journey of his hero to include encounters of other heroes, from Jason who travels east, to Odysseus who gets lost in the west. And so Aeneas encounters both the Cyclopes as well as the Harpies. Like these past heroes, Aeneas also travels to the land of the dead across the Styx.

Pygmalion

The journey to what would eventually be his home was not an easy one for Aeneas, since the goddess Hera was still angry with the Trojans, smarting from the fact that Paris had judged Aphrodite more beautiful than her. And the fact that Aeneas was Aphrodite's son and a Trojan only served to compound her hatred. So she asked the wind god Aeolus to cause the Trojan ship to crash against the rocks.

The sea god Poseidon did not appreciate

Hera's interference in his realm. So he countered Aeolus's move and ensured Aeneas's ship did not crash. Instead it reached Carthage, a city on the northern shore of Africa, ruled by the lovely Dido.

Dido, princess of Phoenicia, and her brother, Pygmalion, were supposed to jointly rule the kingdom as per their father's wishes. But an ambitious Pygmalion had claimed the throne for himself and then killed Dido's husband, hoping to lay his hands on his hidden treasure. Guided by her husband's ghost, Dido found the treasure and sailed with it, and her many followers, to Africa.

The rulers of Africa told Dido that for her wealth they could give her as much land as could be enclosed by the hide of a bull. So Dido sacrificed a bull, got its hide cut into thin strips and joined the strips end-to-end to enclose a vast tract of land.

The Africans were impressed by Dido's intelligence and let her stay. Her kingdom, Carthage, became a major trading port, rivalling, and even overshadowing, the ancient trading ports of Phoenicia.

- The more famous Pygmalion is a sculptor who carves a statue of what he considers to be the most beautiful woman in the world, and falls in love with it. Amused, the Olympians give the statue life and a name, Galatea, and she marries her creator.
- The story of Dido claiming land using strips of hide has given rise to a perimetrical problem in mathematics popularly known as 'the Dido problem': What is the closed curve which has the maximum area for a given perimeter?
- Carthage and Rome were rival cities that were competing for control over the Mediterranean.
- Hannibal, a great general of Carthage, took a roundabout route to cross the Alps and enter Italy with elephants; he conquered and occupied Italy for fifteen years. He was eventually defeated by Scipio, a Roman general who incorporated Hannibal's war strategies and acknowledged him as one of the greatest generals in the world after Alexander and Pyrrhus.
- In the ancient world, there was no such entity as Europe. Civilization thrived around the Mediterranean, with ancient cultures such as the Greek and Roman in the north, Carthage and Egypt in the south, and Phoenicia in the west. The creation of Europe, Asia and Africa happened much later in history, probably with the rise of Islam which led to the Arabs occupying much of Africa by the eighth century. Their northward march was resisted by a united Europe, led by kings of what is now France and Germany, whose ancestors were considered barbarians by the Romans and the Greeks.

Dido

On his arrival, Aeneas told Dido his story, and Dido told Aeneas hers. They spent hours telling each other about the tragedy of losing old homes and seeking new ones; of their families and losing loved ones. Before long, they were talking about each other, gazing into each other's eyes, and falling in love.

Aphrodite orchestrated this love between her son and Dido to ensure her son's safety. But Zeus was clear that Aeneas would have to leave Dido eventually and make his own home elsewhere. And so, he sent Hermes to remind Aeneas of his destiny: Carthage was his lover's home, not his. He had to fulfil his destiny, and make a new home for the Trojans. For that his love would have to be sacrificed.

Not having the courage to break Dido's heart, Aeneas planned to slip out of Carthage secretly with his sailors and his ship, laden with provisions. But Dido was no fool. She had sensed Aeneas's hesitation. She came to the harbour just as Aeneas's ship was about to set sail, but she did not stop the Trojan prince. Instead, she ordered her servants to set up a huge bonfire: she threw in all the gifts Aeneas had given her, and cursed him that his descendants would forever suffer the enmity of her descendants. Finally she stabbed herself in the heart and hurled herself into the flames.

- The idea of women killing and burning themselves on the pyre of their dead husbands, to protect their honour or prevent their abuse, is found in many Hindu stories. Many male heroes also threaten to burn themselves to death if they fail to keep a promise. Voluntary death by fire was seen as heroic.
- The story of Dido and Aeneas is clearly inspired by the tension between Rome and Carthage that peaked during the Punic Wars which took place about 150 years before Virgil.
- The people of Carthage were called Punic by the Romans.
- While the Egyptians lived in the Nile valley, the Berbers lived on the north African coast, in what was known as Lybia. The Punics descended from the Phoenicians as well as the Berbers.
- In medieval times, the story of Dido and Aeneas inspired many ballads and plays. The idea of a powerful woman aware of her own desires made people uncomfortable and so she was portrayed as barbaric, even demonic, not in control of her passions. In Dante's *Divine Comedy* written in the fourteenth century in Italian, the 'lustful' Dido is imagined as being in Hell, eternally blasted by fierce whirlwinds.
- In the twentieth century, under Mussolini, when streets in Rome were being named after characters from Virgil's epic, Dido was conspicuous by her absence as she represented feminine desire, Semitic origins (Phoenicia) and Africa; hence she was demonized by the fascist powers.

Sibyl

Guided by Hermes, Aeneas crossed the ocean from Africa to Europe and reached the coast of Italy, where lived the famous Sibyl.

'Unless you go where the Sibyl tells you to go, you will not find your home,' Hermes told Aeneas.

The Sibyl wanted to see if Aeneas was indeed the man prophesied to establish the city of Rome. She pointed to a golden oak tree in her sacred grove and asked Aeneas to break off a branch. Only if he was worthy, if he was the chosen one, would he be able to do it.

Two doves led Aeneas to the golden oak tree.

When Aeneas broke off a branch, a new branch grew in its place; a good sign, said the Sibyl.

With that golden branch, Aeneas entered the Sibyl's cave. She directed him to go deep down where he found himself on the banks of the River Styx. He realized, like heroes before him, that he had to journey to the land of the dead before he could find a new home in the land of the living.

Aeneas paid a silver coin to Charon and was ferried across. He fed honey cakes to the three-headed Cerberus and with the permission of Hades and Persephone met the ghosts of his wife and those who died in Troy, and those who had perished at sea on the way to Italy. He saw Dido there too, but she turned away from him. The ghost of his father told him that he would establish a great city of leaders who would rule the world.

- Since Hindus believe in rebirth, there are not many tales of heroes travelling to visit their ancestors in the land of the dead. However, hermits do dream of ancestors suffering in the land of the dead: hanging upside down over a bottomless crevice (a hell called Put for childless people) into which they risk falling because they are unable to be reborn, as their descendants have become hermits and practise celibacy, refusing to father children.
- Underworld journeys are a recurring theme in Greek mythology. Heroes such as Heracles, Odysseus and Theseus all go to the underworld where they see visions of the past and the future, and then return to the land of the living.
- Sibyls or oracles were popular in the ancient Mediterranean world. The most popular lived in Delphi, Greece. They were known for mouthing the words of the gods in a state of frenzy. These words were in the form of puzzles mostly, cryptic and often prophetic. They were known not by personal names but by the places where they lived.
- While prophets in Abrahamic mythology are mostly male, Greek mythology continuously refers to female prophets, like the Sibyls.
- In 1890, the Scottish anthropologist Sir James George Frazer published a book called *The Golden Bough: A Study in Comparative Religion*. It is a wide-ranging, comparative study of mythology. The title is based on the story of Aeneas being asked by the Sibyl to take a branch of the tree to prove his worthiness as king. It refers to an ancient practice, pre-Roman, of priest-kings who were married to a goddess and eventually killed by their successors. Their life and death mirrored the sowing and harvest cycles of agriculture.

Lavinia

On returning from the underworld, Aeneas continued his journey along the coast of Italy. After many days of sailing, he came to a river's mouth that was lined with trees full of fruit and berries.

Aeneas weighed anchor so his sailors could rest and eat in peace. It was here that the people 'ate their plates' as the Harpies had predicted: they were so hungry that they ate the dry stiff bread on which the women served the fruits they had collected and the meat they had cooked. It was also here that Aeneas and his son, who were exploring the countryside, came upon a gigantic white sow suckling thirty piglets, as Helenus had foretold. This was Italy. This would be their home. Here, Aeneas would build the city that would eventually become Rome.

But before that there would be marriage, a war and an unlikely alliance.

When Aeneas met King Latinus, who ruled the land, the King immediately knew that this stranger of regal bearing was the man the oracle had told him about, the stranger from a distant land who would marry his young daughter, Lavinia. He requested Aeneas to accept the hand of his daughter in marriage and Aeneas agreed, knowing that marriage to a local princess would grant him legitimacy and enable him and his people to make a home in Italy. Unlike the union with Dido, this union was blessed by Zeus.

Unfortunately, the queen Amata wanted Turnus, king of the Rutuli, to be her son-in-law. She was angry and this anger served Hera well. The goddess got the queen to fill Turnus with hate for the Trojan, and he went around rallying a vast army of all the people who lived in Italy including the Etruscans and Sabines. Soon a confederacy of Italian tribes declared war on the Trojans.

It was a terrible war that saw the death of the warrior-maiden Camilla, priestess of Artemis, raised by her father, suckled on a mare, who, like Atlanta before her, could run over water without getting her feet wet, and could run over a field without breaking a single ear of corn.

There was bloodshed all around and everything was spinning out of control. Finally, the angry Olympians, led by Zeus, told Hera to forget her anger against the Trojan race. 'Only if,' said Hera, 'Aeneas forgets the Trojan way of life and embraces all things Italian, and makes friends with a Greek.'

This was communicated to Aeneas. Henceforth, he declared, he would refer to

Zeus as Jupiter and Hera as Juno. Hermes would be called Mercury, Artemis would be Diana, Apollo would be Phoebus, Eros would be Cupid, Poseidon would be Neptune, Hades would be Pluto, Aphrodite would be Venus, and Athena would be Minerva.

Aeneas then scoured the island looking for a Greek ally. He came upon Diomedes, the Greek warrior, who had fought in the Trojan War.

When Diomedes had returned home to Greece, he had found that his wife had taken another husband and started a new life. So he had turned away from his city and sought a new home. But wherever his ship had stopped, he was pursued by birds—the ghosts of the men who were once his companions. They wailed all day and all night, forcing him to set sail again, shunning land, until he reached the shores of Italy. Here the birds told him to wait for a Trojan and to give him the image of Athena, the Palladium, that he and Odysseus had stolen from Troy. Only then would he find peace, and a home.

Said Diomedes to Aeneas, 'I will neither fight for you nor stand against you. I have had enough of war. But here, take this image I stole from your father's city and place it at the centre of your new city.'

Diomedes then directed Aeneas to Evander, who was also Greek, but who had left Greece long before the Trojan War. Evander decided to support Aeneas and put an end to this hostility against immigrants. In the battle that followed, Evander lost his son Pallas, but Turnus was also killed and Aeneas declared victor.

'Let there be peace,' begged Aeneas. He was tired of war. Did not all residents of

a land descend from refugees from other lands? Everyone agreed. So the Trojans, Greeks and Italians embraced one another. Everyone drank to the marriage of Aeneas and Lavinia, and the friendship of Aeneas and Evander.

Together they built a temple to enshrine the ancient Trojan Palladium, and around it eventually rose a great new city: Rome.

- In the Mahabharata, after being cast out of the house by his father, Yadu finds shelter with the Naga people whose king, Dhumravarna, invites him to marry his five daughters. From this union is born the race of Yadus, who rule Mathura. In another story, a childless king finds the blind sage, Dirghatamas, floating on a river clinging to a log of wood, and sends him to his wife so that she can have children by him. Thus are born the kings of Anga, Vanga, Kalinga, Pundra and Suhma. Thus, homeless warriors and sages end up founding royal dynasties in Hindu mythology too.
- Is Latinus, who befriends Aeneas, the son of Telemachus and Circe as mentioned in Hesiod's *Theogony*, or the son of Telemachus and Circe as mentioned in *Fabulae*? In Roman writings, Latinus is said to be the son of Faunus, the horned god of the woods, the local version of Pan, and Marica, the nymph, who was probably the local version of Artemis.
- Livy, who wrote in the time of Augustus Caesar, documented Roman mythology. While Greek mythology focuses on heroes, Roman mythology speaks of chaste wives like Lucretia who kill themselves when raped to protect their husband's family from shame, and of great heroes like Scoevola who burn their own hand to prove to the enemy, the Etruscans, that even under torture he would never betray Rome.

- If the Greeks were associated with contemplation, the Romans were associated with action. If the Greeks were focused on tragedy of the human condition, the Romans spoke of triumph and honour more than anything else. It is in Roman mythology that we see the early traces of the concept of nationalist patriotism, for it is about loyalty to a city state and not to a clan. The latter is expected of women and children.
- Remus and Romulus, twins who were suckled by a she-wolf, are the most famous descendants of Aeneas. Their mother was a mortal woman, a Vestal Virgin, and their father was Mars, the Roman god of war. The story goes that Remus saw six eagles and Romulus, soon after, saw twelve. Romulus claimed Zeus favoured him as he had seen more birds, while Remus argued that since he had seen a vision first, he was the favoured one. When Remus jumped over the walls built by Romulus to show how strong and capable he was, Romulus killed Remus, and became king of Rome. Unable to find wives, Romulus and his men were forced to abduct women of the Sabine tribes who eventually learned to love their captors, and had to forcibly stop war between their fathers, brothers and husbands. These Roman tales show the dangers of sibling rivalry and the importance of women as peacemakers and homemakers.
- Britain too owes its origin to Troy. Briton, a descendant of Aeneas, was exiled from Italy for accidentally killing his father, and he made his way to the island of Albion that would eventually be called Britain.
- Graeco-Roman philosophy played a key role in the founding of the American republic, as we can see in American state architecture and the use of words like 'senate' in the political system. But the 'pagan' pantheon of Greece and Rome was not embraced; instead, the Christian God prevailed.

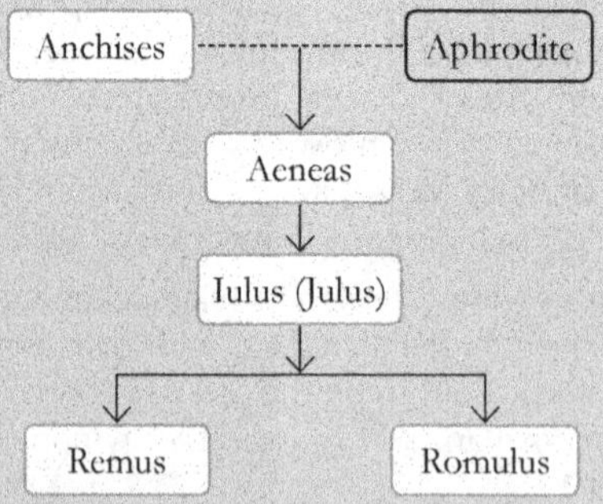

House of Aeneas

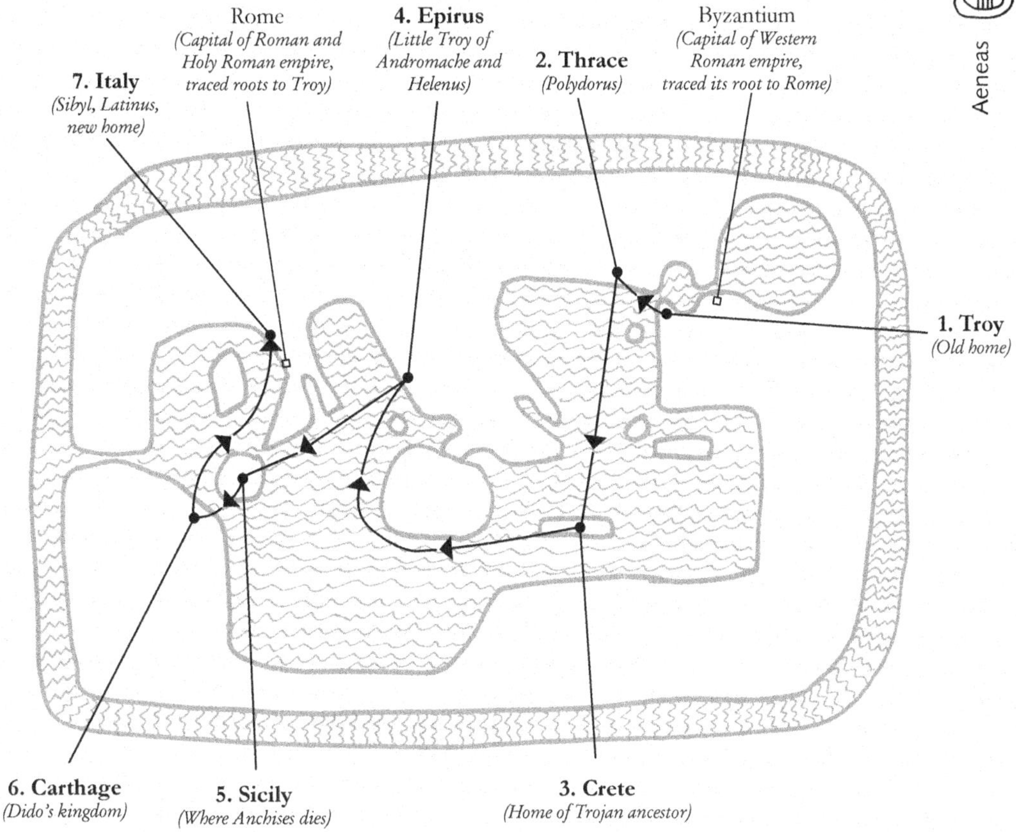

Aeneas's Expedition

(Probable route as per Virgil's *Aeneid*: representational, not drawn to scale)

EPILOGUE

The Indian Headshake

As the stories came to an end, the gymnosophist smiled. 'Such wonderful stories. Of heroes who go on adventures, kill monsters, rescue damsels, and eventually return home, or establish new cities. What about you, Alexander? You have killed monsters and rescued damsels. Do you wish to go home now, or create a new home?'

'Olympus it shall be for me,' Alexander replied. 'Onward I shall go . . . To the edge of the world, where no man has gone before, and there I shall earn the love of the gods. But I fear that my life will end as it did for Theseus and Oedipus and Heracles and Jason and Achilles and Agamemnon—in tragedy.'

'So it has been before. So it will be again.'

'What do you mean?' asked Alexander.

'Every hero thinks his path is unique and original. Tragedy is discovering that all paths have existed before. This land you are about to enter is named after Bharat, a great king, who conquered the world and then climbed the tallest mountain in the world to hoist his flag and declare to the world his great achievement. But on reaching the peak he found there hundreds of flags, of kings before him, each one assuming he had conquered the world.'

'I have never heard of this Bharat. Are you saying he conquered the world before me? When? Why have I never heard of him? I don't believe you. I don't think this Bharat existed,' Alexander argued, his temper rising.

'You have never seen Olympus. Yet you believe that Olympus exists. You and I, we believe in different things.'

'That's not true. We are not so different. We believe in the same things. Like Olympus, don't your people also speak of a city of gods where heroes are entertained? And of a place of punishment and suffering, after death, like Tartarus?'

'Swarga! Naraka! You are right. You have indeed heard much. But not all,' said the gymnosophist calmly. 'In Swarga, one's hunger is indulged. In Naraka, one experiences eternal hunger. But then there is Kailasa, the abode of Shiva, where one outgrows hunger. And finally, there is Vaikuntha, where attention is paid to other people's hunger. Different heavens for different lives.'

'Different lives? I don't understand.'

'You told of me of the Styx, the river that separates the land of the living from the land of the dead. You cross this river just once. There is another river, the Vaitarni, that separates the land of the living from the land of the dead. You must cross her many times, so that you live many lives, and experience different destinations. In Swarga and Naraka, one's stay is temporary. In Kailasa and Vaikuntha, you can live forever.'

'Great feats grant us a place in Elysium. What takes you to Kailasa and Vaikuntha?' asked Alexander, curious.

'Understanding,' replied the gymnosophist.

The sky turned golden, and a hundred green parrots descended on nearby trees. Alexander did not respond for some time, distressed by what he was hearing. Did achievement not matter at all? The leader of the Greeks finally spoke. 'Action, I feel, matters more than understanding. I still don't believe our worlds are as different as you claim they are. Surely Vishnu on his eagle is like Zeus, as is the thunderbolt-wielding Indra, and Shiva who dances wildly is like Bacchus, and Krishna who fights the bulls and lions and multi-headed snakes is Heracles. Surely Kartikeya is your Ares, and Kama your Eros.'

'You look at the flesh, not beyond, at the literal meaning of the word, not its metaphor.'

'Don't you want to change the world—make it a better place?' asked Alexander.

'What is better for you may not be better for me. Why do you presume to know my needs? Every plant is different. Every animal is different. Every human being is different. Our worlds are different. You see your world as chaotic and so strive for order. I see my world in a flux, like the sea, changing endlessly, maybe not at my pace, or to my will, but always changing. You wish to control change, because you are convinced you can. I don't wish to control this changing world, because I know I can't,' said the gymnosophist. 'Who is right? Can't we both be right?'

'The point of life is to be remembered for our extraordinary deeds,' insisted Alexander. 'The value of our life is the sum total of our achievements.'

'When you live only once, the denominator of your existence is only one, and so what you say is true. When you live many lives, the denominator of existence is infinite, and achievements have no intrinsic value. Eventually, we will all be forgotten.'

'I will be remembered forever, till the end of time,' roared the mighty Greek warrior.

The gymnosophist shook his head this way and that with a smile, annoying Alexander who asked, 'Why are you bobbing your head that way?'

'It's the Indian headshake. It means you are probably right, or probably wrong. Who knows? Varuna has but a thousand eyes, Indra a hundred, you and I only two.'

Alexander, who found comfort in certainty, did not like the answer. He walked away, determined to inspire his army and take them further east.

But Alexander's men had other plans. They were tired, restless and wanted to go home.

'Then by a different route! We shall not retrace our steps,' insisted Alexander, when he finally conceded. And thus the great Greek army sailed down the River Sindhu to the sea and then along the coast back to Babylon, from where they would make the journey to Greece.

As he moved down the river and along the coast, Alexander thought of the Styx and Vaitarni. One which you cross only once, and another which you keep crossing again and again. Was his life predetermined by karma, or by the Fates, or by the gods, or was it a consequence of his own hubris? Would he return again?

As they pressed onwards, Alexander's beloved friend and companion, Hephastion, died of fever. Alexander wept for days. A huge bonfire was lit to cremate his body. The flames touched the skies. 'Will I meet him in Elysium? Will I be alone in Olympus? Will we return here again, as birds or kings, always together like Achilles and Patroclus?' he wondered.

Alone on his throne, surrounded by angry Greeks who refused to bow to him, and confused Persians who wanted to bow to him, the great student of Aristotle felt like the Greek heroes, despondent after an adventure.

Was this it? Yet another frontier, yet another edge of the world, yet another war? Would he, like Icarus and Phaeton and Bellerophon, be cast down to earth for daring to rise up to the sky? Or would he be carried up, with his beloved like the Discouri, or alone like Heracles, Ganymede and Odysseus? Why did he not feel in control?

Slowly, as the sun rose, Alexander realized that no matter how much he wanted to determine the course of his life, the world often took decisions for him. He had conquered the world, almost. And the world had conquered him, almost.

Alexander shook his head this way and that, imitating the gymnosophist, and smiled.

- Unlike Greek plays, Sanskrit plays are never tragedies. In fact, in principle, they embrace the idea of sukhant, or happy ending. But the Ramayana and the Mahabharata were composed a few centuries before the first Sanskrit plays, when Indo-Greek influence was widespread in north India. Perhaps that is why, unlike Sanskrit plays, the epics have tragic endings like most Greek epics, with the abandonment of Sita in the Ramayana, and the destruction of the Kuru and the Yadava clans in the Mahabharata.
- While the sage Dandamis declined the invitation to travel with Alexander, declaring that he was content with his life in India, the sage Calanus did travel with the king. Sadly, the sage, who enjoyed perfect health in India, fell ill in Persia and finally after much suffering decided to mount a funeral pyre and burn himself to death, an idea that shocked and fascinated the Greeks. Alexander gave him many gifts that, as per Greek tradition, would have been burned on the pyre. But Calanus distributed all these to people around him and without any fear mounted the pyre, singing songs

to the gods, and embraced death. Before he died, Calanus predicted the death of Alexander in Babylon.

- After the death of Alexander, the Indus valley came to be ruled by his satrap, Seleucus. Legend has it that his daughter, Helen, was given in marriage to Chandragupta Maurya, on the advice of the political strategist Chanakya, who then orchestrated the fall of the Nanda dynasty in Magadha, and eventually established the Mauryan Empire that stretched across much of South Asia. The alliance suited both as Seleucus was more interested in the West than the East.
- The Mauryans gave 500 elephants to Seleucus which helped him defeat his rival, Antigonus, at the Battle of Ipsus and establish the Selucid Empire that lasted for nearly 300 years, controlling much of the Middle East.
- Megasthenes, the Greek envoy, visited Chandragupta Maurya after the king established Pataliputra as the capital of his vast empire. In his book *Indika*, Megasthenes noted how the Indian emperor had a contingent of female warriors (Amazons?) as his bodyguards.
- Just like Alexander, Chandragupta was strongly influenced by a gymnosophist, the Jain monk Bhadrabahu, and eventually gave up his royal title and became a naked ascetic himself.
- The Mauryans introduced many of the empire-management techniques established by Persian emperors, including using the written word to communicate the will of kings to remote corners of the empire. This led to the creation of the indigenous Brahmi script, which enjoyed royal patronage. It was carved in stone during the time of Ashoka, the grandson of Chandragupta. Until then, Indians avoided writing and preferred transmitting ideas orally.
- Roughly 2200 years ago, the Yavana or Gandhara or Indo-Greek Empire was established by Demetrius, stretching from the Indus to the Gangetic plains. But this was not a united empire and was full of many warlords, whose capitals included Taxila, Pushkalavati (Peshawar?) and Sakala (Sialkot?), all currently in Pakistan.
- The most famous Indo-Greek ruler was Milinda or Menander, a patron of Buddhism. The Greek geographer Strabo wrote that Menander conquered more tribes than even Alexander the Great. His coins bear images of Athena.
- Indo-Greek ideas contributed to many Hindu practices in later times, including giving a human form to the gods. They were the first to create the image of Buddha, as well as those of Shiva and Vishnu, who until then were represented only as symbols—umbrellas or conch shells or wheels—or simply as rocks or mounds.
- During Alexander's time, the earliest versions of the Ramayana, the Mahabharata and the Puranas were probably being orally transmitted. They were written down in the centuries that followed, and they reached the form that we currently receive them in, over 500 years later. How deeply Greek thought impacted the narration remains a matter of speculation.

Gods of Greek, Roman and Hindu mythologies

Greek name	Roman name	Closest Indian equivalent
Aphrodite	Venus	Rati
Apollo	Apollo	Vishnu
Ares	Mars	Kartikeya
Artemis	Diana	Revanta (male)
Athena	Minerva	Saraswati
Cronus	Saturn	Shani
Demeter	Ceres	Bhu-devi
Dionysus	Bacchus	Shiva
Castor and Pollux	Castor and Polydeuces	Ashwini Kumar
Eos	Aurora	Usha or Aruna
Eris	Discordia	Kalaha (Alakshmi)
Eros	Cupid	Kama
Gaia	Terra	Prithvi
Hades	Pluto	Yama
Hephaestus	Vulcan	Vishwakarma
Hera	Juno	Sachi
Heracles	Hercules	Vasudeva and Baladeva
Hermes	Mercury	Budh
Hestia	Vesta	Yogini
Persephone	Proserpine	Patala-Lakshmi, Shakambari
Poseidon	Neptune	Varuna
Rhea	Ops	Aditi
Uranus	Uranus	Dyaus, Brahma
Zeus	Jupiter	Indra

Bibliography

- Bhattacharya, Sukumari. *Indian Theogony.* Cambridge: Cambridge University Press, 2007.
- Callaso, Roberto. *Marriage of Cadmus and Harmony.* London: Viking, 1994.
- Campbell, Joseph. *The Hero with a Thousand Faces.* Princeton, N.J.: Princeton University Press, 1949.
- Campbell, Joseph. *The Masks of God* (4 volumes). New York: The Viking Press, 1959–1968.
- Coupe, Lawrence. *Myth.* London: Routledge, 1997.
- Danielou, Alain. *Gods of Love and Ecstasy: The Traditions of Shiva and Dionysus.* Rochester, Vt.: Inner Traditions International, 1992.
- Eliade, Mircea. *Myths, Dreams, and Mysteries.* London: Collins, 1974.
- Ferry, Luc. *A Brief History of Thought.* New York: Harper Perennial, 2011.
- Ferry, Luc. *The Wisdom of the Myths.* New York: Collins, 2014.
- Flood, Gavin. *An Introduction to Hinduism.* New Delhi: Cambridge University Press, 1998.
- Frazer, Sir James. *The Golden Bough.* London: Wordsworth, 1993.
- Freeman, Philip. *Oh My Gods: A Modern Retelling of Greek and Roman Myths*. New York: Simon & Schuster, 2013.
- Graves, Robert. *The Greek Myths.* Baltimore: Penguin Books, 1955.
- Jayakar, Pupul. *The Earth Mother.* Delhi: Penguin Books, 1989.
- Kosambi, Damodar Dharmanand. *Myth and Reality.* Mumbai: Popular Prakashan Pvt. Ltd., 1994.
- Mani, Vettam. *Puranic Encyclopaedia.* Delhi: Motilal Banarsidass, 1996.
- Zimmer, Heinrich. *Myths and Symbols in Indian Art and Civilization.* Delhi: Motilal Banarsidass, 1990.

Index of Greek and Roman names, places and terms

Index of Indian names, places and terms

YOU MAY ALSO LIKE

YOU MAY ALSO LIKE

ALSO BY DEVDUTT PATTANAIK

JAYA:
An Illustrated Retelling of the Mahabharata

'Devdutt Pattanaik is a master story-teller'—Bibek Debroy

High above the sky stands Swarga, paradise, abode of the gods. Still above is Vaikuntha, heaven, abode of God. The doorkeepers of Vaikuntha are the twins, Jaya and Vijaya, both whose names mean victory. One keeps you in Swarga; the other raises you into Vaikuntha. In Vaikuntha there is bliss forever, in Swarga there is pleasure for only as long as you deserve. What is the difference between Jaya and Vijaya? Solve this puzzle and you will solve the mystery of the Mahabharata.

In this enthralling retelling of India's greatest epic, the Mahabharata, originally known as Jaya, Devdutt Pattanaik seamlessly weaves into a single narrative plots from the Sanskrit classic as well as its many folk and regional variants, including the Pandavani of Chattisgarh, Gondhal of Maharashtra, Terukkuttu of Tamil Nadu, and Yakshagana of Karnataka.

Richly illustrated with over 250 line drawings by the author, the 108 chapters abound with little-known details such as the names of the hundred Kauravas, the worship of Draupadi as a goddess in Tamil Nadu, the stories of Astika, Madhavi, Jaimini, Aravan and Barbareek, the Mahabharata version of the *Shakuntalam* and the Ramayana, and the dating of the war based on astronomical data.

With clarity and simplicity, the tales in this elegant volume reveal the eternal relevance of the Mahabharata, the complex and disturbing meditation on the human condition that has shaped Indian thought for over 3000 years.

ALSO BY DEVDUTT PATTANAIK

SITA:
An Illustrated Retelling of the Ramayana

'Outstanding'—*Indian Express*

It is significant that the only character in Hindu mythology, a king at that, to be given the title of *ekam-patni-vrata*, devoted to a single wife, is associated with the most unjust act of abandoning her in the forest to protect family reputation. This seems a deliberate souring of an uplifting narrative. Ram's refusal to remarry to produce a royal heir adds to the complexity. The intention seems to be to provoke throught on notions of fidelity, property and self-image.

And so the mythologist and illustrator Devdutt Pattaanik retells the *Ramayana*, drawing attention to the many oral, visual and written retellings composed in different times, in different places, by different poets, each one trying to solve the puzzle in its own unique way.

This book approaches Ram by speculating on Sita: her childhood with her father, Janaka, who hosted sages mentioned in the Upanishads; her stay in the forest with her husband, who had to be a celibate ascetic while she was in the prime of her youth; her interactions with the women of Lanka, recipes she exchanged, emotions they shared; her connection with the earth, her mother, and with the trees, her sisters; her role as the Goddess, the untamed Kali as well as the demure Gauri, in transforming the stoic prince of Ayodhya into God.

ALSO BY DEVDUTT PATTANAIK

MYTH=MITHYA:
Decoding Hindu Mythology

'The book delves into virtually every important myth and story associated with these gods/goddesses . . . from a host of original and secondary sources from the Vedas to the Puranas'—*India Today*

Hindus have one God, and also 330 million gods: male gods, female gods, personal gods, clan gods, household gods, gods who reside in plants, animals, images, designs and objects; and a whole host of demons, not all bad; but no Devil-like character or the concept of 'evil'. Explore all this and more in this classic work by mythologist Devdutt Pattanaik that has revolutionized everyone's understanding of Hinduism and mythology.

'Folklore hasn't been written with such simplicity, economy of words, even humour . . . recommended to every kind of reader—uninitiated or expert'—*First City*

'Mythology demystified but not dumbed down'—*Times of India*

ALSO BY DEVDUTT PATTANAIK

THE BOOK OF RAM

'Ram's story as a metaphor for human strengths and weaknesses and as a window to inner divinity'—*Tehelka*

Ram is maryada purushottam, the supreme upholder of social values, scion of the Raghu clan, jewel of the solar dynasty, seventh avatar of Vishnu. Reviled by feminists, appropriated by politicians, he remains serene in his majesty, the only Hindu deity to be worshipped as a king. Join Devdutt Pattanaik as he explores the relevance of Ram in modern times, peeling back the layers of metaphors and meanings in the many retellings of his tale.

'A good summation of the many Ramayanas, showing how the story has been adapted over the centuries to suit the needs and perspectives of different people'—*Sunday Guardian*

'Pattanaik is a consummate writer . . . his engaging and easy style will appeal to and charm both the lay as well as the serious reader'—*Mail Today*